RENEWELS 691-4574

DATE DUE

DEC 2 2	JUL 1 4		
FEB 2 1			
MAR 2 1		NOV 2 3	
APR 1 9			
AUG 0 8			
SEP 1 6			
NOV 2 1			
MAR 2 6			
APR 1 1			
NOV 1 5			
OCT - 1			
NOV 1 5			
FEB 2 1			
AUG - 4			

Demco, Inc. 38-293

BUILDING THE

COMPETITIVE WORKFORCE

INVESTING IN HUMAN CAPITAL FOR CORPORATE SUCCESS

BUILDING THE
COMPETITIVE
WORKFORCE

INVESTING IN HUMAN CAPITAL
FOR CORPORATE SUCCESS

**Based on the groundbreaking Louis Harris and Associates
"Laborforce 2000" Survey**

Philip H. Mirvis
Editor

John Wiley & Sons, Inc.

New York • Chichester • Brisbane • Toronto • Singapore

Library of Congress Cataloging-in-Publication Data

Building the competitive workforce : investing in human capital for corporate success / Philip Mirvis, editor.
    p.   cm.
  Includes bibliographical references and index.
  ISBN 0-471-59257-9 (alk. paper)
  1. Personnel management—United States. 2. Human capital—United States. 3. Competition—United States. I. Mirvis, Philip.
HF5549.2.U5B865 1993
658.3–dc20   92-42165

Printed in the United States of America
10 9 8 7 6 5 4 3 2 1

Foreword

Readers of this book may be surprised to find that it was sponsored by the Commonwealth Fund, a private foundation best known for supporting innovations in medical care. Yet the subject of this study based on the Harris Laborforce 2000 survey—the dilemmas facing America's companies and workforce—has proved a compelling foundation investment. The Commonwealth Fund, like most foundations, is in the business of developing human potential. The workplace, as we learn here, is one of the nation's prime arenas for enhancing individual growth and collective capacity. Supporting efforts to better understand and ultimately improve conditions of work promises to benefit working people and the communities in which we live. This purpose inspired and guided the authors whose analyses and recommendations stock the chapters of this book.

In their efforts to develop human potential, foundations typically enlist partners from voluntary organizations, educational institutions, and governmental agencies or programs. Few foundations have viewed the workplace as fertile soil for reaping knowledge or have seen corporations as partners in cultivating it, perhaps because the terms of employment seemed relatively fixed and few of the societal ills that foundations seek to redress seemed dependent on them. But today these terms are in transition as American business undertakes its largest restructuring since World War II. And changes in work opportunities and work conditions are leading to dramatic changes in the life circumstances of tens of millions of Americans.

The workplace of tomorrow could unleash more of our nation's human potential. Alternatively, it could undermine prosperity and incite the divisive urges latent in our society. To inform those who lead or work in business, government, and unions of where things stand and to guide future decisions, this book provides an up-to-date picture of what is behind the changing workplace conditions that are already reshaping our lives. It also highlights what lies along the path to the twenty-first century. Readers learn of the varied ways in which businesses are coping with a vastly more competitive environment and how their actions both create and preempt opportunities for different groups of American workers.

Corporate responses to several major petitions for developing human potential are investigated in this volume. Basic needs for steady employment, a living wage, and fair treatment are, of course, requisites for human development. So are jobs that make use of our talents and a work environment that encourages responsibility, initiative, and personal growth. Beyond these, the petitions on the doorstep of business are more diverse than at any time before: They come from working women who seek improved pay and more opportunities for advancement; from parents who seek relief from the problems that their children can encounter without suitable, stable alternatives to parental supervision during working hours; and from young adults with limited scholastic success who need training and entry level jobs.

People today expect that business should insist on adequate academic preparation of students and that it should help communities undertake the difficult changes required to improve student performance. The majority of Americans without health insurance are employed adults (or their dependents) who cannot get affordable coverage through their employers. At the same time, millions of insured workers fear the loss of their financial protection as employers pass on to them steep yearly increases in the costs of insurance. Still other workers avoid changing jobs, afraid they will not be able to replace the insurance protection they now have.

Meanwhile, older workers seek part-time or rescaled employment throughout the sixth decade of life. Armed with the best educations, work histories, and health status of any generation of senior Americans, today's older workers regard continued work as vital to their happiness and well-being. This change in expectations alone could transform the workforce within a decade, once the baby boom generation begins to swell the ranks of seniors.

There are also petitions from former welfare recipients who now actively seek employment. Welfare is no longer viewed as a lifelong means of support. Redefined, it is a program aiming to transform temporary recipients into self-sustaining employees. Finally, there is a growing number of people laid off via corporate downsizing who need retraining to be reemployed and assistance during a period of worrisome transition. The nation's economic health and civil harmony depend on whether these individuals, too, can find productive employment.

The public continues to look to business, more than to government, to devise solutions for this list of workforce petitions. Business is believed to have the opportunity, the motive, and the competency to get the job done. *Opportunity*—business creates wealth and jobs; it commands half the waking time and attention of most adults; it determines who gets hired, retrained, and promoted; and it sets the terms of the health insurance, retirement benefits, and vacation and leave policies that protect and facilitate family life. *Motive*—business can reap the benefits of responding to these petitions if, in so doing, it increases the value of the workforce, boosts productivity, and advances the competitive agendas of individual firms. *Competency*—business has its own considerable shortcomings in the minds of the public, but local action developed through private initiative, rather than through government policies, continues to be seen by most Americans as the better path to improving our individual and collective lot.

Devising solutions to these petitions is a formidable challenge. The competitive position of American business is in decline, and the nation's standard of living is severely threatened. The basic dilemma for business explored in the chapters of this book is this: American industry is confronting a competitive struggle for its very existence at precisely the moment when the public has heightened its demands for more and better responses to human-potential challenges in the workplace.

Business is dealing with unprecedented global competition by restructuring and reinventing itself on a massive scale. This enormous task is preoccupying, and many senior managers and human resources officials have little time left for sustained attention to human-development petitions. Even worse, restructuring efforts are exacerbating many of the very problems the nation has been appealing to business to improve. Massive layoffs, a much-larger part-time-only workforce, tens of thousands of jobs moved overseas, a fractious and rough-edged corporate atmosphere: These are the effects on employees of deploying the tactical weapons of the new, globally competitive era.

The dynamics are manifest in individual firms. Forging a new spirit of employee commitment is considered crucial for succeeding in today's competitive environment. Yet the very covenants on which commitment has historically been based have been broken. Gone, or at least significantly eroded, is business's commitment to provide lifelong employment, guaranteed annual raises, comprehensive health insurance, and substantial retirement benefits.

Yet there are strategies and practices identified in this study that present workable alternatives to the continuous retreat from corporate paternalism. They are brought to life by companies that believe that developing human potential is a competitive necessity and that take seriously the importance of investing in human resources. These firms, as described throughout this book, set the pace by investing in new work designs and other workplace innovations, by aggressively training and retraining their employees, and by responding genuinely to the requirements of the *new workforce.*

The covenants of the new competitiveness will doubtlessly place more responsibility on the individual worker. It will come as an irresistible union: Business necessity will join the worker's prevailing faith in individual liberty and responsibility. Business can use to its advantage the prevailing ethos that, through individual choice and striving, each of us can control our own destiny. The message of the 90s will sound like this: Keep your own skills marketable and see to your own financial security. Already, there are whispered exhortations to be more self-reliant and individualistic.

Each of us must increasingly invest in ourselves. To be globally competitive, our workforce must undergo periodic skills upgrading on a scale much larger than the nation yet comprehends. Technological innovation is dramatically outpacing the training currently available. Methods for financing and providing the requisite training will have to be devised and put in place.

Although the public embraces the idea of individual striving and financial self-sufficiency, its behavior lags far behind. For example, most baby boomers report they do not expect to collect adequate social security payments to sustain a decent retirement—yet few have increased their woefully inadequate savings levels to prepare for tomorrow. The majority of workers fail to understand that their fringe benefits are an earned part of their total compensation, just like the cash in their pay envelopes. Instead, they tend to view fringe benefits as benevolent gifts from their employer, gifts that they are watching their employers take back. Today, few employees have choice over which benefits give them real value, and few press for the kind of choices that well-stocked "cafeteria" plans offer.

The public has another dilemma to consider. Even as people campaign for those new work rules that will improve their own well-being, they realize that their neighbors' needs may be precluded and that satisfying immediate desires may jeopardize the standard of living that the nation's children will inherit. They understand that business must put its shoulder to the competitive wheel and steer the tough course. But whether our collective behavior will be self-interested and short-sighted or be generous-minded and future-directed is still up in the air. The workforce is struggling to come to grips with its priorities and values.

Forging new workplace covenants will test the ingenuity and tenacity of businesses, government, foundations, and academe; and coalitions of these groups may produce society's best response to the dilemmas. For instance, businesses are reluctant to shoulder the burden of entry level education and worker retraining alone. Most do not have the scale of operation large enough to conduct continuous skills training or the extra resources to finance the substantial ongoing expense. Moreover, firms that can underwrite training fear the loss of their investments as employees are lured away by high-wage bids from competitors who do not pay for training. Other resource-strapped firms are likely to limit skills building to those with the greatest potential to increase profitability: up-and-coming executives and professionals who are already highly skilled, such as engineers and scientists. This response is logical for an individual firm, but such a response will not improve the skills of the tens of millions of Americans looking for upward mobility. The promise of upward mobility has been the workplace covenant that has most helped to hold together our diverse nation.

It is plausible to ask employees to meet some of the costs needed for their periodic skills building by providing tax incentives. And perhaps the cost of retraining classes taken at a community college could be paid through a fringe benefit option. Or perhaps the release time necessary to attend such sessions would be provided at the employer's expense. Many such *new covenant* possibilities, including business–public school partnerships and European-style apprenticeship programs, merit careful analysis. This book examines several of them.

Health care reform offers another opportunity for collaborative action. Corporate America has neglected to use its market muscle to insist that affordable, competitive health care plans to be made available to employees. Nor has business yet endorsed the reform proposals that would facilitate cost-sensitive purchasing on the part of the individual employee. Caught in a philosophical muddle between providing for employees and letting them fend for themselves, employers have simply let standard insurance coverage erode. Isn't it time for business to work more directly with government, education, and foundations as partners in order to find a better means of financing cost-effective health care?

Then there is the vital goal of building a corporate spirit of cooperation, interdependence, and teamwork. Some fear that the widespread celebration of ethnic, gender, and cultural diversity is an upsurge of "tribalism" that threatens to dissolve the values that hold Americans together. Building one workforce out of many diverse groups of workers is an increasingly precarious task. To take diversity seriously requires respecting the separate preferences, customs, and beliefs of each subgroup. The task before us is to reconcile different notions of teamwork and good process into common core values. Can diversity be synthesized into a competitive strength for America's economy?

The authors of this volume launch every reader on a voyage to the twenty-first-century workplace, by charting significant shifts that influence how we work and live. They describe the vast challenges we will confront on the course to a better life and the routes that companies will follow as they make their way. The authors' expert commentary underscores just how complex but fulfilling the journey could be.

Major credit for this achievement goes to Philip Mirvis, who has skill-fully woven the dozens of critical observations the authors have made into this engaging, purposeful document; to Michael Barth, who has steadfastly captained both this work and the Commonwealth Fund's efforts in search of better solutions to workforce dilemmas; to William McNaught, who—as an expert on the workforce aspirations of older Americans—now places them in the context of the twenty-first-century economy; and to Penny Duckham, who has contributed handily to the content and structure of this project, which she so capably managed on behalf of its sponsor.

Full partners in the success of this venture include Arlene Johnson and Fabian Linden of the Conference Board, each of whom has brought key perspectives and energies to the development of this project. Humphrey Taylor, Robert Leitman, and Ron Bass of Louis Harris and Associates have brought their years of experience in the surveying of business executives about laborforce issues to bear, refining the direction and improving the caliber of this project. Dennis Ross has lent skillful assistance to the data analysis and preparation of chart materials in the book.

Finally, we thank the Commonwealth Fund's board of directors for their expansive view of the health of the American people. The support of this work has opened up grand vistas for achievement. May many more founda-tion officials and business executives learn from this work and take up the vital challenges it inspires.

THOMAS MOLONEY
Institute for the Future
New York, New York

Contributions

A broad agenda of human resources issues will compete for the attention of business and its leadership in the decade of the 90s. Each contributor to this volume considers specific laborforce issues and how companies are responding to them based on in-depth interviews of top human resources executives by Louis Harris and Associates in 406 randomly sampled Conference Board companies.

Chapter 1   A Competitive Workforce: The Issues and the Study

Philip Mirvis—the editor, a private researcher and consultant—presents the framework underlying the research and details the data base and sample of the Laborforce 2000 study. He looks at the key competitive strategies of the studied companies and what current and future laborforce issues mean for their success. This chapter also examines the changing contours of the American laborforce and how the studied companies rate the impact of several human resources issues.

Chapter 2   Strategic Human Resource Management

Edward Lawler, Susan Cohen, and Lei Chang—specialists in human resources management trends and strategies at the Center for Effective Organizations of the University of Southern California—hone in on the priorities and positioning of human resources management in the sampled companies. They compare the human resources philosophy of "cutting edge" organizations, which lead change in the corporate world, with more traditional outfits, which tend to lag behind. Their findings provide a clear distinction between firms that are well positioned to deal with future challenges and those that are at risk.

Chapter 3   Restructuring and Downsizing

Mitchell Marks—an expert on change management with William M. Mercer Incorporated, an international human resources consulting firm—examines corporate restructuring and downsizing. He discusses the overall impact of deindustrialization and corporate consolidations, including what has caused them and why they will continue through the rest of the decade. He also describes the manner in which companies have downsized and how many people have been affected.

Chapter 4   Company Policies on Education and Training

Michael Useem, a professor of sociology from the Wharton School of the University of Pennsylvania, looks at the needs of business for skilled workers, professionals, and managers—today and tomorrow—and whether or not the needs can be met. His data highlight the necessity of more training and retraining. The chapter describes the training methods used by the studied corporations: whom they reach and how effective they have been.

Chapter 5   Workplace Flexibility: Faddish or Fundamental?

Victoria Parker and Douglas (Tim) Hall, experts on careers and workforce planning from the School of Management at Boston University, focus on the question of corporate flexibility: Do companies understand the issues posed by increasing diversity and the conflicts between work and family life? And are they responding genuinely and effectively? The authors find that most companies are doing something about these matters, but they see sharp differences between leaders and laggards in these areas.

Chapter 6   Corporations and the Aging Workforce

Michael Barth, Senior Vice-President of ICF Incorporated; William Mc-Naught, former Research Director for the Commonwealth Fund; and Philip Rizzi, with ICF, focus on the employment of workers over age 55, the fastest-growing segment of the workforce. Based on the data collected, they report that a majority of employers think that workers over 55 are more reliable and have better work attitudes than younger employees. Yet the authors find a pervasive gap between attitudes and practices and make a case for investing in older workers.

Chapter 7   The Changing Nature of Employee Health Benefits

Karen Davis—a specialist in public health, health care management, and corporate health insurance, and Executive Vice-President of the Commonwealth

Fund—finds U.S. businesses making dramatic changes in their health coverage. Health care costs seriously threaten competitiveness. Hence almost all companies studied have cut back on their health care benefits in the late 80s. But few think that further changes will bring costs under control. Her analyses show that business is seemingly ready for government-mandated cost containment.

Chapter 8 The Findings and Their Implications

In this concluding chapter, Mirvis reviews key findings from the Laborforce 2000 survey and shows how the practices of "cutting edge" companies set an example for business to follow. He notes that fundamental issues—regarding the future compact between employees and companies, the diffusion of change management skills throughout business, and the urgent need for investment by business and government in human capital—will require vigorous attention if America is to build a truly competitive workforce.

Harris Surveys

Throughout the text Ron Bass, Vice-President, Louis Harris and Associates, presents results of American's attitudes about public education, the skills and attitudes of young people, health insurance and the American health care system, and other relevant subjects.

Contents

1

A Competitive Workforce: The Issues and the Study

Philip H. Mirvis

The headlines today portend trials tomorrow for corporations and their leaders. Intense global competition, pressures to cut costs and reduce staff, declines in the nation's skill bank, growing diversity in the workforce, an aging population, health care costs that are running out of control—all of these factors promise to make competing claims on the resources and imagination of business executives for the rest of the decade. In this Laborforce 2000 study, leading experts examine the priorities and practices of 406 companies in order to highlight where industry is keeping pace with the demands of change and where, in some cases, it is seriously behind.

The following list highlights some of the issues that we examine:

- Many companies do more than pay lip service to the value of people. But given competitive pressures, is there any evidence that human resource management is a top priority of senior executives?

- Most firms downsized in the decade past. Will periodic downsizing become a fact of life in the years ahead? Are companies prepared to handle massive retraining and redeployment?

- High-skill jobs require high-skill workers. Do firms foresee critical skill shortages? Will they change their recruiting and retention strategies? Or will they move more employment offshore?

1

- The skills of entry workers are suspect. Are businesses able to provide the necessary basic and remedial training? Will apprenticeship programs and corporate involvement in public schools become essential in the years ahead?

- Demography could be destiny. Are companies poised to capitalize on diversity in the workforce, to deal with work/family issues; or will most just muddle through?

- The population is aging. Are more workers over age 55 destined to be considered deadwood, or can they find a meaningful place in corporations?

- The health care cost crisis looms large. Are more cutbacks in health benefits coming? Does industry expect government to intervene?

The need for authoritative knowledge about the ways that companies perceive and manage these issues is urgent. Anecdotal accounts of "excellent" companies or the "100 Best Firms" portray corporations as traveling the yellow brick road to Oz. By comparison, daily news stories about corporate cutbacks in staffing, training, and health insurance and about indifference to the needs of their workforce and society show firms to be shortsighted and self-serving. Both of these caricatures of business are misleading. This study of 406 corporations—large and small, public and private, from many different industries—presents a truer picture of corporate conduct today. It shows where business is at its best and at its worst—and all the points in between.

HUMAN CAPITAL

John Kenneth Galbraith declared in the late 1950s that America had successfully "solved the problem of production."[1] Another decade and a half of steady increases in productivity, rising standards of living, and dominance in the marketplace seemed to affirm such bullish confidence in U.S. industry. Since the mid-1970s, however, the nation has experienced declines in annual productivity growth, income stagnation among its wage earners, and a flood of imports from Japan, Pacific Rim nations, and Europe, coupled with an erosion in the U.S. share of world trade. Hence the problem of production has reappeared as a vital issue on the nation's agenda.

America's economic rise following WWII and its relative decline over the past fifteen years are clearly reflected in investments in physical capital, technology, and labor. Put simply, in the 60s and 70s the country and its industries invested a much larger proportion of the gross national product (GNP) than they do today in infrastructure, plant and equipment, research and development, and, importantly, working people. Currently, the United States lags in capital formation with country and companies burdened by heavy debt. Japan, as a comparison point, invests twice as much as America does as a percentage of GNP. Furthermore, the nation is losing ground in basic science and its applications. One indicator is that the percentage of U.S. patents granted to American corporations and citizens dropped from 62% to 53% from 1980 to 1990. Moreover, studies find that the United States is behind in the development of 33 out of 94 emerging growth technologies such as high-speed machining and genetic engineering.[2]

Education and Training

Our concern is with the nation's human resources. It was economist Theodore Schultz who first equated skills and knowledge with human capital and argued that investments in education and training were crucial to the nation's productivity growth.[3] Experts estimate that between 1929 and 1982, one-quarter to one-third of the increase in the nation's productive capacity was due to investments in public education. Furthermore, on-the-job learning accounted for over one-half of the productivity increase.[4] Michael Porter's studies confirm that industries that spend the most on employee development and training are typically the most competitive ones in every developed country in the world.[5] He goes on to argue that spending on education and training is decisive in a nation's competitive advantage. However, even as education levels continue to rise in the United States, there is growing concern that monies spent on students and public schools are not yielding a competitive return. U.S. high school students test two to three years behind their Japanese counterparts of the same age, and in the important areas of science and mathematics, U.S. school children rank near the bottom when compared with students in other developed countries.

This has placed new demands on companies to provide remedial and basic skill training for entry workers. The introduction of computers into offices and plants, changes in work designs and processes, and the move from *brawn* to *brain* industries in the United States all require a general "upskilling" of the workforce and massive retraining. Yet U.S. firms overall invest about ten times more in new plant and equipment than they do in education and training. And while they spend about 10% of the purchase price of machinery to maintain it, they spend less than 2% of the purchase price to maintain the skills of their workforce.[6]

Management and Organization

The value of human capital is not determined solely by how much money is spent on educating and training *individual* workers. Companies also invest to coordinate and integrate work in the production of goods and services. Itami calls these organizational skills "invisible assets."[7] Naturally, there is a tendency to associate them with top managers who design, direct, and oversee the organization. However, Dennison, in a series of case studies and surveys of the management practices in over a thousand companies, finds that high-performing companies coordinate work through extensive employee participation and shared cultural values.[8] This being so, he contends that efforts to increase employee participation and enhance the company culture all serve to increase the *collective* human capital of an enterprise.

Rensis Likert, pioneer in the field of human resource accounting, first argued that the return on investment in human resources is, to a large extent, influenced by practices within the workplace.[9] Longitudinal studies have since confirmed that investments in work redesign, participative decision-making, and ongoing career development all contribute to increased employee productivity and quality workmanship. These also translate into fewer accidents, less absenteeism, and lower rates of voluntary turnover.[10]

What is the value of American industry's collective human capital? Japanese politicians sneer that American workers are "too lazy" to compete while top U.S. executives are chided for getting "too much pay for too little performance." Stereotypes aside, there is worrisome evidence that U.S. firms have lagged elite competitors in the adoption of innovative work designs and management practices.[11] Moreover, cross-national surveys find that most U.S.-based companies do not have as much employee commitment or cultural cohesion as those based in Europe and Japan.[12] Studies by various special commissions and governmental agencies, by academics and research firms, and by businesses and unions make it plain that to remain competitive the country and its industries have to invest more monies and manage more wisely in the decade ahead. These, and other calls to action, have been heeded by some companies, in some instances, to the point that model efforts in employee training and development, and in work redesign, quality improvement, and work/family programs, are featured in books, periodicals, films, and seminars.

Still, every corporation makes its own decisions about how much to invest in human resources, which activities and employee needs to fund, and toward what ends. The purpose of this Laborforce 2000 study is to identify how U.S. companies appraise their current problems and opportunities, set their human resource priorities and directions, and prepare their employees and organizations for the future.

FRAMEWORK FOR THE STUDY

As a starting point, consider that human resource management is influenced by three *external* forces impinging on business today (see Exhibit 1.1). First, companies have to contend with massive and rapid changes in the marketplace. These include increased competition, demands for higher-quality products and services, earnings pressure from investors and Wall Street, and, in many cases, the need to establish or enhance an international supply, manufacturing, and distribution capability. This focuses

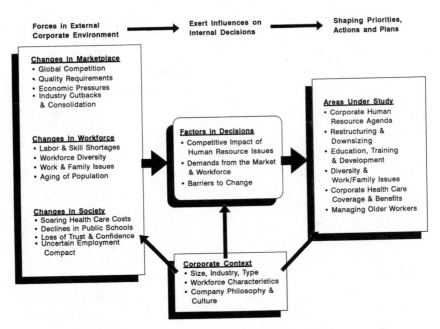

Exhibit 1.1   Laborforce 2000 study: Research framework.

our attention on how companies perceive the competitive impact of investing in people and the workplace.

Second, firms are being confronted with significant changes in their workforce, including the aging of the working population, the entry of more women and minorities into their ranks, and the need to help employees address work/family conflicts. These different employee groups are stakeholders, whose interests have to be considered whenever companies make human resource decisions.

Finally, companies have to respond to changes in society, such as the decline in the quality of schools, soaring health care costs, and a roster of environmental and social problems. To address these issues, firms must reach beyond their boundaries to schools and communities and often need guidance and assistance from policymakers at all levels of government.

Why do firms choose to make human resource investments? On what criteria do they base their decisions? This framework shows that human resource issues are assessed, calibrated, and translated into action via *internal* decision-making processes in a corporation. Here we examine how much importance executives assign to human resource issues and how they are being affected by changes in the labor market and their own workforce. We also look at how companies weigh competing priorities and deal with barriers to changing their practices, including the costs and a lack of support from management, employees, or unions.

Finally, the framework hones in on the specific human resource priorities, programs, and future plans that emerge from this decision-making context. Our aim is to identify what human resource issues companies take action on and why. A good example is the issue of staffing and training: Firms may choose to hire and train new graduates to fill future jobs, retrain and redeploy current staff, involve themselves in apprenticeship programs with local schools, or tap into the growing number of early retirees seeking full- or part-time work. Each strategy has pluses and minuses. Here we will see how firms appraise the relative value of each investment and what factors predict favoring one or some combination of options.

In addition to education and training, the other subjects covered in this Laborforce 2000 study are staffing and downsizing strategies, movements toward flexibility in response to work/family issues and increased diversity in the workforce, employment practices with regard to older workers, and what companies plan to do about health insurance for their workers. We will also examine the positioning and direction of human resource management within corporations.

Predictors of Human Resource Strategy

Naturally, the relevance of particular human resource issues and the perceived payoff of taking action vary from company to company. Old-line industrials, for example, are confronted by different competitive and workforce challenges than upstart biotech firms. A company's philosophy and culture also play a role in its human resource management. Hewlett Packard, for instance, hires engineers straight out of college and grooms them in the cooperative values that define the "HP Way." By contrast, Apollo Computer, a former competitor in the computing workstation business, paid top dollar for experienced talent and encouraged engineers to compete with one another for projects and staff. Here, then, are two firms in the same industry with very different human resource strategies. When Hewlett Packard acquired Apollo, insiders described it as the "Stepford Wives" meet the "Hell's Angels"![13]

Throughout this volume, contributors will be searching for patterns in the way that firms in different competitive environments, or who are more or less future-oriented, assess human resource issues and set their action agendas. Some firms, we will see, are boggled by competitive pressures and a myriad of business problems, to the point that they have adopted a strictly short-term, cost-cutting approach to managing people and running the business. Others appear to have found a workable middle ground between selective cutbacks in people and strategic investments in quality and productivity improvement. And still others have concluded that investing in human resources is essential to competitive advantage and long-term success.

What differentiates these firms? Three kinds of predictors of the human resource management will be examined.

Organizational Structure. Companies vary in their approach to human resource issues based on their industry, sales, number of employees, private versus public ownership, and international scale and scope. These structural factors are typically predictive of a company's general business strategies, technologies, and resource base. Here we will examine to what extent they also predict patterns of human resource management.

Workforce Composition. Another predictor is the composition of a company's workforce. Firms with a larger proportion of women or more college graduates, for instance, are likely to have somewhat different human resource priorities than firms employing more men or mostly blue-collar workers. Authors will examine how the makeup of a company—by age, gender, race, education, collar color, and so forth—factors into its human resource agenda.

Human Resource Orientation and Culture.   Finally, the framework shows that the ways in which companies see and act on human resource issues are influenced by their philosophy about change and by their company culture. Here we will compare firms that position themselves at the *cutting edge* of human resource management with those that lag behind as they wait for new ideas and practices to prove themselves. We will see that the top management in innovative firms seems to champion human resource improvements with the strong support of middle management, line workers, and, where present, unions. By contrast, laggards in this arena find top management indifferent and lack support from middle management and the ranks. They also see their company culture and values as inhospitable to innovation.

This introductory chapter examines in more depth the forces of change bearing on business and their impact on the sampled companies' outlook and strategy. The chapters that follow describe in detail how the firms in this cross-section respond to current human resource challenges and what they plan to do in the decade ahead.

Data Base and Sample

The data for this study come from face-to-face interviews with top human resource executives in a sample of 406 randomly selected Conference Board member companies. The interviews were conducted by staff from Louis Harris & Associates between September 3 and October 22, 1991, and lasted an average of sixty minutes. The interview began with several open-ended questions about issues facing the company and its response to them. These were followed by questions asking respondents to rate their human resource priorities and programs in the areas of interest.

As a follow-up to the interviews, companies were asked to complete a detailed questionnaire about their staffing profile, training and development expenditures, and other pertinent information needed for comparative analyses. A total of 304 of these self-completion forms were returned. Another 31 studied companies provided partial information via a telephone call or fax.

It is important to note that this sample is not representative of the full spectrum of U.S. or multinational corporations. First, the sample was drawn from Conference Board companies, a business research consortium composed of firms more interested in data on economic and organizational trends than perhaps the "typical" firm. Second, the sampled companies are larger than the norm in the United States (28% have more than 10,000 employees with the median being 4,050 domestic workers), have more total sales, and are more likely to have international plants and offices (one-third have substantial overseas sales, marketing, or production facilities).

The appendix at the end of this chapter provides full details on the composition of the sample. It shows that the sample represents manufacturing (35%), financial services (27%), and other service industries (27%) as well as firms in mining, construction, and elsewhere. Three out of every five firms are public companies. There is also variability in the staffing profile of the sampled firms. For instance, about half of the employees in these companies are white-collar workers (technical, professional, or clerical) and 17% are managers. The bulk hold high school diplomas and more than two-fifths have college degrees.

Interviewees were all experienced human resource professionals with 57% carrying the title of vice-president or above and another quarter holding the office of director or manager of human resources. Two-thirds reported to a CEO, executive vice-president, or senior vice-president in their firms. The average length of time that interviewees had been working in human resources was 19.4 years.

THE TOP STRATEGIC PRIORITIES OF CORPORATIONS

This survey of corporate human resource officials began with a simple question: "What would you say are the two or three dominant strategic issues—of any kind—that are of most concern or interest to your top management?" Their answers demonstrate the force of the marketplace on strategic priorities.

Global Competition

The most important strategic concern in corporations today is global competitiveness. Some 34% of the interviewees cited this as their firm's dominant concern. Its significance increases in larger companies (cited by 43% with over $1 billion in sales), those with substantial overseas operations, and those in the manufacturing sector.

Economic data amply justify this concern. During the 1980s, for instance, the United States imported $920 billion more in goods and services than it exported (although exports have increased in the early 1990s). Overall, the U.S. share of the total world export market has shrunk to 12% today from a base of 17% in the 1950s. The nation's share of world manufacturing, in particular, has declined with steady erosion in core industries like aerospace, chemicals, machine tools, and motor vehicles; in the high-tech fields of computers, electronic components, and telecommunications equipment; and even in pharmaceuticals. The United States remains the leading economic power in the world with twice the GNP of Japan, but the shifting balance of trade has had a substantial impact on domestic employment and earnings. *Business Week* estimates that the proportion of the U.S. workforce employed by U.S.-based multinationals declined 20% in the 1980s and that the real earnings of people employed outside the export sector dropped 6%.[14] The upshot is that, directly or indirectly, foreign competition has reduced the number of higher-paying U.S. jobs.

Certainly the public feels the press of competition. Nine of ten Americans polled by Louis Harris and Associates in early 1992 were very (57%) or somewhat (32%) concerned that U.S. industry is becoming less competitive in the global economy. Harris has reported that Americans are worried about becoming the third most important world economic power, after Japan and Germany. The Laborforce 2000 data show that the public's worries are echoed in the top echelons of corporations.

The Economy

The state of the economy and the current recession are a second strategic concern of note. These are the chief worry in privately held companies and smaller businesses (cited by 44% of firms with 1,000 or fewer employees, versus 31% overall). The recent recession has led to a loss of 1.1 million jobs in the manufacturing sector and has slowed growth dramatically in services. Moreover, traditional measures to combat recession, chiefly government spending, has been constrained by the daunting deficit, which has tripled in size since 1980. Indeed, federal spending on physical capital, nondefense R&D, and education declined from 9.5% to 6.5% from 1980 to 1990. As a result, the nation's productive infrastructure—from roads to research to schools—has suffered.

Cost Cutting

The economic environment has a direct bearing on corporate priorities. A third strategic concern among top executives in this sample is the need to cut costs (cited by 17%) and improve profitability (15%). This means trimming staff, reducing hiring, shutting down facilities, and making more use of consultants and the contingent workforce—points that are documented in this research. Of course, current cost cutting continues a wave of depressed wage increases and job elimination in manufacturing. The consequences ripple through the workforce: U.S. workers are putting in more hours and earning less take-home pay than a decade ago. To maintain their standard of living, American families have had to borrow more and increasingly depend, where feasible, on the earnings of two incomes. The data here demonstrate that economic pressures weigh heavily on top executives and influence their firms' strategic decisions. Almost all the firms studied have made cutbacks the past five years. The implication for human resource management is that many companies are being forced to do more with less.

Productivity and Quality

A final major concern of top executives encompasses quality (cited by 13%), productivity (10%), and customer service (10%). The need to make improvements in these areas proves to be an across-the-board issue, in companies of every size and in every sector of industry—again, with good reason. Growth in productivity in the U.S. service sector was anemic in the 1980s, and the overall rate of productivity increase per year in Japan and Germany has been higher than that of the United States in the past ten years. The public perception is that the quality of American goods and services has dropped precipitously over the past two decades, and "Made in the USA" no longer guarantees quality or durability in consumers' eyes.

Yet there are signs that American industry has responded to demands for increased productivity and quality. Manufacturing productivity, for example, rose substantially in the late 1980s and early 90s, the best performance since WWII. Firms like Xerox, Motorola, Corning, and General Electric have been literally made over and regained lost market share by putting a strong emphasis on quality improvement. The wide following given W. Edwards Deming and other quality gurus and the quest to win the Malcolm Baldrige quality prize finds many companies aspiring to world class standards in quality and efficiency. The Laborforce 2000 survey shows top executives still very much concerned with winning in these areas.

HOW CORPORATIONS RESPOND TO COMPETITIVE PRIORITIES

Companies have adopted four major strategies in response to their competitive environment (see Exhibit 1.2).

Restructuring and Downsizing

Over five of six companies studied undertook some form of downsizing over the past five years, the chief ones being to shut down some operating units, combine functions, impose a hiring freeze, or sell off business units. Nearly half laid off a substantial number of workers. All told, this eliminated an average of 12% of the jobs in downsized firms.

The 1980s witnessed widespread corporate restructuring. Nearly 40% of the Fortune 500 companies disappeared from the Big Board via mergers and acquisitions. Half of the nation's largest retailers, 60% of the largest transportation firms, and nearly all of the tire and rubber companies changed hands. The "feeding frenzy" has abated, but the merger wave is likely to continue through the 1990s as firms try to achieve the size and scope needed

Exhibit 1.2   How companies respond to competitive priorities.

Businesses are dealing with competitive priorities through downsizing and the computerization of the workplace. Percentage that	
Downsized in past few years	85
Introduced advanced computer technology in offices and plants	73
Many firms are involved in work redesign, employee involvement, and total quality programs. Percentage who have made *substantial* investments in	
Redesigned work processes	44
Employee involvement programs	39
Total quality programs	37
Global expansion is also a factor in competitiveness. Percentage with	
Over 20% of workforce outside the United States	23
Plans to open or expand plants or offices abroad in the early 1990s	57

to compete in the world market. Moreover, international deals—U.S. acquisitions overseas and foreign firms buying U.S. companies—are growing in number and prominence.

Two human resource issues related to restructuring and downsizing are considered in this study. First, what has been the impact of these corporate upheavals and cutbacks? Studies confirm that they have had a substantial impact on those who have been laid off or had their jobs eliminated. Estimates are that only one-quarter of the managers and professionals who lost their jobs in mergers or downsizings have been reemployed by large corporations, and the majority of those who have found new jobs have had to take 20–50% pay cuts.[15] But less is known about the impact of downsizing on corporate staffing plans, departmental operations, and the morale and motivation of the remaining workforce. We will see that there has been a substantial *downside* to downsizing among companies in this sample.

Second, have restructuring and downsizing become facts of life in corporate America? We will find that most firms plan to continue to reshape and resize themselves in the next five years. However, there is a stark difference between those who are cutting back feverishly to control costs and improve profits versus those who are aiming to increase productivity or gain competitive advantage. In the first instance, employees are simply "costs" to be reduced. In the second, people are "assets" to be retrained and redeployed. Our analysis shows that much hinges on the reasons behind restructuring and the human resource philosophies of the companies involved.

New Technology

Another competitive strategy adopted by three of four companies studied has been to make substantial investments in advanced computing systems for offices and plants in the late 80s and early 90s. Today the majority of the nation's office workers use computers on their jobs and nearly half of the factory workers operate computerized equipment ranging from numerical control machinery to robots. Although the computer revolution has not yet spread as dramatically or effectively into business as once hoped or yielded its projected economic payoff, many experts think that the 1990s will see industry realize substantial productivity gains from better network technology and new software developments.

Plainly some companies have used automation to replace labor. However, fears that computerization of the workplace would result in widespread job loss have proved largely unfounded except in segments of heavy industry, and the specter that jobs would become "deskilled" and workers turned into "robots" has also proved illusory. But this begs the question: Will firms have the talent available to develop, adapt, and operate increasingly "smart" technology? A shortage of scientists, engineers, technicians, and skilled blue-collar workers already racks a segment of American industry. Furthermore, the introduction of advanced technology requires a substantial upgrading of the skills of the American workforce. Here we will consider whether or not companies will be able to recruit the technical talent needed to capitalize on technology and can offer the training and retraining that blue-collar workers need to make them equal to the task.

Work Redesign, Quality Improvement, and Employee Involvement

A third strategy that companies have adopted to improve productivity and quality has involved massive change in the workplace. Some 44% of the firms in this sample redesigned their work processes in recent years to exploit new technologies and make use of new production and service delivery concepts. In some cases, companies have created *work cells,* where a team of production workers manufacture or assemble a whole product or where clerical and service workers team up to manage customer accounts. Other redesigns move technical and staff work—accounting, quality control, and personnel management—into hands of line workers who themselves may operate as a self-managing work team. In addition, nearly two out of every five firms (39%) undertook programs to promote employee involvement in work planning, problem solving, and decision making. These programs emphasize participatory management, through either joint labor-management committees or employee teams, and typically shift authority and responsibility down in the organization. Finally, nearly as many firms made significant investments in total quality management practices.

These innovative work redesigns and employee programs reverse long-standing traditions in organization and management. Since the onset of scientific management at the turn of the century, industry has divided complex tasks into simple operations, drawn clear lines between the authority of management and labor, and separated quality control from production work. The new programs, by contrast, put challenge and responsibility back into the job, promote cooperation between workers and management, and emphasize that quality has to be built into products and services, rather than checked and corrected later on. Manufacturing companies have been the leaders in implementing these programs, followed by financial service firms. The remainder of the service industry lags behind.[16] Here we will examine the different factors that predict corporate activity in work redesign, total quality management, and employee involvement and their implications for employee training and retraining.

Global Expansion

Global expansion is a fourth way that firms are responding to competitive challenges. Nearly one out of every four of the companies in this study has over 20% of their workforce located outside the United States. Looking ahead, over half report that they are very likely (37%) or somewhat likely (16%) to expand their overseas operations in the near future.

Significantly, the chief reasons companies give for the current overseas activity and planned expansion are to be global competitors and to be closer to markets. Lower labor and transportation costs are a consideration for some manufacturing firms as well. By comparison, taxes, government regulation, and the skills and work ethic of foreign versus U.S. employees are not considered very important criteria in global expansion (see Exhibit 1.3).

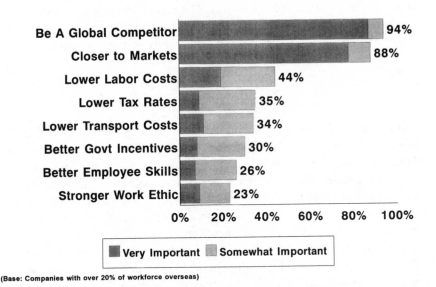

(Base: Companies with over 20% of workforce overseas)

Exhibit 1.3   Why companies employ people in other countries.

Putting corporate priorities and strategies together, it seems that top companies have tried to extend their reach and improve productivity and quality, while all the time controlling costs. The winning formula involves strategically motivated restructuring and downsizing coupled with introducing advanced computing systems, redesigning work processes, incorporating quality management techniques, and involving employees at all levels in decision making. Yet it was baseball manager cum philosopher Casey Stengel who noted, "If you ain't got no animals, you ain't got no zoo." The question at hand is whether or not firms will have the employee talent and managerial know-how to make these strategies pay off.

AN EMERGING PRIORITY: THE QUALITY OF THE WORKFORCE

One in five human resource executives interviewed regards the caliber of the workforce and availability of qualified people as dominant concerns of their top management. This figure increases to 33% in companies that employ a highly educated workforce (over 50% college graduates). Furthermore, human resource managers themselves rate this as their top priority in the next five years.

However, there are complex changes in the labormarket facing businesses in the United States as well as abroad. The success of companies that try to produce *faster, better, and cheaper* depends, to a large extent, on how they respond to changes in the availability and quality of the workforce.

Labor Shortages

The Bureau of Labor Statistics projects that the U.S. laborforce will grow slowly in the 90s. The big growth decades of the 70s (19% increase in the workforce) and 80s (29% increase) saw baby boomers making their way into corporations. With the appearance of the "baby bust" generation, the workforce will grow only by 13% in the 90s, even accounting for immigration. This has led to the prediction that industries will face labor shortages in entry level workers in 90s and thereafter.

Although labor shortages are evident in selected small businesses and services where Help Wanted notices abound, predictions of widespread shortages have proved inaccurate. On the contrary, the nation has experienced job drought.[17] The Fortune 500 industrial companies employ 3.7 million fewer workers today than 10 years ago, a loss of about one job in four. Moreover, forecasters predict extensive downsizing in the service sector in the 1990s.

A combination of extensive downsizing coupled with slowdowns in hiring has forestalled labor shortage problems for most companies in this sample. Only one out of every six regards labor shortages as a serious problem today and some 80% expect to be able to pay enough to attract the qualified job entrants they need in the next five years. A recent study of the hiring outlook of large U.S.-based multinationals came to this same conclusion.[18] However, that study found multinationals deeply concerned about a shortage of skilled workers for technical positions. Such concerns prove to be broader-based in the Laborforce 2000 sample.

Skill Shortages

Indeed, some 37% of the companies studied report that they have had trouble recruiting technical staff the past few years. And 30% have had difficulties recruiting skilled labor. As an example, New York–based Chemical Bank has had to interview 40 job applicants for every 1 found suitable for training as a bank teller. And NYNEX has had to test 60,000 applicants to fill 3,000 open positions.[19] The mismatch between the high-skill demands of today's jobs and the qualifications of job applicants is well documented in the Labor Department/Hudson Institute's Workforce 2000 study.[20] That study projects that the bulk of jobs created in the 1990s will require more education of jobholders than current ones and higher levels of language, math, and reasoning skills. Meanwhile, the educational preparation of high school and college graduates is declining, and the percentage of students graduating with degrees in science and engineering is falling well behind demand.

Many firms surveyed in our study anticipate that a shortage of skilled talent will make it difficult to recruit for selected positions (see Exhibit 1.4). Three of four firms that employ scientists and engineers say it will be very (26%) or somewhat (48%) difficult to find and recruit them. And over half say it will be very (15%) or somewhat (40%) difficult to hire skilled blue-collar workers. These projected shortages are most acute in manufacturing firms.

About half the sampled companies also anticipate problems in recruiting top managers and clerical and office workers. This is most pronounced in financial and nonfinancial service businesses. There is even some level of

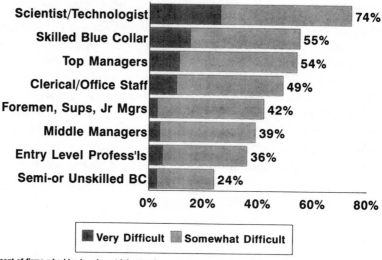

Exhibit 1.4   Difficulties finding qualified people for jobs.

concern about finding qualified supervisors, middle managers, and entry level professionals during the mid-90s among segments of the sample.

Skill shortages are recognized as a pressing human resource issue in companies in this study. And the stakes are high: Nearly half of the companies having trouble recruiting qualified people expect that productivity will suffer if they cannot find the right people, and 37% say that work quality will decline (see Exhibit 1.5). Smaller firms (65% of them) are especially vulnerable on these counts and report that they are most likely to aggressively expand

Exhibit 1.5   Consequences of not finding the the right people for jobs. (Base: Firms that have trouble recruiting.)

	Percentage That Project This Problem
Lower productivity	49
Reduced product quality	37
Higher training costs	28
Morale problems	22
Higher labor costs	21

their recruiting and training efforts. Other potential problems cited include lower morale, higher labor costs, and higher turnover, all contributing to a general lack of competitiveness in the marketplace.

The larger conclusion from these findings is that it is not so much a shortage of people but a *skills gap* that is of concern to industry. Firms need more mental rather than manual labor. Yet the two issues are not fully separable: With fewer new entrants to the workforce, companies will be forced to dig deeper into the less well educated and trained segments of the workforce to fill their ranks. It is questionable, then, whether or not the expectation of eight in ten companies that they can pay enough to attract qualified people will prove realistic. Thus we will explore, in some depth, corporate plans to reduce the skills gap in their workforce.

THE CHANGING CONTOURS OF THE WORKFORCE

Any discussion of the availability and quality of the workforce must also take into account projected changes in the makeup of the working population in the years ahead.

Workforce Diversity

Although the workforce overall will grow slowly over the 1990s, African-Americans, Hispanics, and Asians will be the faster-growing groups in the employee mix. African-Americans are expected to account for 13% of the new entrants to the laborforce, Asians and Native Americans for 6%, and Hispanics for nearly 16%, to the point that nonwhites will account for roughly 27% of the U.S. workforce by the year 2005. Interestingly, African-American women will outnumber African-American men in the laborforce by the turn of the century. The net result is that the white (non-Hispanic) share of the laborforce is projected to decline from 78.5% to 73% from 1990 to 2005.

Increased minority participation raises a key issue for industry: Will companies hire more women and minorities into higher-paying, higher-status jobs, or will they be content with the status quo? Over one-third of the new jobs created in the 1990s will go to American-born minorities. Yet, as things stand, a far larger proportion of minorities than whites, as a result of education and opportunity, are slotted into lesser paying service jobs. It is likely, as well, that minorities will constitute a disproportionate share of the nation's unemployed. Some 46% of the companies sampled in this study expect there to be a significant increase in the number of minority women they employ in the next five years, and 36% anticipate a significant increase in the number of minority men. But there are, as we will see, notable differences in the ways in which the sampled companies approach the issue raised by increased diversity. Some firms regard it as an *affirmative action* issue; others believe it can be handled as simply part of *good management*; while still others see learning to capitalize on diversity as a *competitive opportunity* for their businesses. This has a bearing on whether or not companies institute training programs for managers and take other measures to assist in the entry and assimilation of minorities.

Another important change in the workforce is the steady increase in the number of working women. Women will constitute nearly three-fifths of the new entrants to the workforce in the 90s and by 2000 will account for 47% of all employed Americans. This compares to 33% in 1960. Furthermore, women entering the workforce in the 90s will be as well educated as men. While diversity programs address the needs of working women as well as minorities, questions about the significance of the *glass ceiling* and other barriers to the employment of women in traditionally male jobs remain of concern. Hence these issues, and women's demands for equal work and equal pay, are likely to move up the corporate human resource agenda in this decade.

More Working Parents

The dramatic rise in employment of women in the workforce means an increase in the number of working parents. Nearly three-fourths of employed women are of childbearing age, and 60% have school-age kids. In turn, nearly 60% of employed men have wives who work. This makes work and family issues a matter of concern to more and more couples in America.

Furthermore, divorces and changes in life-style have increased the number of single working parents in the workforce. About 25% of children in the nation live in single-parent homes, and estimates are that three out of every five children will do so for a significant period of time before they are age 18. Polls show that, whether workers are heading one-provider or two-provider households, an ever-increasing number of them want, need, and expect their employers to offer them more flexible work schedules and help and support

Worker Desires for Flexible Work Arrangements

Ron Bass

A 1991 survey of U.S. office workers reveals that more flexible work arrangements are deemed quite important by many in the workforce:

	Percentage Who Rate Very or Somewhat Important
Flexible hours	81
Financial support or child care facilities	51
Spend some work hours at home, not at office	46
Chance to work part-time	39
Chance to job share	32

In all instances, there was a large gap between the number of office workers rating a flexible arrangement as important and the number who had such flexibility in their workplace.

In a 1990 Harris survey of women executives, nearly one-third said that the failure of their company to recognize women's special family needs was an obstacle to the success of women executives in their firm.

Source: The Steelcase Office Environment Index. Louis Harris and Associates, 1991.

in caring for their children when they are at work. Here we will see what companies are doing in response.

An Aging Workforce

Finally, the U.S. workforce is aging. The segment of the workforce that is age 50 and older will grow faster than any other age group in the 1990s as the first wave of baby boomers matures. In addition, the life span of adults is expected to increase over the next decades meaning that, if current trends continue, more and more older workers will *want* to remain employed in their companies or else find another job. Furthermore, trends in real earnings, pensions, and health insurance coverage imply that older people will simply *need* to work longer. These trends fly in the face of the corporate downsizings that have led to the early retirement of large numbers of workers age 50 and older. Here we will consider what companies are doing in the way of "phased retirement" and how many are creating new career tracks or part-time work options for older workers whose skills may be needed in decades hence that portend slower growth and maybe even labor shortages in certain disciplines and regions of the country.

CHANGES IN SOCIETY

There are also changes in society that must be factored into a company's decision-making process. Several have a direct bearing on human resource management.

Health Care Costs

The United States spends nearly 13% of its gross domestic product on health care: Far more than Europe and Japan spend. Business spending on health insurance and care has increased from 14% of corporate after-tax profits in 1965 to 100% in recent years. Not surprisingly, we will see that health care costs are a major competitive concern among companies in this sample.

Cost containment has led to increases in the employee share of health care costs and an emphasis on having them join managed-care programs—points detailed in this study. But there are also 36 million Americans, two-thirds of them in families with the head of the household holding a full-time job, who have no health insurance. Of interest, then, is companies' outlook on the role of government in the health care coverage and cost containment equations.

Education

We have highlighted the skills gap facing American industry. A closer look at the failings of our educational system reveals that 25% of the nation's high school graduates read at the eighth-grade level while 50% of high school science and mathematics teachers are not qualified. Indeed, while industry offers more "knowledge-intensive" jobs, today's high school graduates score one year behind graduates of the class of 1966.

Harris surveys capture the public's concern with the educational system. Over three-fourths (79%) believe that how well the United States educates its laborforce will make a major difference in whether or not America maintains a leading economic position in the world. In turn, nine-tenths say that it is very (61%) or somewhat (29%) important for business to help fund public schools, provide equipment, and have businesspeople serve as mentors to students. Here we will see how many corporations have responded to this outcry and which ones take an active role in public schooling.

Public Views on Problems in the Public Schools

Ron Bass

A 1991 Harris poll reveals that the American public is extremely concerned about the current state of the educational system. When asked how well they would rate teaching and helping students to learn the skills needed to hold down a job, only 30% said schools were doing an excellent or pretty good job. Two-thirds said schools were doing only fair or poor in this regard. Other questions reveal just as much doubt about the educational system:

How good a job are schools of this country doing in teaching and helping students	Percentage Responding Only Fair or Poor
To learn to solve complex problems?	76
To really understand math, science, and technology and be able to use what they know?	67
To read, write, and reason well?	64
To learn how to communicate well and work successfully with other people?	60

Source: School Reform: Public Perceptions. Louis Harris and Associates, 1991.

Declining Confidence and Trust

Next there is the matter of employees' attitudes toward their employers. Longitudinal Harris surveys show there has been a steady worsening of public attitudes about business leaders. Some 55% had high levels of confidence in business leaders in 1966, compared with 29% in 1973, 21% as recently as 1987, and 11% today. Although public confidence in the people running most institutions—including colleges, the government, and television news—has dropped considerably since 1966, confidence in no other institution has declined as much as confidence in business.

Rising levels of cynicism in the workforce are widely documented.[21] Over half of the American public believes that the leaders of big business are more interested in their own power and status than in the needs of their company or their workforce. Nearly as many mistrust their own company executives and doubt the truth of what they are told by their employers.

This is one backdrop against which companies must make their human resource decisions. Certainly it makes it difficult for managers to have an open dialogue among employees about problems, tradeoffs, and constraints. It also makes cutbacks suspect, however economically justifiable, and casts doubts on any newly proposed investment, whether in employee training, total quality management, or even child care assistance.

The Changing Employment Compact

Finally, there are questions of the employment compact underlying human resource decisions. Plainly, notions of cradle-to-grave job security have been abandoned by most employers in this study and the broad base of American industry. And expectations of what constitutes a fair day's pay for a fair day's work have also been adjusted. Accordingly, we will ask about how downsizing and reductions in health insurance have affected employees in the sampled companies. More broadly, we will also discuss how human resource investments and actions taken by these firms affect the compact between employer and employee.

Whereas the 80s gave society young urban professionals who were upwardly mobile (yuppies), the 90s may offer downwardly mobile urban professionals (dumpies). It seems doubtful, in the decade we have entered, that corporations will offer as many employees the kinds of pay increases and benefits that they need to purchase homes, provide for their children's education, or satisfy their full range of consumer aspirations.

Trust and Confidence in Companies

Philip Mirvis and Donald Kanter

A 1990 national survey administered by Diagnostic Research Inc. of a sample of 1,115 employed adults in the United States revealed widespread cynicism about the leaders of big business. The survey also showed that many employed persons mistrust the management of their own companies and feel that they are not being treated fairly.

	Percentage Who Agree	Percentage Who Disagree
Management of my company will take advantage of you if given a chance.	49	28
I often doubt the truth of what management of my company tell us.	41	33
Management of my company never lets employees know the real reasons behind decisions that affect them.	39	36
Management of my company is more interested in profits than in people.	36	40
Management of my company makes an unfair salary versus the average employee.	34	40

Compared with data collected on worker attitudes in the early 1980s, the current findings show even more doubts about the trustworthiness of management.

Source: Diagnostic Research, Inc. Full study, based on prior data, reported in Kanter, D. L., and Mirvis, P. H., 1989. The cynical Americans. San Francisco: Jossey-Bass.

Still, very few of the companies sampled find that the wage expectations of high school or college graduates will prevent them from hiring as many as they need. Interestingly, however, nearly one-third say that the skyrocketing wage expectations of MBAs may limit their employment (see Exhibit 1.6). This is one group, then, that may face a decade of downward mobility.

Many firms, as we will see, are also planning to limit the health insurance coverage offered to retirees and to hire more contingent workers without health insurance. Many also expect to downsize further. Does this portend more of a dog-eat-dog atmosphere within companies? Or are there strategies

Exhibit 1.6 Whether wage expectations of graduates prevent companies from hiring as many as needed. (Base: Percentage with a firm opinion.)

	Prevent Hiring as Many as Needed	
Wage expectations of	No (%)	Yes (%)
High school graduates	96	4
College graduates	87	13
MBAs	68	32

and practices that at least provide a common ground between people and their firms? Each author speaks to how projected changes in human resource management will affect employees—for better or worse.

THE COMPETITIVE IMPACT OF HUMAN RESOURCE ISSUES

To conclude this overview of human resource issues facing industry, consider how the sampled companies rate the competitive impact of the subjects under study (see Exhibit 1.7).

- More than nine out of every ten companies studied say that the cost of health insurance has an impact on their competitiveness. The impact is most pronounced in larger companies and those in the manufacturing sector.

- Eight out of ten say that the poor quality of education of entry workers has competitive implications. Again, this is most notable in larger employers and those having trouble recruiting.

- Some eight out of ten also say that the family responsibilities of workers have competitive implications. This is most pronounced in firms employing a larger percentage of women workers.

- Nearly six out of ten are concerned with the poor work attitudes of entry workers. Interestingly, this concern is most prominent in smaller employers.

- Over half say that the aging of the laborforce has competitive implications—most notably in firms employing a larger percentage of workers over age 50.

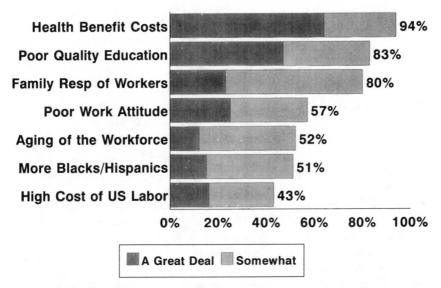

Exhibit 1.7 Human resources issues: Impact on competitiveness.

- About half are concerned with the impact of the growing proportion of African-Americans and Hispanics in the laborforce. No differences were found across firms in this regard.
- Finally, some 43% say that the high cost of U.S. labor relative to that in other countries has a bearing on competitiveness—even more so in highly unionized manufacturing firms that employ a larger proportion of blue-collar and older workers.

Clearly this makes for a broad agenda of issues competing for the attention of business and its leadership in the 90s. Exhibit 1.8 highlights the key managerial and policy implications of each human resource issue under study. In the chapters that follow, the contributors consider how companies are responding to these issues and appraise the companies against their tested experience.

The chapters show that some firms, at the leading edge of innovation and experimentation, have ideas, models, and projects underway that can serve as benchmarks to forward-looking businesses. Others, by comparison, are fixated on short-term problems, hobbled by unimaginative management, and threatened by change. Who leads? Who lags? Each expert looks at a profile of leaders and laggards and at what predicts leadership on specific human resource issues.

Exhibit 1.8 Human resource issues: Implications for action.

Human Resource Issues	Implications for Action
Costs of health benefits	Cost containment: higher deductibles and premiums, managed care programs; look for government interventions.
Poor quality of education among new job applicants	Remedial employee education and training; involvement in schools, apprenticeships.
Family responsibilities of workers	Flexible schedules and employment options; child and elder care assistance.
Poor work attitudes of entry level job applicants	Mentoring, careful supervision, and corporate socialization.
Aging of the workforce	Maintenance of skill base; retraining/redeployment; part-time work options, phased retirement.
Growing proportion of African-Americans and Hispanics in workforce	Valuing diversity programs; mentoring, career management.
High cost of U.S. labor relative to other countries	Careful staffing, cost containment, productivity and quality improvement.

Although much of the emphasis is on fact-finding, the contributors also identify the best practices of American business and offer recommendations—addressed to top executives, human resource managers, and policymakers—about what *should be* on the corporate agenda and why. In some areas, they call for the continued development of current strategies. In others, they make the case for a complete overhaul of management outlooks and company human resource practices. What is at stake, they contend, is the long-term viability of many firms as well as the employment prospects and job satisfaction of large segments of the American workforce.

To the extent that the current sample is representative of corporate opinion, business is ripe for fresh thinking. Of the 406 companies studied, three in every four (77%) said that they have to make major changes in their human resource policies to attract, retain, and motivate the qualified people they need in the 90s.

NOTES

1. Galbraith, J. K. 1958. *The new industrial state.* Boston: Houghton Mifflin.
2. Stewart, T. A. 1991. The new American century. *Fortune,* Spring/Summer, 12–23.

3. Schultz, T. W. 1962. Reflections on investment in man. *Journal of Political Economy* 70 (5): 1–8.

4. Carnevale, A. P. 1989. The learning enterprise. *Training and Development Journal* 58, 64–92.

5. Porter, M. 1990. *The competitive advantage of nations.* New York: Free Press.

6. Reich, R. B. 1991. *The work of nations: Preparing ourselves for 21st century capitalism.* New York: Alfred A. Knopf.

7. Itami, H. 1986. *Mobilizing invisible assets.* Cambridge, MA: Harvard University Press.

8. Denison, D. R. 1991. Organizational culture and "collective" human capital. In *Socioeconomics: Toward a new synthesis,* ed. A. Etzioni and P. R. Lawrence, 263–274. London: M. E. Sharpe.

9. Likert, R. 1967. *The human organization: Its management and value.* New York: McGraw-Hill.

10. Mirvis, P. H., and Macy, B. A. 1976. Accounting for costs and benefits of human resource development programs. *Organizations, Accounting and Society* 1: 179–194; Mirvis, P. H., and Macy, B. A. 1983. Assessing the costs and benefits of organization change program. In *Assessing organizational change,* ed. S. E. Seashore, E. E. Lawler, P. H. Mirvis, and C. Cammann. New York: Wiley Interscience.

11. Cole, R. 1982. Diffusion of participatory work structures in Japan, Sweden, and the United States. In *Change in organizations,* ed. P. S. Goodman. San Francisco: Jossey-Bass.

12. Wolff, M. 1992. *Where we stand.* New York: Michael Wolff & Co.

13. Mirvis, P. H., and Marks, M. L. 1992. *Managing the merger.* Englewood Cliffs, NJ: Prentice-Hall.

14. *BusinessWeek.* 1990. Can you compete? December 17, 62–93.

15. *BusinessWeek.* 1992. Downward mobility, March 23, 56–63.

16. Lawler, E. E., Mohrman, S. A., and Ledford, G. E. 1992. *Employee involvement and total quality management: Practices and results in Fortune 1000 companies.* San Francisco: Jossey-Bass.

17. O'Reilly, B. 1992. The job drought. *Fortune,* August 24, 62–74.

18. Loveman, G. W., and Gabarro, J. J. 1991. The managerial implications of changing workforce demographics: A scoping study. *Human Resource Management* 30 (1): 7–29.

19. *BusinessWeek.* 1988. Needed: Human capital, September 19, 100–141.

20. Johnston, W. B., and Packer, A. E. 1987. *Workforce 2000.* Indianapolis, IN: Hudson Institute.

21. Kanter, D. A., and Mirvis, P. H. 1989. *The cynical Americans.* San Francisco: Jossey-Bass.

APPENDIX: CHARACTERISTICS OF THE SAMPLE

Profile of Organizations		Profile of Workforce	
Primary Industry $n = 406$		**Gender of Workforce** $n = 299$	
Manufacturing	35%	Women	45%
Financial services	27	Men	55
Other services	27		
Other/Not sure	11	**Age of Workforce** $n = 289$	
		24 years or under	10%
Annual Sales $n = 406$		25–39 years old	43
$100 million or less	14%	40–49 years old	27
$101 million–$250 million	7	50–59 years old	15
$251 million–$500 million	8	60 years and over	5
$501 million–$1 billion	11		
Over $1 billion	43	**Race of Workforce** $n = 293$	
No answer	17	White	78%
		Black	12
Number of U.S. Employees		Hispanic	6
$n = 335$		Asian-American	4
1,000 or less	23%	Other	—
1,001–5,000	31		
5,001–10,000	16	**College Grads in Workforce**	
Over 10,001	28	$n = 294$	
Not sure	2	25% or less	21%
		26%–50%	28
Ownership of Company		51%–75%	14
$n = 322$		75%–100%	10
Public	61%	Not sure	27
Privately held	34		
Not sure/No response	5	**Unionization of Workforce**	
		$n = 158$	
Substantial Overseas Sales,		25% or less	43%
Marketing, or Distribution		26%–50%	32
Facilities $n = 296$		51%–75%	18
Yes	35%	76%–100%	4
No	62	Not sure	3
Not sure/No response	3		
		Contingent Workforce $n = 292$	
Positions in Workforce $n = 301$		5% or less	59%
Managers	17%	6%–10%	12
White collar	50	11%–15%	8
Skilled blue collar	22	16% or more	10
Unskilled blue collar	11	Not sure	11

2

Strategic Human Resource Management

Edward E. Lawler III, Susan G. Cohen, and Lei Chang

The strategic management of human resources is an important idea whose time has come. Many of the critical competitive issues facing business require changes in traditional human resource policies, practices, and capabilities. Chapter 1 has shown that over three-fourths of the companies in this study agree that they must make major changes in order to attract, motivate, and retain a quality workforce. But talk is cheap. In this chapter we examine to what extent corporations are truly linking their business and human resource strategies.

Developing an appropriate human resource direction in an organization is a complex process. The actions of competitors, demands from customers and the marketplace, and changes in organizational structure and technology all can and should influence staffing, training, and compensation decisions within a corporation. Changes in the workforce and changes in the job mix within a firm need to come into play. In addition, management values and the company culture can affect how a company decides to compete and whether its organizational design and human resource management practices are used to advance business strategies.

Historically, few corporations based in the United States have used human resource management as a source of competitive advantage.[1] Instead they

31

have relied on technology, financial acumen, and access to markets.[2] As a result, the human resource department has not typically played a key role in the business. Nor have U.S. firms been particularly change-oriented or innovative in managing people. Today, however, foreign competitors match U.S. technology and are making gains in marketing strength. Given demands for high quality, cost competitiveness, and faster time to market, how organizations manage their human resources may become the key difference between economic success and failure.

Certainly the role of the human resource department has changed over time. The old-line personnel department was charged with processing people and paperwork. It handled routine employment functions and lacked corporate influence. Over the past some twenty years, however, personnel work has become more professionalized. Specialists in compensation, benefits, legal matters, and employee relations now staff the function. Moreover, many personnel departments have been renamed *human resource* departments, reflecting an increased awareness of the monies spent on employees. On the one hand, these developments have given the human resource department a major responsibility in controlling labor costs, chiefly through salaries and benefits. On the other, they have given it a role in developing human assets through recruiting, training, and career development. Still, the work of the human resource department is often treated as separate from mainline management. And in many cases, "people programs" do not address central needs of the business.

Increasingly, experts contend that human resource management is key to competitive advantage. Indeed, the argument has been made that because new human resource management practices are hard to duplicate, they offer a business the chance to gain a significant and lasting competitive advantage.[3] To compete successfully through human resource management, however, requires a further shift in the operations of human resource departments and in the attitudes of management. It means that a company's business and human resource strategies must be in sync. It also means that human resource managers need to be *partners* with line managers in guiding the business.

Some studies of the outlooks of human resource officials, academicians, and consultants show that the human resource department is evolving from an era of functional specialization to such a partnership model.[4] But a closer look at human resource management today will show where things stand: To what extent are human resource departments becoming strategic partners in the management of the business? Changing their practices to adjust to the realities of global competition? Adapting to changes in the U.S. domestic workforce in order to increase organizational effectiveness? When does rhetoric match reality? And critically, are there signs that corporate human resource management is adding to competitive advantage?

The Laborforce 2000 survey of 406 human resource (HR) executives enables us to address these questions. The first section of this chapter compares the strategic priorities of businesses with the responsibilities of human resource departments. We next highlight the factors that influence human resource policies and attitudes and barriers to changing these policies and attitudes. Then we compare the practices of human resource innovators with the practices of those organizations that lag behind. The conclusion explores firms' readiness to deal with current laborforce issues and examines their plans for the future.

BUSINESS STRATEGIES VERSUS HUMAN RESOURCE PRIORITIES

The introductory chapter showed that global competition and the state of the economy are the two most significant strategic concerns of the top management in companies in this sample. Nested within these strategic concerns are needs to control costs and improve profitability; to improve productivity, quality, and customer service; and to ensure the caliber of a company's workforce. Meeting these needs is central to organizational effectiveness and hinge on management's ability to organize and utilize people.

Research shows that organizational effectiveness is critically influenced by human resource (HR) management practices. Improvements in productivity, quality, and customer satisfaction do not occur simply through changes in accounting systems or technology; rather they typically depend on changes in multiple management systems. Changes in staffing, training, and compensation form an integral part of a coordinated change effort. Because HR management systems are critical drivers of behavior, they must be in alignment with other management systems. Otherwise, change efforts are met with resistance and often fail. In short, it is very difficult to improve organizational performance without paying attention to HR management. Accordingly, the HR department must be a central player in a company's competitive efforts.

Human Resource Priorities

One test of the strategic orientation of a human resource department is the degree to which it assumes responsibility for the top priorities of the organization. It is an indicator of how central is the role of the department in overall operations. After naming the most significant strategic issues, survey respondents were asked, "which, if any, of these issues are a major responsibility of the human resource department?"

Exhibit 2.1 contrasts top executives' central priorities with responsibilities of the HR department at their firms. Note the substantial gap between management's concern with competition and the current recession and the

Exhibit 2.1   Most important competitive issues in corporations: Top management views versus HR department responsibilities.

	Top Management (%)	Human Resources (%)
Key Issues		
Competition/Global competitiveness	34	6
Economy/Recession	31	5
Caliber of workforce	20	15
Cost management	17	6
Profitability	15	4
Quality control	13	4
Productivity	10	4
Customer satisfaction	10	4
Other Mentions		
Government regulation	14	4
Medical benefits	13	7
Technology	6	2
Changing business climate	6	1
Management development	3	1
Acquisition/Buyout	3	1
Workforce diversity	3	2
Employee motivation	3	3
Restructuring	3	2
None	—	21
Not sure	—	6

finding that few HR departments consider them to be major responsibilities. It can be argued, of course, that the HR function is not chartered with primary responsibility for global strategy and the corporate financial plan. However, nearly one-third of the companies cite improved quality, productivity, and customer service as the chief competitive concerns of top executives. By contrast, only 12% of the HR executives regard them as a major responsibility of their department.

The gap narrows when it comes to the availability and caliber of the workforce. Some 20% of the companies see workforce caliber as a dominant concern of top executives, and 15% of the human resource departments identify it as a major responsibility. This agreement is hardly surprising given that selection, training, and development are the historic responsibilities of the human resource department. But note that 21% see no relationship between the priorities of top executives and the work of the HR department, and another 6% are not sure where the HR function fits into company strategy. This means that over one out of every four HR departments says that *none* of their company's business strategies are a major responsibility of their department.

What emerges is a picture of the HR department as disconnected from mainline business concerns in the majority of the companies studied. Even when it comes to such traditional personnel areas as cost containment, medical benefit costs, and the impact of regulation, there is a gap between management's concerns and the responsibilities of the HR department.

Interestingly, firms in the manufacturing sector seem to have much more alignment between the executive and HR priorities. This fits with research that shows U.S. manufacturers' consensus about the importance of human resources in global competitiveness and intent to compete through employee involvement and total quality management. No doubt, offshore competition is one stimulus to such innovation: Manufacturers in the United States have also made it a point to study the HR practices of their Japanese and European competitors, and many have understood the need to connect HR efforts to business strategies. The manufacturing sector may be leading the way in strategic human resource management.

Differences in company size, the nature of the workforce, public versus private ownership, and geographical location were not predictive of the strategic fit between the HR department and the business. Many possible explanations exist for these findings. For instance, a pervasive emphasis on cutbacks and cost cutting dominates some companies in the sample. This often puts human resources in a reactive mode—to simply implement downsizing decisions and deal with the fallout. Increased specialization also may hamper the HR department's overall strategic posture. Finally, we see a smattering of departments assuming major responsibility for technology implementation, diversity programs, employee motivation efforts, and the integration of acquisitions. This situation suggests that few HR departments have an integrated mission to serve the needs of the business.

The Best Strategic Human Resources Decision

Further evidence of the diffuse mission of human resource departments emerges when respondents identify the best strategic HR decision that their company made to prepare itself for the mid-90s (see Exhibit 2.2). Over 20% identified changes and improvements to benefit and compensation plans as their best decision. These included installing flexible benefit plans, tying pay to performance, and creating new pay systems. Other frequently cited decisions were investments in training and development (14%), restructuring or reorganizing management (10%), and employee participation and empowerment (7%).

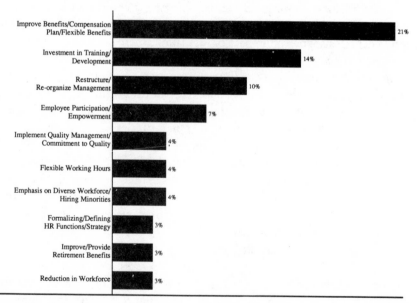

Exhibit 2.2   The best strategic HR decision made by companies to prepare them for the mid-90s.

We cannot determine to what extent these decisions fit into a coherent strategic thrust in the companies studied. Improvements in pay and benefits, and in training and development, can have strategic intent but also fall within the traditional purview of HR departments. Involvement in organizational restructuring and in employee empowerment can be strategically oriented, but only a modest number of firms cited them as key competitive decisions. Indeed, what is most notable is that HR executives point to many and varied decisions as emblematic of the "best" ones their company made to prepare itself for the next few years. This reinforces the point that specialized contributions drive HR activity in the majority of surveyed firms. This "programmatic" approach to HR management often falls short when it is not aligned with the central priorities of the business.

Is Human Resources a Strategic Partner?

Based on these findings, we can conclude only that most HR departments have a long way to go before they become business partners in the enterprise. Clearly, many do not see productivity, customer satisfaction, and quality improvements as major responsibilities. Nor is there a strong strategic coherence to human resource programs and initiatives in many firms. Apparently, human resources is asked to recruit and hire qualified employees but is not systematically involved in how they are managed. Hence there is a real gap between the need for more strategic management of employees and the ability of the HR department to deliver. Are firms taking actions to bridge this gap?

CLOSING THE HR DEPARTMENT'S PERFORMANCE GAP

It is widely accepted in organization theory that senior-level management leads significant corporate change. Thus, high-level attention to human resource concerns elevates their importance and can give a boost to the HR department. In response to a question about upper management's time and energy devoted to human resource issues over the preceding five years, 86% of the respondents said that their company's upper management had increased its involvement, with half citing a significant increase (see Exhibit 2.3). This suggests that HR issues are gaining in prominence and that more

Exhibit 2.3   Upper management's time and energy devoted to HR issues.

	Percentage of Companies
Increased significantly	51
Increased somewhat	35
Stayed the same	11
Decreased	1
Not sure	1

companies view people as a competitive factor. The increased activism of corporate executives in this area could be a step toward transforming the role of human resources.

We found some notable differences between firms in the involvement of senior executives:

- Senior-level managers from companies employing over 10,000 people were more likely to have significantly increased their time and energy on human resource issues than those from smaller firms.

- Senior managers from companies expecting changes in their workforce were also more likely to have significantly increased their involvement, when compared with managers whose firms expect their workforce to remain stable.

Specifically, 61% of the companies employing over 10,000 employees say that upper management has significantly increased its involvement in HR issues, and only 4% say that upper-management involvement has stayed the same. By contrast, 41% of the companies employing under 1,000 employees say that upper management has increased its involvement, and 17% say involvement has remained the same. Interestingly, larger companies are the most concerned with global and domestic competition, which may account for the increased attention of top management.

In turn, 58% of the companies that expect significant change in their workforce find that upper management has increased its involvement in human resource issues, compared with 45% of the companies that do not expect change in their workforce. We can speculate that top managers who are versed in demographic trends in the workforce understand the importance of involving themselves more fully in HR matters.[5]

Another factor that can elevate human resource issues in corporations involves the reporting relationship of the top HR official. We found that 46% reported directly to the president or chairman of the company. This gives them more clout in strategic decisions and allows for a better dialogue about the role of human resources in the plans of the business. In sum, the increased top-management attention to HR issues and the elevation of HR executives to top-level posts both promise to add to the strategic management of people.

FACTORS SHAPING HR POLICIES AND ATTITUDES

Of course, upper management's involvement in issues is only one factor shaping policies and attitudes within a company. Respondents were asked to rate the impact of various internal and external factors on their company's human resource directions. Based on statistical tests, we group these into three clusters: (1) changes in the market—including customer demands, competitive pressures, and technology changes; (2) changes in the workforce and company staffing requirements; and (3) changes in a company's culture and management.

1. Changes in the Market

Companies differed in the significance they assigned to market factors and the specific issues that comprised them (see Exhibit 2.4). Over 70% said that various external changes in the marketplace had some or a great deal of impact on their HR policies and attitudes, with demands from customers or the marketplace exerting a great deal of influence in over one-third of the sample.

The attention that companies give to the demands of customers and the practices of competitors can be a real boon to more strategic human resource management. Many manufacturers, as noted, have begun to benchmark their HR efforts against those of foreign competitors. Financial service firms also say that the actions of domestic competitors and the demands of new technology influence their approach to HR management. A body of research shows that an awareness of market needs and competitors' responses prompts change and innovation in organizations.[6]

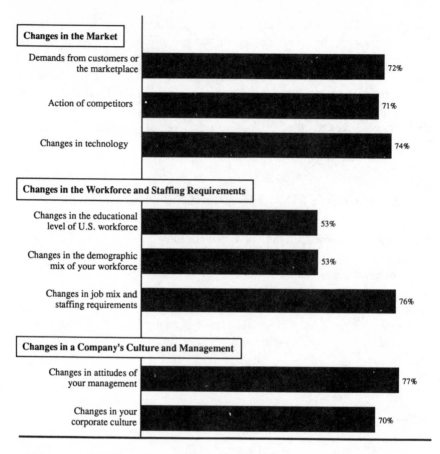

Changes in the Market

Demands from customers or the marketplace — 72%

Action of competitors — 71%

Changes in technology — 74%

Changes in the Workforce and Staffing Requirements

Changes in the educational level of U.S. workforce — 53%

Changes in the demographic mix of your workforce — 53%

Changes in job mix and staffing requirements — 76%

Changes in a Company's Culture and Management

Changes in attitudes of your management — 77%

Changes in your corporate culture — 70%

Exhibit 2.4 Factors influencing HR policies and attitudes (percentage of respondents indicating some or a great deal of impact).

2. Changes in the Workforce and Staffing Requirements

Relatively fewer interviewees see changes in workforce education and demographics as having an impact on their HR policies, with just one of every ten saying they have a great deal of influence. What explains this discounting of the effects of a changing population? Perhaps many companies, because of downsizing and hiring freezes, are not experiencing the brunt of changing workforce demographics. Furthermore, most companies expect to be able to pay enough for recruiting and hiring the qualified people they need. Still, we believe that firms are underestimating the potential impact of the changes. In any case, most say that changes in their job mix and staffing requirements have a bearing on HR policies and attitudes.

3. Changes in Culture and Management

Finally, over 70% of the companies say that changes in management's attitudes and the company culture figure into their HR practices. However, the influence exerted by management attitudes and the corporate culture can be a mixed blessing. On the one hand, support from management and a congenial corporate culture can aid human resource innovation. Aligning policies and attitudes with those of management may give human resources a better focus on business requirements. On the other hand, a fixation on current management attitudes and mores can prove to be a barrier to change. The risk is that HR executives become too internally focused and rely solely on signals from management when setting their HR direction. This concern is softened by signs that the sample companies see *both* marketplace demands and internal changes as shaping their HR efforts.

Several analyses were done to determine whether any patterns existed across companies in factors influencing HR policies and attitudes. Two characteristics (see Exhibit 2.5) seemed to differentiate firms in the sample:

- Larger companies were more likely than smaller companies to see their HR policies influenced by changes in the marketplace and in the workforce.
- Companies that expected changes in their workforce were more likely than those that did not expect changes to say that their HR policies were strongly influenced by changes in staffing, in the market, and in their company's culture and management.

These findings indicate that larger companies, more so than smaller ones, pay close attention to external conditions in their business and labor markets when planning their HR strategies. Experience suggests they are also more likely to systematically assess and react to changes in business conditions when developing new initiatives or elaborating programs already in place. By contrast, smaller companies may not have the time, inclination, or staff to do more than basic personnel administration. Indeed, other research suggests that having a strategic HR orientation may be, in part, a function of company size and stage of development.[7]

Exhibit 2.5 Factors influencing HR policies and attitudes: Key comparisons.

Comparitive Variables	Changes in the Market	Changes in the Workforce and Staffing Requirements	Changes in a Company's Culture and Management
Larger companies	Customer demands Action of competitors	Educational mix Demographic mix	
Companies with expected workforce changes	Demands from customers or marketplace	Changes in demographic mix of workplace Changes in education level Changes in job mix and staffing requirements	Attitudes of management Changes in corporate culture

Furthermore, we find that companies that expect significant changes in the makeup of their workforce by the mid-90s are more likely to view changes in the demographic mix of their workforce, changes in the educational level of the U.S. workforce, and changes in their job mix and staffing needs as having a greater impact on their HR policies and attitudes. These companies also see other external and internal factors as having a stronger bearing on their direction. Perhaps, firms that expect their workforce to change are simply more attuned to their HR environment and more responsive to variety of stakeholder groups—customers, managers, and employees.

BARRIERS TO MAKING STRATEGIC CHANGES

Certain barriers may prevent companies from making needed changes in their human resource policies and practices. Interviewees were asked to rate the significance of seven potential barriers. Our analyses revealed three categories of barriers: (1) an efficiency and crisis orientation—the costs of making changes, the company's need to address more immediate issues, and a focus on short-term goals; (2) a lack of support from employee constituencies— middle management, employees, and unions; and (3) corporate culture and management—a culture that does not emphasize human resources issues and an inability to get the attention of top management.

As Exhibit 2.6 shows, a company's orientation to efficiency and crises re- sults in the most significant barrier to desirable strategic HR change. Specif- ically, 82% of the companies surveyed viewed the cost of making changes as a barrier, with 32% describing it as a major barrier. Similarly, 73% of these companies perceived the need to address crises or more immediate issues as a barrier, with 29% citing it as a major barrier. Somewhat fewer described their focus on short-term goals as a major (14%) or minor (33%) barrier to change.

By comparison, the other two factors—one measuring a lack of support from middle management, employees, and unions and the other covering an unresponsive corporate culture and management—were seen by fewer than one of every five companies as being a major barrier to strategic change. Still, 69% said that a lack of support from middle management was at least somewhat of a problem, and over half saw an unfavorable culture as another impediment to change.

There were notable differences across the sample among those who rated a lack of support as a key barrier to change. Exhibit 2.7 shows, for instance, that larger manufacturing companies, having a bigger proportion

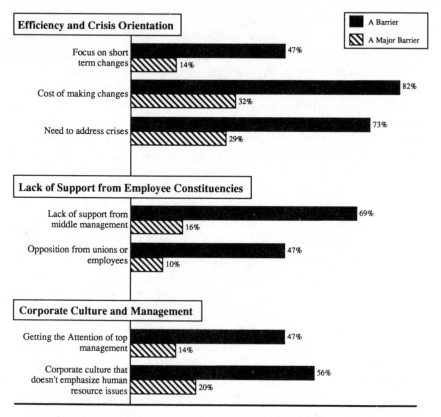

Exhibit 2.6 Barriers to making strategic changes in HR policies.

of unionized workers, are more likely to experience a lack of support from middle management and from unions or to experience employees as obstacles to change than are smaller companies, those in the service sector and those who are not unionized. This lends credence to the war stories coming from old-line industrials about problems of introducing change in HR management. Privately held companies are more likely than the publicly held to name their organizational culture as a barrier to change.

Workforce composition also influences companies' perceptions of obstacles to change. Companies with a greater percentage of women find the lack of support by middle management and the opposition from unions and employees to be less of a barrier to HR change than companies with more men. Again, this highlights the problems that male-dominated industrial firms are having in coping with change. Companies with racial diversity faced no more or fewer obstacles to change than firms with less diversity.

Exhibit 2.7 Barriers to making changes in HR policies: Key predictors.

Predictors	Efficiency and Crisis Orientation			Lack of Support		Culture and Managment	
	Focus on Short-Term Goals	Costs of Making Changes	Need to Address Crises	Lack of Support from Middle Managers	Opposition from Unions and Employees	Get Attention from Top Managers	Culture Not Emphasizing HR
Company Characteristics							
Privately held *vs.* publicly held						+	+
Manufacturing *vs.* service				+	+		
Unionized *vs.* not				+	+		
Size (no. of employees)				+	+		
Size (total sales)					+		
% of domestic sales				+			
% of overseas sales							
Workforce Composition							
% of women employees				−	−		
% of men employees				+	+		
Predominantly white *vs.* racially diverse workforce							
Expected Future Workforce Composition							
Expect workforce demographic changes	+			+	+		+

Note: For all the categorical variables (such as private *vs.* public), the relationship is with the first variable.

Key: The plus and minus signs indicate positive and negative relations between the predictor variable and barrier statistically significant at $p < .05$.

We have shown that companies who expect significant change in their workforce are more attuned to change in their business and labor markets. At the same time, they seem to encounter more resistance to change from middle management, employees, and unions. Note that these firms are hobbled by their focus on competing short-term goals and by corporate cultures that do not emphasize HR issues. The paradox here is that such firms seem to be more aware of the need for change and yet are less able to effect it.

Perhaps their awareness of the need for change makes these companies more cognizant of the resistance by middle managers and employees and of potential problems in assimilating larger numbers of women and minorities into the workforce. Conversely, companies that already have a larger proportion of women and minorities find such barriers less formidable; maybe they have already overcome resistance from middle managers and employees and have seen their culture accommodate workforce diversity.

PHILOSOPHY ABOUT ADOPTING
NEW HUMAN RESOURCES POLICIES

In order to get a better fix on how companies go about making strategic changes in HR management, respondents were asked to describe their company's approach to adopting new HR practices as either: (1) at the *cutting edge*—usually trying to lead; (2) *advanced*—adopting policies to stay ahead of other companies; (3) *thoughtful*—adopting policies when a consensus is developed; or (4) *prudent*—adopting policies after they are proven effective. This distribution depicts the typical diffusion pattern for innovations. Those at the front edge of innovation are the first to adopt new ideas and practices, followed by those guided by logic and theory, then by evidence and demonstrated success, and finally by the need to survive.

In this sample, cutting edge companies gravitate readily to new ideas about HR management and the latest developments in practice. They typically have a coherent HR philosophy. Advanced firms, by comparison, are "fast followers," who respond to competitors' actions and the apparent merits of the leader's experimentation. Those classified as thoughtful generally wait for new ideas to prove themselves in a broader base of companies, whereas the prudent firms innovate when there is widespread evidence of success and, as a result, lag behind.

Exhibit 2.8 depicts the distribution of companies surveyed in these dimensions. The sample sorts out in a normal distribution along this continuum, with a small proportion of firms describing themselves either as

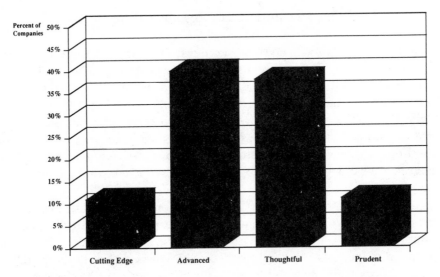

Exhibit 2.8   Company philosophy on adopting new HR policies: From "cutting edge" to "prudent."

leaders (11%) or laggards (11%) and the majority describing themselves as either advanced (39%) or thoughtful (37%).

Research on the spread of innovations—whether among peoples, countries, or companies—shows that new ideas are gradually adopted along this continuum. What Exhibit 2.8 suggests in this case is that the proven practices of the most innovative companies will eventually be adopted by firms who follow and lag on the innovation cycle. What is a human resource innovation today may be common practice in the years ahead. It is important, therefore, to understand which, if any, organizational factors are associated with leading, following, or lagging on the innovation cycle.

Interestingly, whether or not a company leads or lags in its adoption of human resource innovations is *not* related to specific company characteristics or the contours of its workforce. Small companies do not differ from large companies, manufacturing from service, unionized from nonunionized, and so on, in terms of their willingness to innovate. Similarly, the makeup of a firm's current or expected future workforce has no relationship to its willingness to take the lead in implementing new HR policies. We can conclude, therefore, that the diffusion of HR innovations is not likely to be sped up or constrained by any structural or demographic factors.

Influences on Human Resource Policies

Cutting edge companies, however, are much more attuned to change in their environment. For instance, cutting edge firms are more likely to view customer demands and changes in technology as having a greater impact on HR policies than companies that are slower in adopting HR innovations. Over half of the cutting edge firms say that demands from customers and the marketplace influence their HR strategies as compared with one-third of the followers and laggards. In turn, over 40% say that they are influenced by changes in technology compared to one-fourth of the rest of the sample.

Cutting edge companies (23%) are also far more likely to say that changing demographics exerts an influence on their HR policies than are the other firms (7%) studied. Overall, this means that cutting edge companies pay *more* attention to the factors that influence competitiveness in their business and labor markets. Interestingly, they pay somewhat *less* attention to changes in management's attitudes and their corporate culture.

Barriers to Human Resource Changes

Human resource leaders have different perceptions of barriers to change than do followers and laggards on the innovation cycle (see Exhibit 2.9). Cutting edge companies are less likely to consider a focus on short-term goals, the cost of making changes, and addressing other needs or crises as significant or even modest barriers to change, as compared to the rest of the sample. Moving along the continuum, advanced, thoughtful, and especially prudent innovators view these as increasingly important impediments to change.

Cutting edge firms are less likely to see opposition from employees and unions as a barrier to change. Significantly, however, there is scant difference among firms in their outlook on resistance from middle management. A lack of support from the middle ranks proves to be something of a barrier to change in companies, no matter what their philosophy and approach to human resource innovation.

There is, however, a sharp distinction among firms in their outlook on company culture. Prudent firms are twice as likely to view their company culture as a barrier to change when compared to cutting edge companies. Moreover, some 37% of those companies view it as a major barrier, as compared to 7% of the innovation leaders. The same trend, though not as pronounced, is found in a company's success in getting the attention of top management.

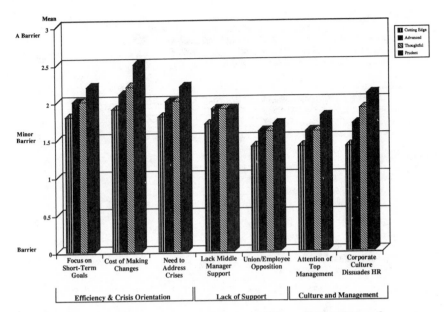

Exhibit 2.9   Barriers to making changes in HR policies: Role of company philosophy.

We are left with the conclusion that what predicts innovativeness in human resource management is not a company's size, structure, or workforce but rather its close attention to the marketplace, its willingness to invest in people and long-term goals, the supportive interest of its top management, and its human resource–oriented company culture. Scholars make the point that culture is a lens through which organizations view the world, a guide to the members' everyday behavior. It is not surprising that values and culture so strongly predict a firm's approach to HR innovation. This plays out, in turn, in what types of innovations firms actually introduce.

Investments of Human Resource Innovators

Human resource innovativeness is related to several practices intended to improve competitiveness. Specifically, companies that lead in HR change are more likely to make significant investments in new computer technology, the redesign of work methods, the advancement of employee involvement practices, and the implementation of total quality programs than those who follow or lag on the innovation cycle (see Exhibit 2.10). For instance, almost

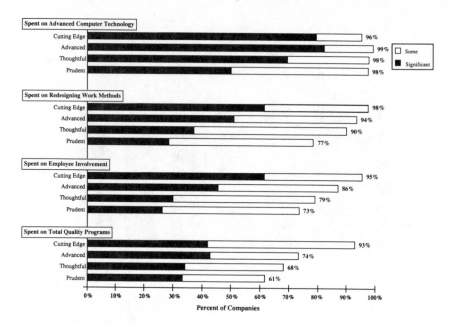

Exhibit 2.10   Spending on HR innovations to improve company competitiveness: The role of company philosophy.

twice as many of the cutting edge companies made significant as compared to moderate investments in employee involvement. By contrast, half as many thoughtful and prudent companies spent significantly on employee involvement, and a number of them spent nothing at all. A similar trend is found for investments in new work designs. Although the trend is not as pronounced, cutting edge and advanced firms also spent more on advanced computer technology and total quality management. These findings give weight to the notion that innovations follow a diffusion cycle. The fast followers spend almost as much as the leaders on practices intended to improve competitiveness, whereas thoughtful and prudent firms lag in their investments.

To complete this picture, we must also consider how influences in the corporate environment factor into innovation decisions (see Exhibit 2.11). Here we see that companies that innovate with new technology are especially attuned to changes in the world of technology. Those who choose to redesign work are also in touch with technological change and watchful of the actions of their competitors. This confirms other evidence that growing acceptance of new work designs—involving self-managing production teams linked by integrated computing systems—is being driven by forces in the marketplace.[8]

Exhibit 2.11   Competitive investments and what most influences HR policies.

Competitive Investments	What Most Influences HR
Technology	Changes in technology
Redesigning work methods	Actions of competitors
	Changes in technology
Employee involvement	Customer demands
	Workforce education level
Total quality	Changes in corporate culture

Employee involvement, by comparison, seems to be related not only to customer demands but also to changes in the education level of the workforce. Of course, the increase in "knowledge work" in industry puts a premium on developing a highly skilled laborforce. Many firms have found, too, that employee involvement programs tap into new levels of creativity and know-how in an employee population. Finally, companies that invest in total quality programs seem to be most affected by changes in their company culture. This reinforces the point made by many quality experts that such programs demand a "thought revolution" in companies and require wholesale changes in how they are managed.

Four Elements in Innovativeness

In sum, we have identified four elements that differentiate cutting edge firms from followers and laggards in human resource innovation. First, there is the fundamental philosophy of and approach to change. Cutting edge firms are self-described leaders in trying out new ideas and practices. The rest of industry arrays itself as advanced, thoughtful, and prudent in approaching change. Second, cutting edge companies are less hampered by a focus on short-term goals, the cost of making changes, and the need to address competing crises. In the same way, they encounter less opposition from employees and unions and have less trouble getting the attention of top management. All of this suggests that there is more of an alignment among stakeholders in cutting edge companies. Third, cutting edge firms seem more aware of and responsive to changes in their environment. All of this, in turn, translates into more aggressive investments in work redesign and employee involvement and somewhat more spending on technology and total quality management. Plainly, cutting edge firms have internalized the idea that people can be a prime source of competitive advantage, and such firms have cultures that are more apt to value human resource management.

HUMAN RESOURCE PROGRAMS AND PLANS

Where do companies in this sample stand on other laborforce issues facing the country? Chapter 1 has shown that most companies are concerned about the impact of health care costs on their ability to compete. Eighty percent or so are concerned about the poor quality of education of new job applicants and the growing family responsibilities of workers. About half say that the poor work attitudes of job applicants, the aging of the workforce, and the growing proportion of women and minorities have an impact on their competitiveness.

In follow-up questions, interviewees whose firms saw these as competitive issues were asked whether or not their companies had plans to address them. Exhibit 2.12 shows that over 90% have plans for dealing with the rising costs of health benefits. Roughly two-thirds have plans for responding to diversity, to the family needs of workers, and to the poor quality of education found among job applicants. Half of the companies sampled have plans for addressing issues of the costs of U.S. labor, the aging of the workforce, and the poor work attitudes of job applicants.

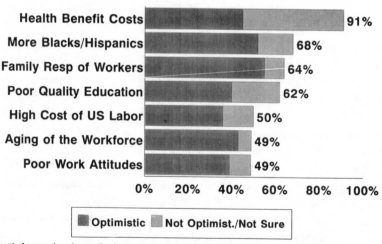

(Base: Percent of companies who say that issues are at least somewhat important to competitiveness)

Exhibit 2.12 Companies with plans to address laborforce issues: Level of optimism.

Consider, next, how optimistic firms are that their programs and plans will succeed (see Exhibit 2.12). Fully half of the firms faced with costly health benefits are not optimistic that their plans will prove effective. Over one-third doubt whether their efforts will address problems in the education of entry workers. These are, of course, societal problems; corporations can only do so much to ameliorate them. By contrast, there is more optimism about addressing work/family issues and the needs of aging workers. As later chapters show, however, most companies have lower ambitions in these areas. Finally, there is a strong concern among multinational businesses, most notably manufacturers, about their ability to compete given the high cost of U.S. labor.

Several factors predict action, if not necessarily success, on these work-force issues. Overall, larger firms and those expecting the most change in their workforce are more apt to have programs aimed at managing diversity, work/family issues, and the needs of older workers. Specific needs also drive plans and activities:

- Companies with a larger percentage of women in the workforce are more apt to have plans for dealing with employees' family responsibilities.
- Those with a larger segment of older workers are more likely to have plans for responding to these employees.
- Those that have more minorities are more apt to have plans for dealing with diversity.
- Firms that are having trouble recruiting qualified job applicants are more likely to have plans for responding to educational deficiencies among their entry level workers.

Finally, cutting edge companies, which are more convinced of the competitive impact of these issues than other firms in the study, are more apt to have plans or programs in place. The details on how companies are responding to these human resource issues are reported in subsequent chapters.

Attracting, Retaining, and Motivating Employees

Beyond specific programs, companies have to stay attuned to the changing needs of their workforce at large. We have seen that attracting, retaining, and motivating a quality workforce is a shared concern of top managers and HR managers within companies. As noted, over three-fourths of the managers interviewed say that their companies must make changes in HR management policies in order to attract, retain, and motivate the quality employees they will need in the 1990s.

The kinds of changes needed are highlighted by responses to a question about the importance of nine factors in attracting, motivating, and retaining quality employees. Exhibit 2.13 shows that respondents rate interesting work as the most important factor, followed closely by compensation and opportunities for advancement. These three factors are highly correlated with a fourth priority: opportunities for participation in decisions. Combined, the four factors make up what companies see as key HR goals. Of somewhat lesser importance are health benefits, retirement benefits, and job security. Finally, the least important factor concerns family support policies and flexible work schedules. It should be noted, however, that these are more important in companies employing a large percentage of women.

One broad conclusion is that companies recognize that bread-and-butter issues are of prime concern to most employees. But they also acknowledge the primacy of interesting work and chances to participate in decisions—factors often given short shrift twenty years ago. These results fit with the findings of many studies that have asked employees to rate the importance of a variety of job factors.[9]

Exhibit 2.13   What companies say is most important to attract, motivate, and retain today's employee. (Scale: 1 [low] to 10 [high].)

	Mean
Health benefits (a)	7.3
Retirement benefits (b)	6.0
Family support policy (c)	5.8
Flexible work schedule (d)	5.6
Job security (e)	7.2
Compensation (f)	7.8
Opportunities for advancement (g)	7.7
Opportunities for participation in decisions (h)	7.4
Interesting work (i)	8.0
Factor 1 (f, g, h, i)	7.8
Factor 2 (a, b, e)	6.9
Factor 3 (c, d)	5.7

Interestingly, companies seem to place equal emphasis on interesting work and on compensation. Recent writings have suggested that challenging work and participation in decision making are more important than financial rewards. Clearly this view is not held by the Laborforce 2000 respondents. In general, the evidence from the research on work motivation supports their view. For most people it is not an issue of high pay versus interesting work, it is a matter of seeking situations where both are present.

Certainly HR departments have a traditional role in pay and benefit decisions in their companies. We would also argue that they should have a role in expanding people's opportunities to gain more interesting work and to participate in decisions. Helping to design and implement new organizational and job designs fits squarely within their charter to attract, motivate, and retain quality people.

There are some predictors of how companies rate what most attracts and motivates people. We have noted the importance of family policies and flexibility in firms employing more women. In addition, the importance of interesting work increases in firms employing a larger share of college graduates. Job security gains in value for companies that have undertaken more layoffs since the mid-80s. And cutting edge companies in general assign more importance to every factor than do later adopters of HR innovations.

Interestingly, companies that have employee involvement and total quality programs have a somewhat different perception of what moves today's employee. Companies active in employee involvement, for instance, put more emphasis on people's chances to participate in decisions than firms having no such programs. Perhaps they have seen how vital participation becomes—once people gain a voice in work decisions. Companies having quality programs, compared to those that do not, rate interesting work (8.3 versus 7.8) and chances to participate (7.9 versus 7.1) as more important, too.

The Rationale for Action

Several conclusions can be drawn. First, companies employing greater numbers from particular "classes" of workers—women, well-educated workers, minorities, older workers, and so forth—seem to better understand how important particular job factors are in motivating *their* workforce. They also see the competitive impact of the needs posed by these workers and are more apt to have plans for satisfying them.

Second, it is clear that perceptions of workforce issues and responses to the issues are influenced by the outlooks and experiences of companies with HR innovations. Cutting edge firms, for example, are simply more likely to rate employees' needs overall as more important than followers and laggards. They also see workforce issues as having competitive implications, and do more in the way of new programs and future plans. Firms having employee involvement and total quality programs seem especially responsive to people's needs for interesting work and involvement in work decisions.

Third, the foregoing should not in any way challenge the emphasis that HR departments give to employee compensation, benefits, as well as training and development. Employees put high value on fair compensation and the chance to advance, and employers need to respond. Human resource departments, however, can do more to make work more interesting and can provide more opportunities for participation in decisions. The needs are recognized; the challenge is to meet them.

HUMAN RESOURCE MANAGEMENT PRIORITIES FOR THE FUTURE

Lastly, respondents were asked to identify their two highest human resource priorities for the mid-90s. Exhibit 2.14 shows that their chief priorities are in the area of medical benefits and the quality of the workforce. The next several priorities—staff training, management development, and dealing with diversity—all have to do with attracting, retaining and developing a competent workforce.

Involvement in organizational redesign and management programs aimed at improving productivity, quality, customer service, and innovation are seen as priorities by a relatively small percentage of companies. This continues the pattern identified earlier whereby HR departments take a highly specialized and programmatic approach to their work and fail to integrate their efforts with the mainline strategies of the business.

Human resource departments typically do not, nor do they plan to, give a high priority to influencing how individuals are utilized and managed. Furthermore, few plan to take a leadership role in programs aimed at improving their organization's effectiveness. This works against the HR department's becoming a full strategic partner in running the business.

STRATEGIC HR MANAGEMENT IN THE FUTURE

Many HR departments are offering new programs aimed at the changing workforce. And more HR activity can be projected. All of this should be of service in their mandate to attract, motivate, and retain a quality workforce through the 90s. We have found there to be leaders and laggards. What

Exhibit 2.14 Priorities of the HR department for the mid-90s.

Issue to Manage	# of Companies Who Rate Issue as First or Second Priority
Medical benefits	131
Caliber of workforce	118
Staff training	94
Management development	75
Retention	59
Diversity of workforce	59
Employee motivation	34
Innovation	34
Productivity	29
Downsizing	18
Government regulation	14
Customer satisfaction	13
Cost management	11
Strategic planning	8
Work/family issues	7
Technology	7
Quality management	6
Women in workplace	6

is especially worrisome is that the laggards—fettered by cost constraints, competing crises, and a lack of support from their management and company culture—may never catch up to their competitors in the management of people.

Our findings suggest that the time of strategic management of human resources has not yet arrived. Despite all that has been said and written, the HR function in most corporations views itself as responsible for traditional HR activities and not as a full strategic partner. On its agenda are reducing the costs of health care benefits, improving the caliber of the workforce, and dealing with the needs of the employee population. Missing from the vast majority of companies surveyed is responsibility for the design and management of practices intended to strategically reduce costs, improve quality, increase speed to market, and add significantly to overall organizational effectiveness.

Moreover, some key responsibilities cited by HR executives will likely demand concerted attention beyond the confines of the firm. Soaring health care costs, for instance, simply cannot be controlled via HMOs and managed care programs, in the opinion of most companies sampled. Considerable pessimism exists about firms' ability to remedy educational deficiencies among entry workers, let alone manage massive retraining of workers. Finally, the social integration of women and minorities will require work on the societal front as much as within corporations. The point here is that addressing the top priorities of HR departments will require strong, proactive leadership deeply engaged with other community and business leaders. Company programs will not be sufficient.

Wickham Skinner has described HR managers as having "big hats" but "no cattle."[10] We see that they have many programs and plans, but not ones that are central to the strategic thrust of their businesses. Nevertheless, these data provide some hopeful signs of change. First, more and more senior-level managers are paying attention to HR concerns. Second, HR issues are being recognized as integral to company competitiveness. Third, some model firms, labeled as *cutting edge* in this chapter, are demonstrating how to innovate in HR management and, importantly, are actively involved in efforts to improve the business. These companies seem to have a progressive HR philosophy and to understand that investments in human capital can increase long-term competitiveness. Given the pattern of diffusion, the innovative practices of the HR leaders today are likely to be practiced by many more companies tomorrow.

We have shown that cutting edge companies consider the design and management of the organization and its HR system as leverage points for gaining competitive advantage. These innovators experience fewer barriers to change in HR policies. And they are more attuned to forces in their environment. Hopefully, their focus on organizational effectiveness, still the exception today, will become more commonplace in the 90s.

This movement of HR managers toward becoming a strategic business partner has been projected in a worldwide study of HR executives, academics, and business leaders by Towers Perrin. The findings point toward a function that is responsive to a highly competitive marketplace and the demands of global business, closely linked to business strategic plans, jointly conceived and implemented by line and HR managers. This would focus HR managers on quality, customer service, productivity, employee involvement, teamwork, and workplace flexibility. The seeming inconsistency between the Towers Perrin findings and the data reported here exists because their study measured *aspirations* whereas ours focused on current practice.

Given the gap between ideals and practice that we have found, efforts to transform HR from a specialized function to a partner in running the business promises to be a challenge. However, it is apparent that an increasing number of human resource executives want the transformation to take place, and in this chapter we have shown how innovators have charted the path leading to a more strategic approach to HR management. In our opinion, the 90s can still be the decade in which a growing number of "followers" discover that competitive advantage can be obtained by linking human resource management to new competitive practices.

NOTES

1. Ulrich, D., and Lake, D. 1990. *Organizational capability*. New York: John Wiley & Sons.

2. Porter, M. 1990. *The competitive advantage of nations*. New York: Free Press.

3. Lawler, E. E. 1992. *The ultimate advantage: Creating the high involvement organization*. San Francisco: Jossey-Bass.

4. Towers Perrin. 1992. *Priorities for competitive advantage*. New York: Towers Perrin.

5. Johnston, W. B., and Packer, A. H. 1987. *Workforce 2000: Work and workers for the 21st century*. Indianapolis, IN: Hudson Institute; Johnston, W. B. 1991. Global workforce 2000: The new world labor market. *Harvard Business Review* 69 (2): 115–127.

6. Porter, M. 1985. *Competitive advantage*. New York: Free Press.

7. Baird, L., and Meshoulam, I. 1988. Managing two fits of strategic human resource management. *Academy of Management Review* 13 (1): 116–128.

8. Lawler, E. E., Mohrman, S. A., and Ledford, G. E. 1992. *Employee involvement in America: An assessment of practices and results*. San Francisco: Jossey-Bass.

9. Vroom, V. H. 1964. *Work and motivation*. New York: John Wiley & Sons; Lawler, E. E. 1973. *Motivation in work organizations*. Pacific Grove, CA: Brooks/Cole; Pinder, C. C. 1984. *Work motivation: Theory, issues, and applications*. Glenview, IL: Scott, Foresman.

10. Skinner, W. 1981. Big hat, no cattle: Managing human resources. *Harvard Business Review* 59 (5): 106–114.

3

Restructuring
and Downsizing
Mitchell Lee Marks

The time-honored notion that sheer size breeds business success has been re-
placed in corporations by an emphasis on adaptability and speed in response
to changing technologies and market conditions. Merging and acquiring,
overseas expansion, and internal restructuring are prominent strategies in
many companies today. These strategic moves and underlying competitive
and profit pressures have led firms to close plants and offices, eliminate layers
of management and staff, and lay off or redeploy line workers. As a result,
the seeming lifetime employment commitment that companies once offered
to many U.S. workers, whereby those who performed their jobs satisfactorily
could expect annual pay increases and an occasional bump up the corporate
ladder, has been abandoned.

Downsizing is the catchall phrase for various approaches that companies
use to reduce and manage headcount (the number of people they employ).
In principle, downsizing enables an organization to improve its competitive
cost position without impairing its ability to execute its strategy. In practice, however, it can exact a heavy toll on organizational effectiveness and
employee well-being. Chapter 1 reported that five of every six companies
surveyed in this Laborforce 2000 study downsized from the mid-80s to the
early 90s. Here we will analyze the reasons behind the downsizing activity,

60

the ways it was accomplished, and the impact it had on companies and people. We will also see sharp differences between firms that downsize for financial versus strategic reasons and show that the practices of *cutting edge* companies lessen postdownsizing consequences.

DOWNSIZING IN CORPORATE AMERICA

Downsizing has occurred on a massive scale in American organizations. During the 1980s, 3.4 million jobs were eliminated from Fortune 500 companies. Many more positions were erased from the payrolls of medium and small firms. Data from this study show that the majority of firms downsize by making changes in their organizational structure such as shutting down some operations, combining operating units, or selling off business units. In other firms, the structure stays intact, but individual positions are eliminated through layoffs, reductions in management staffs, and early retirement programs. Still others downsize by changing employment practices—instituting a hiring freeze or shifting workers to part-time schedules.

Two major reasons for downsizing have been uncovered by this study. In some of the companies studied, downsizing is aligned with broader efforts to redirect corporate strategy or enhance operations. Here it is a proactive and potentially productive method used to build a better organization. However, the data show that the majority of downsizing is financially driven—a reactive response to economically difficult times. These reductions in the number of employees seldom advance strategy or yield expected gains. Indeed, although they generate some savings in corporate expenses, our data show that they produce a large number of underestimated financial costs and untoward employee consequences.

Certainly there is fat to be cut and waste to be eliminated from many corporations, even profitable ones. Moreover, firms wallowing in red ink may have no alternative to a downsizing that could, in the long term, strengthen the job security of the vast majority of employees. Finally, it is imperative for companies to "rebalance" and "rightsize" their workforce in line with technology and the job mix.

Yet downsizing is rarely described as productive or regenerative. On the contrary, it is usually depicted as painful, wrenching, and bloody. Worse yet, despite the pain experienced by organizations and their people, many downsizings fail to achieve desired results. In a cover story on the morale crisis in U.S. business, *Fortune* magazine reported that half of the senior managers surveyed in 275 major companies (representing 26% of the U.S. gross national product) felt that their cost-cutting programs and restructuring had not achieved their objectives. In another study of 1,005 corporations where restructuring had occurred, *Fortune* found that

> most senior executives admitted their companies had missed the mark in one way or another. Fewer than half met their cost-reduction targets, despite much bloodletting. This, they reported, was often because they had cut people without reducing workload, so that pricey outside contractors, and sometimes new full-time hires, had to be called in to take up the slack. Only 32% raised their profits to a level they thought acceptable, and just 21% improved return on investment to any appreciable degree.[1]

In their book on "deindustrialization," political economists Barry Bluestone and Bennett Harrison contend that many U.S. industries, faced with international competition, have protected eroding profit margins through systematic disinvestment in the nation's productive capacity.

> The essential problem with the U.S. economy can be traced to the way capital, in the form of financial resources and of real plant and equipment, has been diverted from productive investment in our basic national industries into unproductive speculation, mergers and acquisitions, and foreign investment.[2]

This does not mean that corporate managers are refusing to invest—only that many are not putting their capital in the basic industries of the country. Bluestone and Harrison cite the cases of U.S. Steel, which paid $6 billion to acquire Marathon Oil rather than use its resources to rebuild steel capacity, and General Electric, which expanded its worldwide payroll during the 1970s by 5,000 but did so by adding 30,000 foreign jobs and reducing its U.S. employment by 25,000.

In sum, the decision to downsize and the manner in which it is executed are important to the firm's future competitiveness, as well as to the economic health of America and the quality of life in its communities. One-half of the human resources executives surveyed in this study say that periodic downsizing will be necessary to maintain an effective, competitive organization. It seems that downsizing is here to stay as a regular and recurring component of modern management. The data here show the downside of downsizing and highlight how, under the right conditions, it can enhance company performance, employees' job prospects, and the nation's economic health.

Downsizing at IBM

In 1985, IBM headed *Fortune* magazine's ranking of America's most admired corporations. Contributing to its high overall score was its second-place position (behind Hewlett-Packard) in ability to attract, develop, and keep talented people.

Then came 1986, and IBM—with a peak employee count of 407,000 and a no-layoff, full-employment tradition spanning half a century—embarked on a massive metamorphosis. The bloated bureaucracy blocked IBM's view of customers' changing tastes. Companies began moving from big mainframe computers, IBM's bread and butter, toward networks of powerful desktop models. Concerned with protecting its core business, IBM came late to personal computers, and the ones it built fell behind the competition in performance. The company conceded such promising niches as laptops and workstations to newcomers. It let costs run away and failed to take full advantage of its acclaimed research prowess. The slow, stodgy organizational giant was weighed down by its massive size.

After earnings fell in 1985 and 1986 following a 1984 record high, IBM put itself through four reorganizations, got rid of more than sixty thousand employees, eliminated huge blocks of its ten layers of middle management, retrained thirty thousand staff bureaucrats for work closer to the customer, closed ten plants, and spun off two divisions into separate business units. Among the waves of downsizing were the following:

1986: Early retirement incentives are offered in hopes of bringing the company's U.S. employment down by 8,000. When the dust settles, 15,000 workers take early retirement, and another 21,000 are either relocated or switched from headquarters jobs into sales.

1988: In its second major consolidation in two years, IBM targets 10,000 jobs to be eliminated by chopping 4,400 manufacturing jobs in Florida and Arizona along with several thousand more jobs at headquarters in Armonk, New York. To maintain its no-layoff policy, all workers affected are offered employment elsewhere. This time, however, early retirement is offered more selectively to keep valued employees from leaving. Displaced workers are offered only one new job rather than a chance to pick and choose among several. This time, 6,500 employees retire, and 20,000 move from staff and laboratory jobs to the sales force.

March 1989: About one thousand people in administrative and support positions at four locations are offered special payments to quit or retire.

December 1989: A cost-cutting program involving plant closings and early retirement incentives is announced with a target of reducing the workforce by 10,000 to 15,000 people, mostly in the United States. Media reports reiterate IBM's past problems with top performers leaving the company in past downsizings and its need to aim early retirement incentives at weak performers.

March 1991: IBM announces another downsizing of 10,000 workers. Like earlier cuts, this year's reductions are made through a combination of attrition and voluntary incentive programs and do not involve layoffs. Unlike earlier cuts, however, this year's reductions involve European operations. In addition, another 4,200 leave the payroll through the sale of IBM's typewriter operations in Kentucky.

November 1991: IBM announces it will cut another 20,000 jobs in early 1992 and overhaul the way it does business by reorganizing into independent business units, in order to be more nimble and better able to adapt to the frantic pace of change in the highly competitive computer business. Again, IBM says it will retain its no-layoff policy and rely on attrition and early retirement incentives to reduce its work force.

January 1992: IBM announces its first ever annual loss—$2.8 billion. The loss is partly attributed to a $3.4 billion write-off to account for the expenses of early retirement benefits and other costs of slimming IBM's staff by 29,000 in 1991.

April 1992: Through voluntary buyouts and attrition, this time primarily in marketing. IBM announces plans to slash more jobs.

January 1993: After a full year of further cutbacks and losses, IBM president John Akers tenders his resignation.

Although no one was officially laid off, allowing IBM to maintain its time-honored tradition, many reports surfaced of employees being strongly urged to voluntarily leave the company. The constancy of downsizing, along with management's not-so-subtle pushing of older workers out the door, has forcefully conveyed to employess that the "hired for life" ground rules have changed. Formerly, company lifers who frequently relocated joked that IBM's initials stand for "I've Been Moved"; today the disgruntled ones grimly joke that it means "I've Been Mislead."

FORCES FOR DOWNSIZING

Several forces in the business environment drive downsizing activity in corporations. Consider their impact on selected industries:

1. **Global Competition.** Global competition emerged as a key strategic concern of top executives in the companies in this study. In some industries, it is expected that a relatively small number of Asian, European, and North American competitors will vie for market share. In large part, this is fueling the current merger wave in the financial services industry where bankers argue that consolidation is essential to competitive advantage on a global scale. For the first time in 50 years, no U.S. bank ranks among the top 20 in the American Banker's annual ranking of the world's largest banks. In the United States, over 250 million people are served by 12,600 commercial banks, 2,000 savings and loans, and almost 16,000 credit unions. By contrast, fewer than 3,000 savings banks, mutual banks, and commercial banking companies serve the entire European Community's 320 million consumers. And, in Japan, fewer than 170 commercial banks serve a population of 125 million. As U.S. banks grow larger, redundant positions and career opportunities have been and will continue to be eliminated.

2. **Government Deregulation.** The impact of deregulation is pronounced in areas such as air transportation where corporate leaders responded aggressively by combining companies and reducing the number of employees. A very few giant-carriers have acquired Piedmont, PSA, Republic, Air California, Ozark, Western Airlines, and others. In addition to corporate identities being tossed aside, thousands of jobs were eliminated through postmerger downsizings. Carriers less active in the merger market, Pan Am, Midway, and Eastern among them, went bankrupt causing the eradication of thousands of jobs.

3. **Delayering.** Recent years also produced a drive to strip away the layers of bureaucracy and managerial excess built up during the high growth years in the United States that stretched from the close of the World War II into the 1970s. As long as markets and revenues grew, corporations erected hierarchies to support managers who managed managers. When growth rates leveled off in the 1980s, top-heavy corporations lost their stability. Growing consumer demands for responsiveness and quality prodded many firms to cut middle management ranks by delayering and getting decision makers "closer to the customer." Middle managers were hit hard in the downsizings of the late

1980s—making up just 6% of the workforce population, they accounted for 17% of all dismissals.

4. **Technology.** Technology continues to become more sophisticated and efficient. The steel industry, for example, produced 100 million tons of output with 577,100 workers in the 1960s. Today, it produces just as much tonnage with 207,700. Often this carries a tremendous human price tag whereby people become surplus because of automation, as when telephone utilities introduce automated switching equipment, or because skill sets become obsolete, as when robotics replace skilled laborers. While some firms offer retraining opportunities, others eliminate people along with jobs.

5. **Economic Conditions.** Economic conditions are another prime concern of top executives in this study. The Bureau of Labor Statistics estimates that some 2.3 million workers are displaced every year in the United States because of the changing fortunes of their businesses. More specifically, pressures to increase earnings and control costs are constant for many companies, leading some to turn to periodic downsizing. This means that when corporate revenues decline, the expense side of the balance sheet is attacked and the number of employees is reduced. Many times, however, the initial cuts are not deep enough to stem losses, resulting in multiple waves of staff reductions.

6. **Corporate Rationalization.** When massive, such cost cutting often accompanies a major corporation restructuring in which plants and positions are *rationalized*, that is, closed or cut to better match supply and demand. Responding to the dismal economy and continuing loss of market share, General Motors in late 1991 announced plans to eliminate 54,000 of 304,000 U.S. blue-collar jobs through early retirement, attrition, and perhaps layoffs, by 1995. Also at risk are 11,000 white-collar jobs on top of 15,000 already slated for elimination. More broadly, as restructuring has entered the mainstream managerial repertoire, shuffling people has taken on the ease of shuffling paper assets. A wave of downsizing and rehiring may enable a firm to adjust to short-term market fluctuations and appear to be more dynamic. But as Robert Reich notes, "This also serves as a deceptive palliative. It allows the firm to avoid undertaking more basic change. And it demoralizes everyone involved."[3]

7. **Human Resources Planning.** However, some firms anticipate economic downturns and try to avoid or minimize layoffs by instituting hiring freezes or offering early retirement and other incentives for voluntary departures. A few firms, responding to changes in their business mix,

also offer retraining to employees whose positions are at risk to provide them with the skills needed to hold jobs in business areas that may be growing or are less affected by negative economic conditions.

PRIMARY REASONS FOR DOWNSIZING

The human resource executives interviewed in the Laborforce 2000 study reported that all these general forces figured into downsizing in their own companies. When asked for the "single most important reason" for downsizing, however, the majority cited the need for cost containment or control (27%) and a lack of profitability (25%). These we label reactive, financially driven motives for downsizing. By comparison, roughly one-third cited a need to improve efficiency or productivity (22%) and to counter competition (12%) as their prime reason for reducing the number of employees. Another 5% downsized because of changes in business strategy, and 3% downsized because of a merger, acquisition, or consolidation. These four motives we classify as strategic and proactive. Finally, a small number of firms (3%) cited the economy as the single most important reason for downsizing (see Exhibit 3.1).

The trend of downsizings that are motivated more by financial considerations than by strategic consideration is consistent across industries (see Exhibit 3.2). The plight of manufacturers in today's economy is vividly seen in the ranking of lack of profitability as the most frequently cited reason for downsizing in that sector. Financial service firms were more likely to downsize to control costs, testimony to the rapid consolidation among banks and other financial service concerns. Furthermore, large firms and public companies were also more apt to cite financial factors rather than proactive, strategic ones as their prime reasons for cutting back.

DOWNSIZING PRACTICES

Companies rely on different tactics to reduce labor costs. One approach involves downsizing through changes in organizational structure—in the basic design of a company, its functions, and physical locations. A second approach alters the organization's employment profile by eliminating positions rather than by changing business units. A third changes employment policies that affect staffing patterns.

1. **Changes in Organizational Structure.** Companies in this study were most likely to downsize by making changes in their basic organizational

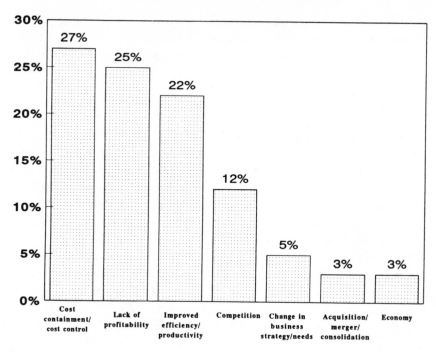

Exhibit 3.1   The single most important reason for company downsizing.

Exhibit 3.2   Downsizing reason by industry group.

	Industry		
Reason	Manufacturing (%)	Financial Services (%)	Other Services (%)
Cost containment/cost control	22	30	27
Lack of profitability	29	23	29
Improved efficiency/production	26	24	17
Competition	13	13	12
Change in business strategy/needs	5	5	4
Acquisition/merger/consolidation	6	6	2
Economy	2	1	3

structure. Nearly two-thirds shut down some operations (64%) and as many combined operating units (62%). One-half of the companies sold off business units. Manufacturing firms were more likely than financial and other service companies to downsize via changes in their structure (see Exhibit 3.3). Over three-fourths of the manufacturers sampled shut down operations, compared to two-thirds of financial services firms and one-half of other service businesses. Similarly, manufacturers were far more active in selling off business units.

By contrast, financial services firms (68%) were somewhat more likely to downsize by combining operating units than manufacturing (63%) or other types of service companies (58%). Here, regulatory changes, including the lowering of barriers to interstate banking, prompted consolidation in the industry. For instance, Bank of America announced that, to eliminate redundancies and reduce debt, it planned to cut 10,000 positions concurrent with its acquisition of Security Pacific. The merger of Chemical Bank and Manufacturers Hanover resulted in removal of 6,500 people.

2. **Changes in Employment Profiles.** Many organizations also downsized by changing their employment profile. Some 47% of companies studied laid off substantial numbers of workers, and 38% experienced significant

Exhibit 3.3   Downsizing measures used by industry groups.

	Industry		
Measures	Manufacturing (%)	Financial Services (%)	Other Services (%)
Some operations shut down	78	68	49
Operating units combined	63	68	58
Hiring freeze imposed	66	59	46
Some business units sold	71	55	33
A substantial number of workers laid off	58	51	36
Early retirement incentives offered	57	35	30
Managment staff significantly reduced	45	41	33
A substantial number of workers allowed to shift to part-time schedules	6	16	10

reductions in their management staff. Four out of every ten companies offered an early retirement incentive to reduce employee ranks. Manufacturers were more likely to lay off substantial numbers of workers, offer early retirement incentives, and reduce management staff than firms in other sectors. In turn, financial service companies were more active in changing their employment profile than other service concerns.

3. **Changes in Employment Policies.** Finally, downsizing through changes in employment policies occurred in varying degrees. While a majority of organizations (57%) imposed hiring freezes to control the number of people they employed, just 10% allowed a substantial number of workers to shift from full- to part-time schedules. Again, manufacturers were more likely than other businesses to impose a hiring freeze, whereas financial service firms were more inclined than others to allow substantial numbers of workers to shift to part-time jobs.

Differences in downsizing were also found in other comparisons:

- The largest employers were the most active downsizers (see Exhibit 3.4). Over 80% of companies with more than 10,000 employees reported shutting down some operations or combining operating units,

Exhibit 3.4   Downsizing measures used by company size.

	Number of Employees		
Measures	1,000 or Under (%)	1,001 to 10,000 (%)	Over 10,000 (%)
Some operations shut down	38	66	82
Operating units combined	55	59	81
Hiring freeze imposed	42	62	62
Some business units sold	19	53	75
A substantial number of workers laid off	34	49	59
Early retirement incentives offered	22	38	59
Managment staff significantly reduced	27	39	52
A substantial number of workers allowed to shift to part-time schedules	8	8	16

and three-quarters sold business units. A majority also imposed hiring freezes, offered early retirement incentives, laid off substantial numbers of workers, and reduced management staffs. Companies with more revenues were as active in downsizing as companies with less revenue.

- Publicly held companies were more active downsizers than privately held firms (see Exhibit 3.5). The most pronounced differences were in their use of structural approaches to downsizing. This reflected their larger size and was also testimony to the continued earnings pressures on public companies to reduce expenses. Privately held firms, subjected to the same general economic and market pressures as public firms but shielded from having to turn out quarterly earnings reports to meet the whims of Wall Street, swung the downsizing ax less dramatically.

Jobs Eliminated

On average, these downsizing measures accounted for the elimination of 12% of jobs in the affected organizations. As Exhibit 3.6 shows, downsizings were limited to 5% of jobs or fewer in over one-third of the companies.

Exhibit 3.5 Downsizing measures used by company ownership.

	Company Held	
	Publicly (%)	Privately (%)
Some operations shut down	72	56
Operating units combined	69	53
Hiring freeze imposed	59	49
Some business units sold	62	41
A substantial number of workers laid off	52	42
Early retirement incentives offered	45	34
Managment staff significantly reduced	43	34
A substantial number of workers allowed to shift to part-time schedules	12	7

Exhibit 3.6 Percentage of jobs eliminated via downsizing.

Jobs Eliminated in a Single Company (%)	Total Companies That Eliminated This Percentage of Jobs (%)
5 or Less	37
6–10	20
11–15	9
16–20	8
21–25	4
26–30	4
Over 30	6
Mean # of jobs eliminated = 12%	

As many eliminated between 6 to 20% of their jobs. And more than one in five jobs were eliminated in 14% of the organizations studied.

Data on the type of downsizing and number of people affected show that two broad trends in American industry are being played out in corporate staffing:

Employment Shifts from Manufacturing to Services.   Downsizing occurs most often in more mature industry sectors. One of five manufacturing firms studied has eliminated 20% or more of its jobs compared with one of seven financial services companies and one of twenty nonfinancial service firms. Manufacturers were more likely to make their cuts via plant closures, layoffs, and early retirement programs. Consistent with this trend, firms with a larger proportion of older workers were much more likely to use early retirement incentives to reduce their staff. Less well educated employees were also more at risk: Companies in which less than 50% of the laborforce graduated from college eliminated one-third more jobs than firms with more than 50% college graduates.

These findings illustrate how downsizing contributes to the continuing movement of jobs away from manufacturing and into services and alters the makeup of the manufacturing workforce. Overall, the number of thirty- to sixty-year olds employed in factory jobs has declined from 30% to 25% of total domestic employment from 1970 to 1990 in the United States. And the proportion of workers under thirty years of age employed in factories had declined from 28% to 19%. It is apparent from survey data that the heavy reliance on downsizing via restructuring, massive layoffs, and hiring freezes in the manufacturing sector contributes to this trend.

The Transfer of Manufacturing Jobs to Foreign Countries. Multi-national corporations were also more likely than domestically based firms to do more in the way of structural downsizing. For instance, three-fourths of the firms with substantial overseas facilities shut down U.S. operations, compared with 59% of those without substantial foreign activity. Similarly, 70% of firms with substantial overseas operations versus 44% of those without much foreign activity sold off business units.

The introductory chapter reported that companies cited the need to be global competitors and closer to markets as prime reasons for their overseas expansion. Interestingly, however, other motives may also figure into their employment decisions. Here we see that firms more concerned about the high cost of U.S. labor relative to foreign wages were significantly more likely to lay off larger numbers of workers than those less concerned with U.S. pay rates (see Exhibit 3.7). This provides evidence of how downsizing patterns in U.S. companies contribute to the movement of jobs to foreign countries.

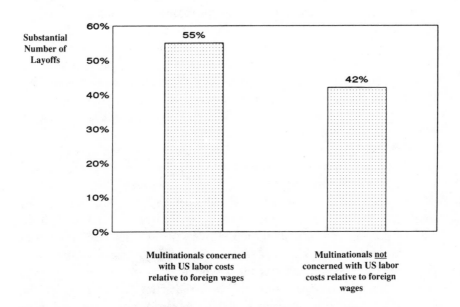

Exhibit 3.7 Corporate downsizing versus overseas activity. (Base: Companies that downsized that have overseas operations.)

REASONS FOR DIFFERENT FORMS OF DOWNSIZING

Analysis of survey data also reveals that companies downsizing for reasons of profitability and cost containment use different measures to reduce staff than those concerned with increased productivity, remaining competitive or making changes in their business strategy. Specifically, the majority of financially driven downsizings involved layoffs of substantial numbers of employees. In 55% of the companies that downsized because of cost containment and 60% of those because of lack of profitability, companies report that a substantial number of employees were laid off. By contrast, when improved efficiency or productivity was the single most important reason for downsizing, a large number of employees were laid off in only 44% of the cases.

Management ranks were reduced to a significant degree in about one-half of downsizings made to contain costs, compared with about one-third of downsizings with the intention of improving efficiency or productivity. In turn, early retirement incentives were offered in 54% of the downsizings for cost containment, but only in 38% of downsizings to improving efficiency or productivity.

These findings show that financially driven downsizings generally eliminate jobs through changes in a company's employment profile. They are more apt to push people out the door by laying them off, eliminating layers of management, or offering people the chance to retire early. Strategically-driven downsizings, by contrast, are less apt to eradicate jobs. Because these downsizings seek to enhance organizational effectiveness and build production capacity, they more often accompany changes in organizational structure. Because many times they are proactively approached, they are often accompanied by hiring freezes, retraining efforts, and opportunities for people to assume part-time positions.

Some selected examples illustrate the differences between proactive, strategic downsizing and more reactive, financial programs. Hallmark, Wm. Wrigley Jr. Company, and Mentor Graphics are three companies where efforts to improve productivity and efficiency and to implement a new strategy were accompanied by downsizing. Hallmark, for instance, whittled 1,300 positions from its 20,000 worldwide staff in a 2½-year continuous retraining process. This truly was the elimination of positions, not people, because the downsizing was integrated with a cross-training program to broaden or replace obsolete skills. At Wm. Wrigley Jr. Company, the chewing gum manufacturer, management coupled a move toward greater efficiency with a plan to let attrition pare its work force from 6,200 to 5,000 over five years from 1986 to 1991. Despite the reductions, output increased 2%

per year during the period. And Mentor Graphics cut its personnel by 15% as it exited the documentation tools, hardware service, and computer-aided software engineering businesses to hone in on its core electronic design automation business.

In contrast to these proactive efforts to align downsizing with broader strategic or operational change, many reductions-in-force are purely cost-containment efforts. American Television & Communications, a cable television operation, needed to remove costs in a maturing business when it cut its headquarters staff nearly in half. And Colgate-Palmolive tried across-the-board staff reductions in the 1980s when it set out to reduce spending at its technology group. However, the cuts did not prove permanent because managers added back the people they needed.

✳ CONSEQUENCES OF DOWNSIZING

Four out of ten companies in this study reported that downsizing efforts resulted in undesirable consequences for the organization. Exhibit 3.8 shows that the most frequently reported problem (in 61% of the cases of downsizing) was the negative impact on the morale of the remaining employees. The next most frequently cited consequences concerned finding ways to do the work that had been performed by former employees. Over four in ten companies that downsized had a greater need to retrain remaining employees, and over one-third increased their use of temporary workers, consultants, and overtime. One-fourth had to contract out the work of entire functions.

Exhibit 3.8 Consequences of downsizing.

Consequences	Total (%)
Lower morale among the remaining workforce	61
More need for retraining the remaining workforce	41
More use of temporary workers or consultants	36
More use of overtime	35
Increased retiree health care costs	30
Entire functions contracted out	26
Wrong people lost	20
Severence costs absorbed that were greater than anticipated	16
Overall, too many people lost	6

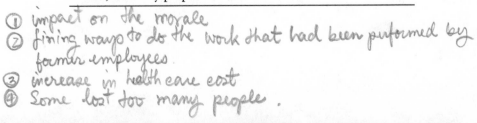

health care cost ↑

The direct financial consequences were that three in ten companies said that retiree health care costs had increased following downsizing, and 16% found that they had to absorb severance costs that were greater than they had anticipated. Another criticism of poorly planned downsizings is that people with critical skills or needed talents take advantage of incentives to leave the company. In this survey, one out of every five companies reported losing the wrong people as a consequence of the downsizing, and a small number lost too many people. There were some notable differences across companies in their postdownsizing problems:

- One-half of the companies in which a substantial number of employees lost jobs reported unfavorable consequences compared to one-fourth of companies experiencing less severe cuts.

- Retiree health costs were far more of a problem in firms employing 30% or more workers over age 55 compared with those having a younger workforce. Firms with older workers also had more need for retraining employees and more undesirable downsizing consequences overall.

- Companies that lost too many people report having trouble recruiting qualified high school graduates. Seemingly, these firms did not adequately plan how to keep valuable contributors from leaving and are now paying the price.

Consequences by Approach

Certain consequences of downsizing were more prominent when particular approaches to reducing headcount were used. Sometimes the relationship between downsizing methods and the consequences was predictable. Firms offering early retirement programs, for example, were far more likely to experience increases in their retiree health costs than those that used other downsizing measures. Firms in which 30% or more of the workforce was unionized had to make greater use of overtime than less unionized firms. This may relate to work rules. Finally, organizations that shut down some operations or sold off business units were more likely to contract out entire functions. Vital resources appear to have been lost along with nonessential jobs.

Downsizings involving large-scale layoffs or the elimination of a layer of management had more unfavorable consequences than in other types of downsizing (see Exhibit 3.9). Firms that eliminated jobs and layers of man-

Exhibit 3.9 Consequences of downsizing by changes in employment profile.

Consequences	Overall (%)	Laid Off Substantial Number of Workers (%)	Reduced Management Staff (%)
Lower morale among the remaining workforce	61	80	79
More need for retraining the remaining workforce	41	51	56
Increased retiree health care costs	30	39	43

agement were more likely to have morale problems, to have increased needs for retraining, and to absorb higher retiree health costs. It may be that they simply hacked away at positions rather than carefully analyzing and justifying these reductions in light of a forward-looking corporate strategy.

Consequences by Reason

Completing the picture of downsizing practices, Exhibit 3.10 compares the consequences experienced by firms that downsized for financial-reactive

Exhibit 3.10 Consequences of downsizing by reason.

Consequences	Cost Containment/ Cost Control (%)	Improved Efficiency/ Productivity (%)
Lower morale among the remaining workforce	67	64
More need for retraining the remaining workforce	37	33
More use of temporary workers or consultants	45	30
More use of overtime	46	27
Increased retiree health care costs	33	24
Entire functions contracted out	30	21
Wrong people lost	24	5
Overall, too many people lost	10	3

reasons versus those experienced by firms that downsized for strategic-proactive reasons. In this figure we see that downsizing for reasons of profitability or cost containment had no more or less of an impact on morale than downsizing aimed at increasing efficiency or beating out competitors. Both increased needs for retraining in one-third of the cases. Ironically, many more financially-driven downsizings resulted in the increased use of temporary workers or consultants, more overtime, higher retiree health care costs, and the need to contract out entire functions. Companies that downsized to control costs were also more likely to report losing the wrong people or losing too many people than those that aimed to improve efficiency or productivity. Clearly, when downsizing is planned and used as a tool to build organizational capacity, the unfavorable consequences are less prominent than when downsizing is a reactive financial move.

✳ THE HUMAN TOLL ✳

No matter what the reason, downsizing extracts a human toll, hitting hard at the financial, psychological, and physical well-being of laid-off employees, their families, and their communities. Although the are not measured directly by this study, the human consequences of job loss are usually severe. For instance, evidence from a broad array of case studies reveals that one-third of those directly involved in plant closings experience long-term unemployment, and those who do find work often have to settle for a decline in occupational status.[4] One study that tracked a nationwide sample of 4,000 job loss victims found that almost three-fifths of the displaced workers had to settle for jobs with less income or status.[5] Another obvious and immediate impact of job loss is family income deterioration.

Downsizing also has an impact on people's psychological well being. Studies find that job loss victims blame themselves for losing their jobs and even for allowing themselves to get in a situation where their job security is put at risk. As unemployment lingers, depression about future prospects sets in.[6] Anxiety and despair grow, while self-confidence wanes. Evidence shows that aggressive behavior, family conflict, and substance abuse increase. Overall, the suicide rate for laid-off workers is 30 times the national average.[7]

Research also shows that workers who have lost their jobs are more apt to be afflicted by high blood pressure, high cholesterol counts, and a high incidence of ulcers and respiratory diseases. These and other physical health problems are manifestations of the psychological stress endured by job loss victims, but are also exacerbated by the financial effects they experience.[8]

The human toll of downsizing is increased in the case of older workers who suffer more health consequences and have more difficulty gaining another full-time job. A sampling of evidence suggests that older workers are more vulnerable to job loss via downsizing than younger ones as a later chapter reports.

Finally, downsizing has a double-barrelled impact on communities where jobs are lost: Unemployment first reduces tax revenues and second increases the need for additional public expenditures. A downsizing or plant closing is particularly painful in communities that rely on one industry or a primary employer. When a large proportion of a community's working population is put on notice, the impact on both the community's revenues and its expenditures can be debilitating. This potential for community suffering received national attention in early 1992 when General Motors approached the decision to close an automobile assembly plant in either Ypsilanti, Michigan or Arlington, Texas. Mayors, county supervisors, and local chamber of commerce officials, knowing full well the cost of losing jobs in their community during the recession, joined labor leaders in lobbying GM on the decision.

HOW YOU DOWNSIZE MAKES A DIFFERENCE

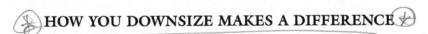

How a downsizing is handled has as much effect on the resulting mindset of employees as why it occurs. At Tenneco, where 1,200 employees were laid off over a six-week period, many learned of their fates when confronted by armed guards carrying boxes for them to use in clearing out their desks. At Allied Bank of Texas, department heads called meetings and then read the names of those to be laid off in front of their coworkers. By contrast, when Donald P. Kelly, then chief executive of Esmark, Inc., personally met with the corporate staff of newly acquired Norton Simon, Inc., he was able to justify staff reductions by fully explicating the financial status of the combined company. Kelly explained the number of redundancies between Norton Simon and Esmark employees and the personnel costs. He went on to describe the attractive severance packages that those asked to leave could expect. Kelly then asked for, and received, people's help in managing the cutbacks.

Memories of how victims of reductions are treated stick in the minds of surviving employees for a long time to come. If they observe that affected employees are treated poorly—given short notice, a piddling severance, and nothing in the way of personal or career counseling—then surviving employees are bound to fear that they are next in line for arbitrary and insensitive treatment. If, on the other hand, unaffected employees see that those who are to be laid off are treated fairly, and given proper notice, decent severance pay, and outplacement assistance, then those who are retained will perceive less threat and have a better opinion of their employer. The implication is that a downsizing must be managed with an eye toward those who remain with the company.

Best Practice

Corporate downsizings are wrenching experiences for all involved, and most managers find it difficult to make cuts; it is one thing to speak of the need to reduce costs in the abstract, but another to make decisions that change the lives of people for whom you are responsible. Offering voluntary approaches to downsizing puts the middle manager in the awkward position of counseling employees on whether to stay or go. No one wants to tell an employee his or her services are no longer needed, even if it is a humane thing to do when a subsequent wave of involuntary cuts looms on the horizon.

Supervisors and managers who lead work teams also find downsizing difficult. They struggle to maintain productivity and find ways to get more work done with fewer bodies at a time when people are emotionally distraught. Human resources professionals become overwhelmed during downsizings. They have not only a staggering load of paperwork in processing terminations and scheduling outplacement services, but the added burden of knowing their own area—a staff function—is likely to be one of the hardest hit. At the same time, employees line up outside their door waiting for a shoulder to cry on.

Overall, an American Management Association study finds that companies are doing a reasonably good job of assisting and supporting people who are being let go: Nearly 90% of the companies surveyed gave employees advance notice of a cutback; 80% continued their health benefits; and 50% provided them with outplacement services.[9] A body of research and practice, however, suggests that there are other steps companies can take to more effectively and humanely manage downsizing.

Preparing People. A primary task during a downsizing is to prepare people for change. The CEO or senior executive in a business unit can best set the tone by acknowledging the human side of downsizing. This is best accomplished by providing a realistic picture of the tough times, rather than being silent or calling for people to tough it out. Distrust and cynicism run deep during a downsizing, and many employees feel they are simply numbers in a master plan. Part of preparing downsizing survivors, then, is to alert them to the fact that the organization is traveling down an uncertain path. There will be false starts and midcourse corrections.

Preparing people for a downsizing also involves acknowledging the human reaction to the trauma of layoffs and letting it take its course. The idea here is to help employees understand that their emotional and behavioral reactions to a downsizing are normal and to be expected, and are not a sign of personal weakness. This is a matter of helping people to understand and control their emotions rather to be controlled by them.

Revisiting Critical Corporate Values. A downsizing provides an opportunity to re-establish the key cultural values and norms that guide employee behavior. A clear statement of the company's operating principles and values tells employee how to succeed in the post-downsizing company. Following a reduction-in-force in a computer distribution company, the CEO presented a statement of "critical success factors" and then charged each senior vice president to translate them into clear principles to guide employee behavior. One critical success factor, "be the easiest company for customers to do business with," led operations to establish a policy that all orders placed by 5:00 P.M. would be shipped the same day. Employees surviving the downsizing were put to work identifying how to implement this principle. Importantly, time was set aside during the work week for problem-solving meetings. Their involvement in helping the company rebound from the downsizing caused employees to feel like architects of change rather than victims. The introduction of more efficient and customer-friendly work methods was a tangible sign that the downsizing would lead to a better organization.

Management Training. Although senior executives set the tone in a downsizing, middle managers are the ones who are seen by and interact with the bulk of the workforce day in and day out. They are typically bombarded with questions about the downsizing and the future of the company, yet they may not have the vision of senior management. As a result, they often avoid contact with employees or offer vague statements that do little to assuage concerns.

This means managers must be trained in strategic approaches to downsizing, the intricacies of implementing change, and the interpersonal skills needed to lead people through a troubling time. After a downsizing at a major brewer, for instance, workshops were conducted with all managers and supervisors to consider human factors in a downsizing and put the issues on the table. Managers discusssed how to use the downsizing as an opportunity to identify and implement better ways of organizing work. They were then given the freedom to choose the way they wanted to present and implement initial plans in their departments. Some opted to mandate certain changes but engage employees in deciding how to implement the changes; others designed processes to empower work teams to make changes on their own. These workshops gave middle managers confidence that they could lead their teams through rough times.

DOWNSIZING IN CUTTING EDGE COMPANIES

As unpleasant and demoralizing as downsizing actions can be, there are ways to ease the pain. To do so, there must be a well-designed, proactive human resources strategy to support the downsizing. Survivors are the real audience for the unfolding drama, and their memories are long and active.

Survivors' reactions to a downsizing are shaped by their leaders' responses to the business conditions that prompt the need for belt-tightening. Many employers make what approaches a classic pattern of mistakes as they begin to step up their response to bad economic news. As their profits erode and they lose market share, they frequently worry first about the investors and focus their communication efforts externally rather than internally. When senior executives freeze hiring and impose spending cuts, the rule seems to be closed-door meetings with little official communication about why the actions are necessary. If the situation escalates to plant closings, layoffs, and the offering of early retirement packages, communication and counseling focus mostly on victims with little attention to survivors.

Likewise, when searching for creative solutions to company business problems, leadership too often declines to discuss their options or offer any kind of outlook for the future. Instead, they lower their profile with their employees as they grope for the right strategy or combination of actions. The result is nervous employees who believe that their own management is either insensitive to their plight or fresh out of ideas. When leaders are finally ready to talk about recovery and offer a fresh vision of the future, they find that their past behavior has earned them an insecure workforce more inclined to look for another job than to stay around and help rebuild the company.

This study confirms a clear relationship between the human resources philosophy in companies and their downsizing activity (see Exhibit 3.11). Over half (54%) of companies classified as having a *prudent* response to new policies downsized because of reactive financial reasons, including lack of profitability or cost containment, whereas only one-third (34%) of companies with a *cutting edge* human resource orientation downsized in a reactive

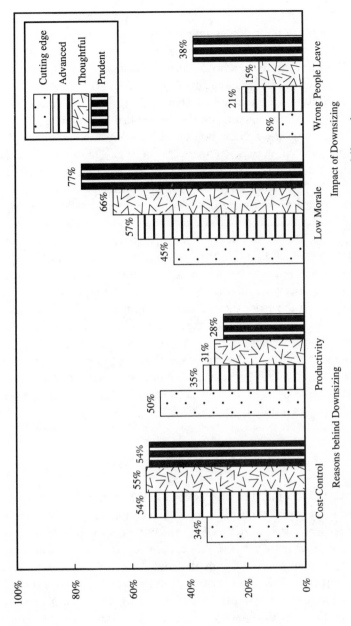

Exhibit 3.11 Corporate downsizing and human resource philosophy.

83

mode. In turn, a need to improve efficiency or productivity was the most frequently cited reason for downsizing among these human resource leaders. The percentage of jobs lost was also higher in companies with "prudent" policies (18%) than in those who describe their philosophy as "thoughtful" (12%), "advanced" (11%), or "cutting edge" (13%).

There were also fewer negative consequences from downsizing in human resource leaders than in laggards. Some three-fourths of the companies that described their response to new policies as "prudent" report lower morale among remaining employees, compared to 66% of "thoughtful," 57% of "advanced," and 45% of "cutting edge" companies. Over one-half of the companies with "prudent" responses to new policies paid the costly price of increased overtime following downsizing, compared to about one-third of "thoughtful" or "advanced" companies, and one-fourth of "cutting edge" companies. In addition, losing the wrong people as a consequence of the downsizing was especially a problem in companies with "prudent" (38%) approaches to new policies, but less so in companies described as "thoughtful" (15%), "advanced" (21%), or "cutting edge" (8%).

The key conclusion from these data is that innovators in the human resource area were more likely to make their downsizing a part of a broad organizational improvement effort and to experience few unfavorable consequences. Indeed, 53% of the executives in cutting edge firms report that their downsizings have fully met corporate objectives with few negative side effects, and another 34% are somewhat satisfied. By comparison, just one in three "prudent" firms fully met objectives.

FUTURE DOWNSIZING

Has downsizing become "business as usual?" While only 5% of human resource executives expect their companies will eliminate a lot of jobs through the mid-90s, nearly two-thirds (63%) project that some jobs will be eliminated. Only about one-fourth (28%) anticipate that no jobs will be eliminated in their companies through the mid-90s. As Exhibit 3.12 shows, manufacturing and financial service companies expect to eliminate more jobs than nonfinancial service companies that are riding a wave of growth. Jobs appear to be safest in the smallest of companies in terms of staff size and revenue. Fewer than half of the companies with less than 1000 employees expect to eliminate jobs as compared to 90% of firms employing over 10,000 people. Similar findings result when companies are measured by revenue. Furthermore, as in the period from 1987 to 1991, public companies expect to do more in the way of downsizing than privately owned firms.

Exhibit 3.12 Expected extent of downsizing over next five years.

	TOTAL (%)	Revenues				Number of Employees			Industry			Company Held	
		100 Million and Under (%)	101 Million to 500 Million (%)	501 Million to 1 Billion (%)	Over 1 Billion (%)	1,000 or Under (%)	1,001 to 10,000 (%)	Over 10,000 (%)	Manufacturing (%)	Financial Services (%)	Other Services (%)	Publicly (%)	Privately (%)
Jobs Lost													
A lot of jobs	5	2	3	2	8	3	4	8	5	7	2	6	3
Some jobs	63	53	57	53	73	43	63	82	69	64	59	70	56
No jobs at all	28	40	38	37	15	52	27	9	23	27	33	21	33
Not sure	4	5	2	7	3	3	5	2	4	2	6	3	8

Comparison with Other Research

To put these findings into context, compare them with data from the American Management Association's annual survey of downsizing among member companies. While the AMA sample suffers from a low response rate and is not reflective of American business as a whole, it does provide an interesting comparison sample and a source of trends over time. Exhibit 3.13 shows that 55.5% of the 1991 AMA sample reported workforce reductions, a substantial jump from the four previous years. The average percentage of the workforce eliminated declined in the 1991 AMA survey to 9.6% from the previous year's 10.9%. The reason cited by AMA researchers was that large companies, frequently engaging in a second or third wave of reductions, had fewer workers left to cut. Only small employers reported deeper cuts in 1991 than before.

In contrast to the AMA results, our sample found that cuts were deeper (an average of 12.2%) and that the largest employers made the deepest cuts. But, the AMA found, as we did, that economic matters were the most important reason for downsizing. A business downturn was cited by 43% of the AMA sample as the rationale underlying downsizing. Other reasons for downsizing—improved staff utilization, result of merger or acquisition, and so forth—were cited in the AMA survey with about the same frequency as in our survey. Interestingly, mergers and acquisitions, while cited by only few human resources executives in both our survey and the AMA survey,

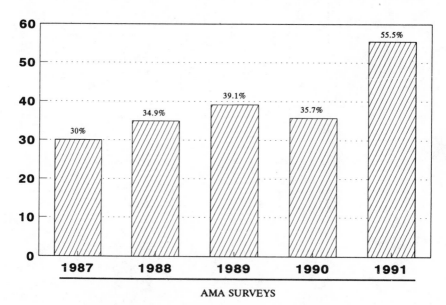

Exhibit 3.13   Downsizing activity 1987–1991.

Exhibit 3.14 Expected versus actual downsizing activity. (AMA survey)

Year	Companies Reporting Plans to Downsize in Following Year (%)	Companies That Downsized in the Following Year (%)
1987	17	35
1988	14	39
1989	17	36
1990	15	56

had been much more frequently cited as a rationale for the reductions in 1990 and preceding years. The onset of the recession changed that.

What is especially important to note in the AMA data is the difference between a company's plans to downsize and its actual downsizing activity. Exhibit 3.14 shows that from 1987–89 the number of AMA member companies that downsized was more than double the number that in the prior year had made plans to downsize. In 1990, moreover, there were 3½ times the number of actual downsizings as planned downsizings. This means that we may expect even more downsizing in the years ahead than is projected by our survey data.

Downsizing versus Overseas Expansion

Furthermore, corporate downsizing projections also have to be considered alongside plans to open or expand overseas plants and offices (see Exhibit 3.15). Here we find that over half of the largest companies sampled, whether measured by employees or revenues, say it is very likely that operations will be opened or expanded overseas. The manufacturers that plan to do the most downsizing (74%) are also most likely to expand abroad (68%). Finally, two-thirds of the firms already having substantial facilities overseas feel that additional expansion is very likely through the mid-90s. This forces us to the conclude that the shifting of jobs from the United States to foreign lands will continue.

In addition, one-half of all human resources executives feel that periodic downsizing is necessary to maintain an effective, competitive organization (see Exhibit 3.16). Interestingly, no significant differences were found across any groups in response to this item. Apparently, a comparable number of human resources executives in all types of organizations have concluded that downsizing is not a one-time event. The question at hand, however, is whether employees in these organizations will accept downsizing as a regular business practice.

Exhibit 3.15 Percentage of companies likely to open or expand plants and offices abroad from 1991 to 1996.

	TOTAL (%)	Company Revenues				Number of Employees			Industry			Substantial Overseas Facilities	
		100 Million and Under (%)	101 Million to 500 Million (%)	501 Million to 1 Billion (%)	Over 1 Billion (%)	1,000 or Under (%)	1,001 to 10,000 (%)	Over 10,000 (%)	Manufacturing (%)	Financial Services (%)	Other Services (%)	Yes (%)	No (%)
Very likely	37	25	25	37	49	18	33	52	50	27	32	64	16
Somewhat likely	16	19	25	19	13	21	16	15	18	15	17	14	15
Not very likely	18	21	18	12	18	16	18	18	17	16	19	15	22
Not at all likely	27	32	30	33	17	42	31	13	13	38	30	4	46
Not sure	2	4	3	—	2	4	2	2	1	4	2	3	2

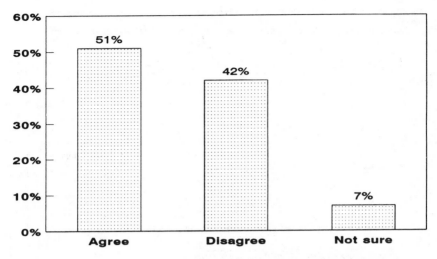

Exhibit 3.16 Whether periodic downsizing is necessary to maintain an effective, competitive organization.

Employee Opinion

Data from an employee opinion study conducted by Gantz-Wiley suggests that the consequences of layoffs are quite pronounced among corporate survivors. Research shows that employees who remain after the cuts experience a set of attitudinal and behavioral reactions known as layoff survivor sickness.[10] Survivors often feel guilty for being spared and become depressed at their inability to control or avert future layoffs. In the short run, surviving employees are distracted from doing their job, and productivity plummets.[11] Over the long haul, those who have been through a downsizing have considerably less confidence and trust in their employers.

Of course, corporate downsizings can have positive consequences, too. Carefully planned and executed, downsizings can prune the organization of unneeded people and business units. Leadership with the right mix of visionary and practical skills can rally employees around the notion that the downsizing is not simply a tactic to cut costs but a turning point at which to examine and improve the very ways work is approached and conducted in the organization. When it comes to employees, however, research suggests that three factors influence postdownsizing attitudes. First, downsizing survivors who cope best feel in control of things that matter to them. They recognize that they cannot manage what is beyond their control and act in areas that they can influence. Second, successful survivors have a greater feeling of

Signs of Survivor Sickness in Companies Following a Layoff

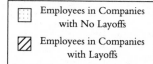

Employees in Companies
with No Layoffs

Employees in Companies
with Layoffs

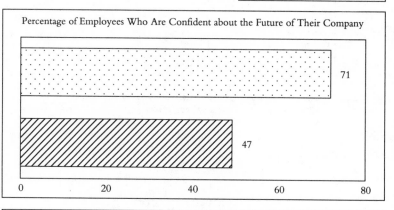

Percentage of Employees Who Are Confident about the Future of Their Company

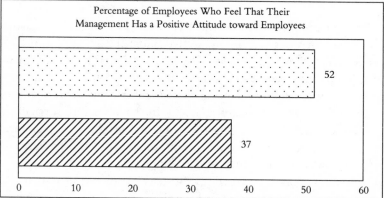

Percentage of Employees Who Feel That Their
Management Has a Positive Attitude toward Employees

Source: Gantz-Wiley Research Consulting Group. 1990 national survey of 2,500 households of employees whose companies have been involved in layoffs in the past twelve months.

involvement in what they are doing. Finally, those who cope best take risks, seek out new challenges, and look for new slants in approaching their work. They recognize that the rules of the game have changed and adapt to new workplace conditions.

IMPLICATIONS

Findings from this survey and other studies, as well as experience in organizations engaged in and rebounding from reductions in the number of people employed, suggest several critical implications for the management of downsizing in business.

1. **Strategic Intent.** Over one-half of the downsizings described in this study were reactive financially motivated events, compared to one-fourth that were proactive efforts to enhance organizational effectiveness and competitiveness. The data show that these cost-containment downsizings have the most negative impact on employee morale and frequently result in costly increases in the use of temporary workers or consultants, in overtime, in retiree health care costs, and in the contracting out of entire functions. In addition, downsizings with the primary objective of cutting costs are far more likely to result in the loss of the wrong people or of too many people overall.

   To minimize unintended consequences, then, downsizing must be closely linked to corporate strategy, nurtured through careful planning, and supported through the dedication of sufficient resources. This can transform downsizing from a reactive crisis management action to a proactive and potentially positive organizational change. As these data show, downsizing to improve productivity and counter the competition is more likely to achieve desired business and human results.

2. **Human Resources Orientation.** Firms with a self-described cutting edge human resource orientation are more likely to downsize to improve productivity and efficiency than those that follow or lag in introducing human resource innovations. They also have fewer unfavorable consequences and problems with postdownsizing morale. This reinforces the point that progressive management practices help to ease the pain of corporate cutbacks.

   Most downsizings do not occur in a vacuum. Many firms have engaged in multiple waves of change the past several years via acquisitions, restructuring, and maybe a change in leadership or strategic direction. As a result, employees can become numbed by so much change, unmotivated by fewer career opportunities, and pessimistic about their management's ability to lead during difficult times. A forward-looking human resource orientation is needed to retain and motivate downsizing survivors.

3. **Retraining and Redeployment.** Another factor in effective downsizings are provisions for staff retraining and redeployment. In this study, we found that the percentage of employees who lost jobs due to downsizing was significantly lower in companies that retrained a substantial portion of their labor force (11%) than the percentage in firms not as engaged in retraining (15%). In the next chapter, analyses show that firms that downsized and also became active in employee involvement or total quality programs had far more success than ones that made cutbacks but did not accompany them with retraining or systematic efforts to improve productivity.

4. **Effective Management.** Our data show that downsizing is here to stay in corporate America. This brings the opportunity to enhance organizational effectiveness and, along the way, rebuild employee relations by carefully structuring downsizings and showing employees explicitly how the downsizing is resulting in a new and better organization. For the downsizing to have positive consequences, the human resources function must educate line management and introduce creative methods for managing the downsizing. Among the imperatives are the following:

- Think through strategically—from a business and human resource perspective—where the organization is going and how it will revitalize its employees, before the actual downsizing occurs.

- Analyze strengths, weaknesses, redundancies, and value-added activities in advance of downsizing, rather than taking the ready-fire-aim approach.

- Provide the talent, time, and other resources to ensure that a broad range of alternative strategies and approaches is being considered in the downsizing planning process.

- Manage the number of employees proactively, by anticipating business changes and cross-training current employees.

- Provide opportunities for bottom-up participation and implementation of downsizing concurrent with top-down strategies.

5. **Managing Survivors.** Most survivors recoup from the trauma of downsizing but they will be more likely to do so if they see some value resulting from the exercise. People can rationalize enduring the pain if they can be shown that there is some benefit for themselves and their organization. This occurs through a committed effort to help teams and individuals regroup following a downsizing.[12] This means addressing both the emotional realities and business imperatives associated with

realigning work after the cuts are made. The challenges for managers are to help their work team members (1) rebound from the psychological trauma of downsizing and realignment, (2) clarify work roles and responsibilities in the new organization, and (3) secure the organizational capability and individual motivation needed for business success.

A downsizing also is an opportunity for an organization to renegotiate its psychological work contract with employees.[13] Most firms can no longer offer so-called womb-to-tomb employment to people, but they are well advised to clarify what they can offer in the way of career opportunities, skills training, retirement programs, and job security and what is expected from employees in return.

Exportation of Jobs

Finally, some comments about downsizing in conjunction with overseas expansion need to be made. Plainly many larger companies, especially manufacturers, plan to continue to downsize their domestic workforce while expanding overseas. Most attribute their plans to the need to be global competitors and to move closer to markets. However, we have seen that the firms most concerned with the cost of U.S. labor have more aggressive plans to expand overseas than otherwise.

Surely this has implications for the preservation and creation of high-skill jobs in the United States. Projections are that 75% of the new jobs created in the 1990s will be in the services. Moreover, the bulk of jobs being exported or eliminated are higher-paying manufacturing jobs. This has a potentially devastating impact on families and communities and the country as a whole. As the United States struggles to pull out of difficult times, public policy must be concerned with the migration of jobs to foreign countries. Downsizing can enhance competitiveness and should not be the issue addressed per se; rather, disinvestment in the nation's productive capacity must come under scrutiny.

CONCLUSION

This study shows that downsizing can be a prudent business move that helps a firm reposition itself, make gains in productivity, reduce costs, and be part of a broadbased effort to get the job done better. It can also be an exercise in politics, pain, and paranoia. The keys to effective downsizing — as measured in both business and human terms — are strategic intention, strong human resource support programs, retraining and redeployment, and constant attention to the management of survivors.

The real impact of how corporations manage downsizing will be measured as the country returns to a period of growth and another set of demands are placed on organizations. Which companies will have a dedicated and well-trained work force? Which ones will have ready-to-go workers? Which will have effective structures and efficient approaches to getting work done? Which will have learned from past downsizings to anticipate and respond proactively to continuing needs to restructure and resize the business? Those firms that base their staffing plans on coherent strategies and that continue to innovate in human resource management will be better positioned for the changes ahead.

NOTES

1. Fischer, A. B. 1991. Morale crisis. *Fortune,* November 18, 70–80.
2. Bluestone, B., and Harrison, B. 1982. *The deindustrialization of America.* New York: Basic Books.
3. Reich, R. 1983. *The Next American Frontier.* New York: Penguin.
4. C & R Associates. 1978. *Community costs of plant closings: Bibliography and survey of the literature.* Report prepared for the Federal Trade Commission.
5. Parnes, H. S., and R. King. 1977. Middle-Aged Job Losers. *Industrial Gerontology* 4(2): 77–95.
6. Jahoda, M. 1988. Economic recession and mental health: Some conceptual issues. *Journal of Social Issues* 44(4): 13–24.
7. Bunning, R. L. 1990. The dynamics of downsizing. *Personnel Journal,* September, 69–75.
8. Kessler, R. C., J. B. Turner, and J. S. House. 1988. Effects of unemployment on health in a community survey: Main, modifying, and mediating effects. *Journal of Social Issues* 44(4): 69–86.
9. American Management Association. 1990. *Responsible reductions in force: An AMA research report on downsizings and outplacement.* New York: AMA Briefings and Surveys.
10. Brockner, J. 1988. The effects of work layoff on survivors: Research, theory, and practice. In *Research in organizational Behavior (Vol. 10),* ed. B. M. Staw and L. L. Cummings, 213–256. Greenwich, CT: JAI Press.
11. Greenhalph, L. 1982. Maintaining organizational effectiveness during organizational retrenchment. *Journal of Applied Behavioral Science,* 18: 155–170.
12. Mirvis, P. H. and M. L. Marks. 1992. *Managing the merger: Making it work.* New York: Prentice Hall; Marks, M. L. and P. H. Mirvis. 1992. Rebuilding after the merger. *Organizational Dynamics.* 21(2): 18–32.
13. Marks, M. 1988. The disappearing corporate man. *Psychology Today* 22(9): 34–39.

4

Company Policies on Education and Training

Michael Useem

Company policies on education and training are shaped by a firm's product markets and production technologies. Managers nonetheless retain considerable discretion to move their companies along varied and sometimes starkly different paths. They face choices about how much to invest in their human resources and how best to capitalize on their employees' skills. Drawing on the Laborforce 2000 survey of human resource practices among 406 firms, this chapter presents information on the varied choices that companies have made about the education and training of both their entry-level and continuing employees.

Concern about the quality of future employees and the need to retrain current employees is widespread. But the corporate response has been uneven, with some firms investing far more than others. Much of the current variation in their education and training practices can be traced not only to company size and workforce composition but also to management cultures and restructuring experiences. When senior managements create an innovative climate for human resources practices, their companies invest more in retraining employees and contribute more to public schooling. When companies redesign their production processes and management practices, they spend more on entry level training and ongoing employee development. In the aftermath of organizational restructuring, however, the record is more mixed: Some companies do more retraining and take extra steps to improve the skills of incoming workers, whereas others pull back.

BACKGROUND

Like most features of corporate organization, a company's human resource policies are shaped by its product markets, production technologies, and business strategies. A newly appointed human resource manager would find many of the basic parameters set, hardly subject to intervention except at those rare moments when a company's direction is questioned and its cultural values and beliefs are subjected to reexamination.[1] Yet many corporations have faced such moments of reexamination in recent years. A number of the surveyed companies have undertaken major restructuring, and most expect that their company's human resource practices will require substantial change in the years ahead. Global competition, a stagnant economy, and demands for improved products and services—also rated as major concerns of top executives in this study—place competing demands on the same limited resources. Still, some companies committed the resources, opting for additional investments and fresh approaches. Others, by contrast, placed priorities elsewhere, preferring to stick with proven education and training practices. Contrasting paths, as a result, coexisted among otherwise similar companies, even those nearly identical in annual sales, workforce demography, and industrial sector.

This chapter argues that the varying paths taken in the area of education and training can be traced to four factors. The first is *management culture,* a company's philosophy and values about human resource practices. The second factor is *corporate restructuring,* defined broadly here to encompass actions ranging from the closing of plants and the reduction of the number of employees to the redesigning of production operations and the enhancment of employee involvement. The third factor is *company size,* and the fourth is *workforce composition.* Company size dictates the resources available for education and training, and employee backgrounds define the education and training needs.

EDUCATIONAL PERFORMANCE
IN THE UNITED STATES

If managements have had the capacity to travel varied paths, they nonetheless have faced common education problems. The quality of public schooling across the nation has seemingly decreased at the very same time that employer demand for well-educated employees has increased. A host of national studies document a widening gap that places intensifying burden on companies to make up privately for the public shortfall. The National Education Goals

Panel, a group of six governors, four members of Congress, and four administration officials, reported, for instance, that less than one out of every five American students enrolled in grades 4, 8, and 12 in 1990 had managed to achieve a national mathematics competency goal. In science, U.S. high school students were found to rank significantly below their counterparts in Japan, the Netherlands, and most other advanced industrial economies. The panel concluded that the "evidence is clear that our educational expectations, efforts, and performance do not begin to approach world-class levels."[2]

Yet we know that to keep up with changing production technologies, information applications, and international challenges our students need a world-class education. One assessment of the future of U.S. manufacturing, for instance, found that "organized smarts" have a decisive bearing on how American companies respond to industry competition from abroad: "An educated, skilled labor force broadens rather than forecloses choice in the competitive development and application of technologies."[3] The U.S. Office of Technology Assessment reached a similar conclusion: "The quality of the U.S. workforce matters now more than ever.... Training goes hand-in-hand with productivity, quality, flexibility, and automation in the best performing firms.... But when measured by international standards, most American workers are *not* well trained."[4]

Related assessments can be found in studies by the National Academy of Engineering and the Competitiveness Policy Council, and in twelve other national reports on educational policy and employment questions published between 1983 and 1991.[5] The source of this gap between employer needs and school performance has been attributed to a host of reasons. On the one hand, Cappelli confirms a significant increase in the skill requirements of production jobs in the United States this past decade.[6] On the other hand, factors as diverse as unqualified teachers, unmotivated students, and inadequate leadership contributed to a decrease in school performance. Bishop and others have also shown that many employers have not been effective communicating the skills they need to education providers.[7]

ENTRY LEVEL EDUCATION

In keeping with the widely reported educational limitations of many entry-level applicants, a substantial fraction of the surveyed companies described problems in hiring qualified personnel. One in four (26%) complained of "trouble in recruiting" qualified high school graduates, and one in six (16%)

Employers' Opinions of Recent New Hires

Ron Bass

A 1991 Harris survey of adults who either supervise or are involved in hiring decisions asked about the educational preparedness of employees hired within the last two years. The findings show majorities rate the preparation of newly hired employees negatively in many areas.

Think of young people who came to work for you. How would you rate the ways their schools prepared them on	Excellent or Pretty Good (%)	Only Fair or Poor (%)
Ability to read and understand written and verbal instructions	51	48
Being capable of doing simple arithmetic	47	50
Having skills that can be easily applied to getting their job done	43	56
Having the capacity to concentrate on the work being done over an extended period of time	40	59
Knowing how to solve problems that come up at work	36	63
Having a real sense of dedication to work	29	70

Source: School Reform, Public Perceptions Louis Harris and Associates, 1991.

reported problems in recruiting qualified college graduates. As noted in the introductory chapter, the problem here is not a labor shortage, but rather a shortage of skilled job candidates. Companies reported that only half (52%) of the high school graduates who advanced to the interview stage were deemed to possess the skills required for entry level positions.

Three-fourths of the firms that employ scientists and technologists anticipate further problems in recruiting them through the mid-90s. Over half of the companies hiring skilled blue-collar workers expect the same. Companies expressed less concern about recruiting other groups, though a number worry about finding qualified managers, clerical workers, and office staff, and even a quarter of the companies worry about finding qualified semiskilled and unskilled blue-collar workers.

The anticipated shortage of qualified employees appears to have as much to do with work motivation as cognitive skills. According to a 1991 survey of those who supervise workers or are involved in hiring decisions, for instance, the inability of many newly hired employees to understand written and verbal instructions, do simple arithmetic, or solve work problems is only part of this skills gap. A majority of the supervisors and recruiters also rated new hires negatively on work discipline, dedication to work, and the capacity to concentrate over an extended period of time.[8] Assessing the results of a number of related studies, Cappelli concludes that much of the perceived skills gap is less about deficits in academic skills and more about deficits in work attitudes.[9]

Of the 235 companies in the Laborforce 2000 study that specifically reported problems in recruiting qualified applicants, the leading solution has been to increase entry-level training, followed by altered recruitment methods and stronger links with schools (see Exhibit 4.1). Much of the entry level training focuses on making up for past deficits. Over half of the companies surveyed asserted that they were either very (24%) or somewhat

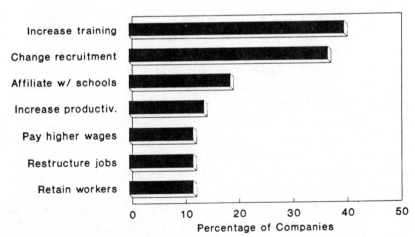

Note: Based on 235 companies reporting problems in recruiting qualified applicants.

Exhibit 4.1 How companies are planning to address problems in recruiting qualified job applicants.

(28%) likely to provide remedial education for some employees. Nearly three-fourths stated that they were very (45%) or somewhat (29%) likely to offer basic skills training.

It is questionable, however, whether companies will apply the resources necessary to bring their newly hired workers up to world-class standards. Already, the training commitment to new employees is relatively substantial: Nearly a fifth (18%) of the surveyed companies' training budgets were allocated on average to training new entrants. A study of one industry in the United States and Japan, however, suggests that American manufacturers are still not investing enough. Japanese automobile manufacturers were found to offer a training program of 320 hours on average for new employees; their American counterparts provided a mere 48 hours. Moreover, the disparities stemmed more from management commitment than the constraints of local markets or production technologies: The average training course for new employees stood at 280 hours for Japanese-owned plants in the United States, more than five times the average for American-owned plants in this country.[10]

EMPLOYEE DEVELOPMENT AND RETRAINING

The bulk of company education and training investments is targeted at upgrading the skills of the continuing workforce. Employee development, generally skewed toward better-educated and higher-ranking personnel, became a significant activity in major firms as they created internal employment markets and came to view their workforces as worthy of long-term investment.[11] The introduction of new technologies generated further demand for continuous upgrading of employee skills. In the present study, for instance, virtually all of the surveyed companies brought advanced computer technologies into their offices or plants during the past decade, technologies that require reasonably well-educated labor forces.

As a result, employee development programs stressing quantitative skills, problem solving, and interpersonal relations were widely in place among the surveyed enterprises. Indeed, the retraining of employees "to keep skills current" was of general concern, with nearly three-quarters (71%) of the companies indicating that it was a *serious* company issue.

Of primary concern was the need to retrain the enterprise's technical, production, and professional workers (Exhibit 4.2). The firms reported that, on average, they had retrained 58% of these main-line workers from 1986 to 1991. The average, however, masks great variation in how *many* workers

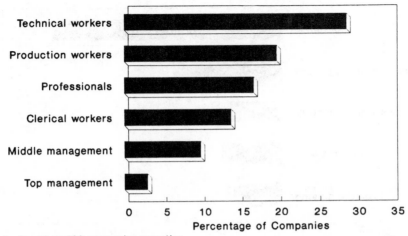

Technical workers
Production workers
Professionals
Clerical workers
Middle management
Top management

0   5   10   15   20   25   30   35
Percentage of Companies

Note: Based on 288 companies reporting
that retraining is a serious issue.

Exhibit 4.2   Employee groups most in need of retraining.

are retrained: Roughly one in four companies retrained 25% or less of their main-line workers, while one in three retrained 75% or more. Firms also varied in how *often* they retrained workers in new technologies or production systems, with the most active retraining every one to three years (25%) or every year (34%). If technological change might be expected to intensify such training, however, the results are not evident in this study: The frequency of training main-line employees is not expected to increase during the 90s.

The lion's share of company training funds is allocated to technical training and management development, as seen in Exhibit 4.3. The allocation of training funds among major subject areas, however, involves significant trade-offs. This can be seen among the 177 companies in the study that provided information on the distribution of their training monies among seven subject areas that included training in new technologies, management training, and training of new employees. Here we find, within this truncated sample of firms, that investing in training new employees can come at the expense of training present employees to use new technologies: These two investments show a negative correlation of $-.34$. Much the same is true for investing in training for new employees or investing in management development: These two investments display a negative correlation of $-.31$. Although training budgets are not strictly zero-sum, this evidence suggests that remedial and basic training for new employees, particularly prevalent among manufacturing and financial service firms, may come at the expense of

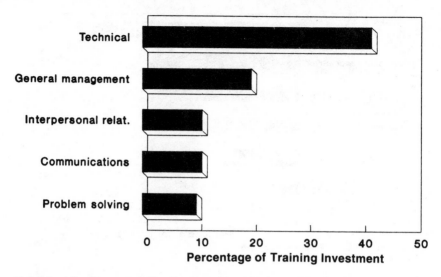

Exhibit 4.3 Expected distribution of company training expenditures among skill areas through the mid-90s.

technological and managerial training for seasoned employees. If so, for some firms, *the hidden cost of a poorly qualified supply of entry level employees may be a shortage of monies to invest in giving current employees training in skills deemed essential for workplace performance.*

Job training and retraining are forecast to increase in the near future: Four-fifths (83%) of the companies reported that they expect to expand such training during the 90s. They also project that more than half of their training expenditure (58%) will be spent on in-house programs, a quarter (28%) will be contracted to outside consultants, and a fraction (14%) will go to community and college programs. The division of the training budget between in-house and outside programs, however, is not related to anticipated trends in training investments: Companies that plan to expand their budget are no more likely than other firms to favor consultants and colleges over internal training programs.

SCHOOL RELATIONSHIPS

Although large companies generally have many years of experience with employee training and development, many have only within the last 5 to 10 years built working relationships with schools as a complementary strategy for workforce development. Some have invested company resources in schools, whereas others have built apprenticeship programs with schools. An example of the first strategy is RJR Nabisco's Next Century Schools Program. Initiated in the wake of a well-publicized leveraged buyout of the company in 1988, the program, through the company's foundation, provided $30 million in competitive grants to innovative educational programs that promised "bold reforms" in public schooling.[12] An example of the second strategy is an apprenticeship program operated by Sears, Roebuck & Co. A select group of high school students receives two semesters of training in appliance repair and related skills, including report writing, computer research, and customer relations. Sears furnishes trainers, appliances, overhead, part-time employment, and full-time employment for some graduates.[13]

Many firms have already cultivated working relations with public schools, according to the surveyed companies, and many more expect to do so during the 90s. A majority (57%) of the companies invest some time and energy in encouraging employees to work with public schools on their own time; a similar fraction (54%) make direct financial contributions or provide equipment to public schools; and about one in ten (9%) provide leaves of absence for employees to teach in public schools. As to the future, more than two-fifths (45%) of the companies expect to increase their efforts to have employees volunteer time to public education, and two-fifths (40%) plan to make more contributions of money and equipment. Nearly a quarter (23%) foresees creating paid leaves of absence for employees to teach in public schools.

More than two-fifths (42%) of the companies reported some familiarity with European apprenticeship programs in which businesses cooperate with secondary schools to provide part-time employment and training to students who receive credit for the experience. Most companies thought that the European scheme would be "good for the U.S.," and two-thirds said that such a program could help companies "maintain a skilled workforce."

Despite widespread company interest in apprenticeship programs, other studies reveal that the United States lags behind other industrial economies. According to one major study, the United States ranked 14th among 16 industrialized countries in apprenticeship enrollment rates.[14] Still, nearly two-thirds of the companies studied here say that they are very (33%) or somewhat (32%) likely to participate in an apprenticeship program during the 90s. Given the paucity of current apprenticeship activity but widespread interest in it, substantial change might be expected on this front during the years ahead. A summary of these concerns and practices appears in Exhibit 4.4.

Exhibit 4.4 Education and training practices of large U.S. companies in 1991.

Entry level education

    18% of a company's training budget on average is allocated to new employees.

    26% report trouble in recruiting qualified college graduates.

    16% report trouble in recruiting qualified college graduates.

    24% are likely to provide basic education to entry workers.

    45% anticipate providing basic skills training to entry workers.

Employee development

    58% of a company's main-line workers on average have been retrained.

    60% of the firms retrain in new technologies or production systems.

    83% expect their investment in job training to expand.

    42% of a company's training budget on average goes to technical areas.

    42% of the training budget on average will be contracted out.

School relations

    57% encourage employees to work with public schools.

    54% contribute money and equipment to public schools.

    9% allow employees to take leaves to teach in public schools.

    81% favorably view apprenticeship systems.

    65% are likely to participate in apprenticeship programs.

    65% see apprenticeships as a means to a skilled workforce.

Forces Shaping Corporate Education and Training Strategies

Corporate education and training strategies are not developed in a vacuum. To assess the forces that shape company priorities in this area, a series of analyses were undertaken to determine relationship between selected characteristics of companies in this sample and their education and training efforts. Among those factors thought to be most predictive of company actions are the following:

1. **Company Size and Workforce Composition.** Here it is expected that differences in the financial resources of companies and in the training needs of employees will influence education and training investments.

2. **Management Culture.** Another factor expected to influence corporate education and training concerns management's philosophy and outlook on change—two key characteristics of a company's management culture.

3. **Corporate Restructuring.** Finally, it is expected that changes in an organization will impinge on its education and training strategies. There is good reason to believe that companies that redesign work and run employee involvement or total quality programs have to do more training and retraining for these investments to pay off. It is less certain, however, what impact restructuring and downsizing have on education and training efforts in corporations.

Company Size and Workforce Composition

Given the substantial expense associated with building training programs, working with area schools, and initiating education programs, we can expect the size of such investments to vary with company resources. Similarly, given the divergent training needs of companies with well or poorly educated workforces, we can also expect the size and type of educational investments to vary with workforce composition. Three measures were created for taking these factors into account. One is company size, gauged by the log of a firm's annual sales. The other two cover workforce composition: The fraction of the company workforce that was managerial or white-collar (rather than blue-collar), and the fraction that held a college degree. These two measures of the workforce are themselves highly correlated (.58).

The relationship of education and training activities to company size and workforce composition is reported in Exhibit 4.5. Smaller and larger firms, as measured by sales, are about equally likely to report trouble recruiting qualified high school or college graduates. Smaller firms are more likely than larger ones to invest in remedial education and the basic training of entry level workers. By contrast, larger companies are more likely to encourage employees to volunteer time in public schools and, especially, to make direct contributions of money and equipment. Larger firms are also more likely to give their people leaves of absence to teach in schools and to value the potential of apprenticeship programs.

The composition of the workforce is also associated with corporate education and training practices. Firms with a primarily white-collar workforce have had less trouble in recruiting qualified high-school graduates than those with a primarily blue-collar workforce. White-collar firms also plan to do less in the way of remedial and basic training for entry workers, put less value on apprenticeship programs, and give less money and equipment to public schools. Companies with a high proportion of college graduates show similar tendencies.

Exhibit 4.5 Correlation of company education and training practices with company size and workforce composition.

Education or Training Practice or Concern	Size	Percentage White-collar	Percentage College Education
Entry level education			
Trouble recruiting h.s. grads		− **	
Trouble recruiting college grads			
Avg. % of training budget to new hires			
Provide remedial basic education	− **	− **	− **
Provide basic skills training	− *	− **	− **
Employee development			
Keeping skills current an issue			
% main-line workers retrained			
Frequency of retraining			
Expected increase in training			
School relations			
Encourage employee-school contact	*		
Direct monetary contribution to schools	**	− **	− **
Excuse employees to teach	**		
Value apprenticeship programs	**	− *	− **

Note: ** denotes correlations that are statistically significant at the .01 level (ranging in value from .18 to .31); * denotes correlations that are significant at the .05 level (ranging in value from .11 to .12). The number of companies on which the correlations are based varies from 133 to 137.

Management Culture

Corporate investments in education and training can also be expected to vary with the culture of company management. Companies with more innovative human resource cultures and less cultural resistance to making change should, other factors being equal, have fewer problems in recruiting employees and have to invest less in remedial training. Having a management culture that fosters innovation and is open to change enables a firm to alter human resource practices more quickly so that the company can adapt to a changing employment market.

Companies with management cultures that are more given to innovation should also be likely to invest more in the retraining and development of their workforce. Moreover, change-oriented companies are more likely to press for better relations with public schools and to see value in starting apprenticeship programs. Apprenticeships can be seen as far-reaching human resource practices with long-term paybacks, and they are likely to be of greater appeal to companies with innovative management cultures.

Two measures were used for taking management culture into account. The first rated a company's commitment to innovating in the area of human resources. As reported in earlier chapters, responding managers placed their firms in one of four categories along a dimension of commitment to innovation. The categories, along with the percentage of companies falling in each, were the following.

- *Cutting edge*—leading in the adoption of new policies and programs (11%)
- *Advanced*—adopting policies to stay ahead of other companies (39%)
- *Thoughtful*—adopting policies when an industry consensus is developed (37%)
- *Prudent*—adopting policies only after they have been proven effective (11%)

It has already been shown that cutting edge and advanced companies have a more strategic view of human resource management than other firms, and we expect that they pursue different policies in education and training as well.

A second measure of management culture, resistance to change, was gauged by asking a question on company barriers to "making desirable strategic changes in human resource policies." Several potential sources of resistance were defined, and one of the factors, "corporate culture that doesn't emphasize human resource issues," was close to our concept. As might have been expected, cultural resistance correlated strongly with four other perceived barriers to change: problems in getting the attention of top management, the cost of making changes, the company's focus on short-term goals, and a lack of support from middle management. The bundling of these factors suggested a culture in which management attention is directed more at financial issues and less at human resource issues, and more on short-term concerns than long-term development.

Correlations reveal some significant relationships between a company's management culture and its education and training activities (Exhibit 4.6). In the area of entry level education, for instance, companies with more innovative practices reported less trouble in recruiting college graduates. When management culture presents a barrier to strategic change, by contrast, companies report more problems in recruiting both high school and college graduates. This could mean that they have to dip deeper into their labor pool to recruit, which in turn may explain why they also plan to offer more in the way of remedial education than other companies.

Exhibit 4.6 Correlation of company education and training practices with management culture.

Education or Training Practice or Concern	Management Culture	
	Innovation Commitment	Company Culture Resists Human Resource Innovation
Entry level education		
Trouble recruiting h.s. grads		**
Trouble recruiting college grads	− *	**
Provide remedial basic education		*
Provide basic skills training		
Employee development		
Keeping skills current an issue		
% mainline workers retrained	**	
Frequency of retraining		
Expected increase in training		
School relations		
Encourage employee-school contact	*	
Direct monetary contribution to schools	**	
Excuse employees to teach	**	*
Value apprenticeship programs		

Note: ** denotes correlations that are statistically significant at the .01 level (ranging in value from .14 to .19); * denotes correlations that are significant at the .05 level (ranging in value from .09 to .10). The number of companies on which the correlations are based varies from 347 to 406.

A company's management culture is, in general, not predictive of the importance it places on employee retraining, the frequency of retraining, or its plans for the future in this area. The one exception concerns the number of employees it retrains. Cutting edge and, to a lesser extent, advanced companies retrained a larger proportion of their workforce than did less innovative firms. Cutting edge companies retrain twice the fraction of employees as do prudent firms:

Type of Firm	Percentage of Workforce Retrained
Cutting edge	84
Advanced	69
Thoughtful	51
Prudent	41

Finally, we find that companies with innovative managements were also those most likely to have fostered working relations with the public school system (see Exhibit 4.7).

Corporate Restructuring

Corporate restructuring is also likely to shape a company's strategy for education and training. Restructuring is here defined to include both redesign of the workplace and redesign of the organization. We can argue, for example, that work redesign presents opportunities for companies to attract a better qualified segment of the labor pool. Repositioning a business may result in the same advantage. Other forms of restructuring, however, especially those

Exhibit 4.7 Which companies invest more in public schools.

Innovation Commitment	Encourage Voluntary Work (%)	Contribute Money or Equipment (%)	Leaves of Absence to Teach (%)
Cutting edge	70	69	14
Advanced	59	56	9
Thoughtful	54	51	10
Prudent	38	40	2

introduced when the company is under duress, could have the opposite effect, making the firm less attractive because of the turbulence and notoriety that can sometimes follow such changes.[15] Furthermore, some workplace redesigns can lead to significant increases in the level of skill needed to perform certain jobs, making entry level deficits more problematic. Here we will examine the relationship between corporate restructuring and the problems companies have with entry-level workers.

Another question concerns the relationship between restructuring and employee development. We can speculate that firms that have redesigned their organizations and work process are also likely to invest more in employee development. This expectation is rooted in the notion of organizational congruence: As firms introduce new work processes, quality control methods, or decision-making procedures, they are also prone to make corollary changes in employee training and development.[16] Again, however, a reverse effect can occur with some forms of restructuring in which cost cutting could lead to downward pressures on the development budget.

The extent of a company's *work redesign* is gauged with information on whether they had invested a "significant amount of time and money" during the late 80s or early 90s to create "significant changes in their office and production areas." As reported in earlier chapters, a substantial fraction of the companies reported making *significant* changes in (1) their work methods and processes (44%); (2) employee involvement (39%); and (3) quality management practices (37%).

The measure of *organizational redesign* draws on information companies furnished about a range of actions often classed together as *downsizing*. Six actions were combined into a single factor by summing the number of such actions that companies had taken: shut down some operations (64%); combined operating units (62%); sold off business units (51%); laid off a substantial number of workers (47%); offered early retirement incentives (40%); and reduced management staff significantly (38%).

Work Redesign and Employee Programs.   Companies that had restructured work—through redesign of the work process, increased employee involvement, and creation of a total quality program—are found to have invested more in entry level education and training (Exhibit 4.8). The complex skills required by job enrichment and quality programs appear to necessitate additional training for new employees, regardless of their initial qualifications.

Companies that redesigned their work processes, promoted employee involvement, and established a program in total quality management also

Exhibit 4.8 Correlation of company education and training practices with work redesign and corporate restructuring.

Education or Training Practice or Concern	Workplace Redesign	Quality Program	Employee Involvement	Company Restructuring
Entry level education				
Trouble recruiting h.s. grads				*
Trouble recruiting college grads				**
Provide remedial basic education	**	**	**	**
Provide basic skills training		**	**	**
Employee development				
Keeping skills current an issue	**	*	*	*
% main-line workers retrained	**	**	*	
Frequency of retraining	**	**	**	
Expected increase in training		*		
School relations				
Encourage employee-school contact		*	*	
Direct monetary contribution to schools	**	**	**	**
Excuse employees to teach	**	**	**	**
Value apprenticeship programs				**

Note: ** denotes correlations that are statistically significant at the .01 level (ranging in value from .13 to .15); * denotes correlations that are significant at the .05 level (ranging in value from .09 to .11). The number of companies on which the correlations are based varies from 347 to 406.

placed more importance on retraining. They retrained a larger proportion of their workforce and planned more frequent retraining of their main-line workers. Work redesigns of these kinds appear to be accompanied by more of an emphasis on continuously upgrading employee skills.

Restructuring and Employee Programs.   By comparison, firms that had restructured their organizations were likely both to experience more recruitment problems and to invest more in entry level education. These enterprises may be less attractive to the ablest new recruits, thus necessitating more entry level training. Staff reductions and de-layering may have also increased the responsibilities of jobs that remained, further intensifying the need for entry level training.[17]

Companies that restructured were no more concerned than other firms with employee development. We know, however, from Chapter 3, that restructuring decisions stemmed from divergent strategies, often with divergent consequences. Whether a company downsized to enhance productivity or simply to reduce costs may thus lead to different human resource practices. This can be seen in the proportions of the main-line workers re-trained by companies that restructured to "contain costs" as compared with the proportion retrained by companies that restructured to "improve productivity." Redesigned companies display a profile almost identical to that of all companies (as seen in the first two columns of Exhibit 4.9). But companies that restructured their organization to cut costs were significantly less likely to retrain large fractions of their workforce than were companies that took such actions to improve productivity (the rightmost two columns).

CULTURE AND RESTRUCTURING
VERSUS SIZE AND WORKFORCE

Although management culture and corporate restructuring predict several aspects of company education and training, they themselves are partially shaped by the size of a firm and the composition of its workforce. For instance, larger companies, as measured by sales, are more likely to have

Exhibit 4.9   Workforce retraining varies by company reasons for restructuring and downsizing.

Proportion of Workforce Retrained	All Firms in the Study (%)	Restructured Companies		
		All Firms (%)	Attempts to Contain Costs (%)	Attempts to Improve Productivity (%)
1/3 or less	29	29	42	27
1/3–2/3	26	25	25	22
2/3 or more	45	44	33	51

restructured their organizations than smaller ones ($r = .20$), and companies with a larger percentage of college-educated workers are less likely to have done so ($r = -.24$). At the same time, companies with a better-educated workforce are less apt to initiate employee involvement ($r = -.15$) or quality management programs ($r = -.22$), and are typically targeted at manufacturing firms with a larger percentage of blue-collar workers.

We have already seen that company size and workforce composition are predictors of some of the education and training measures considered here. We also know from other studies that college graduates are much more likely than high school graduates to receive on-the-job training.[18] To examine the independent impact of culture and restructuring on training and development in companies, we controlled for the impact of company size and workforce composition on education and training by entering them into regression analyses.

The evident impact of management culture and corporate restructuring on education and training is reduced somewhat when we take a company's size and workforce into account. Yet the effects of management culture and organizational redesign remain significant in the regression analyses. The effects of one of the work redesign elements—changes in work methods and processes—also remains significant, but the effects of the other two drop below conventional levels of statistical significance. By inference, companies making changes in work processes also do more retraining than do those that promote employee involvement or quality management programs. This is consistent with other research demonstrating that redesign of the work process often places exceptional demands on employees to master complex skill.[19] Our main conclusions to this point are summarized in Exhibit 4.10.

THE JOINT IMPACT OF MANAGEMENT CULTURE AND CORPORATE RESTRUCTURING

The previous analyses demonstrate that a company's management culture and restructuring activities influence its education and training policies independent of the company's size and the composition of its workforce. It may also be that the joint impact of the two factors, taken together, exceeds the additive contributions of each. When a company especially resistant to strategic changes in human resource practices undergoes restructuring, for instance, its problems with entry level recruitment may be especially acute. When an innovative company restructures, by contrast, it may become exceptionally active in the public schools. These are only two of many

Exhibit 4.10   Company education and training practices: Impact of innovation commitment, management culture, work redesign, and corporate restructuring.

Entry level education

> Corporate restructuring leads to greater difficulty in recruiting graduates.
>
> Restructured firms are more likely to emphasize entry level training.
>
> Cultural resistance to strategic change makes recruiting more difficult.

Employee development

> Companies with an innovative human resource orientation retrain a larger number of their workers.
>
> Companies that have redesigned their work process invest more in employee development.
>
> Companies that have restructured to improve productivity retrain many more workers than those that have restructured to control costs.

School relations

> Corporate restructuring leads to stronger links with schools.
>
> Management commitment to innovation also strengthens work with school systems.

---

potential multiplicative effects, but they will be used here to explore the joint product of management culture and restructuring.

To examine these issues, we modified some of the measures used in our analyses. To gauge the extent of organization redesign, we rated companies as "high" if they used four or more forms of restructuring; we rated them "low" if they used three or fewer. Companies with a high innovation commitment were those classed as "advanced" or at the "cutting edge"; low, those deemed "thoughtful," or "prudent." High cultural resistance included companies for which corporate culture was considered a "major barrier" to strategic change; low, those for which it was deemed a "minor" or nonexistent barrier.

Exhibit 4.11 reports the degree of difficulty in recruiting college graduates found in companies that rated high or low on organizational redesign and cultural resistance. Here we find that firms that engaged in more organizational restructuring in the context of a management culture resistant to change are especially hard-pressed to recruit college students. Still, although they report acute problems, the problems are mainly the additive effects of the two predictor factors, not an especially volatile chemistry resulting from the presence of both. Detailed statistical analyses reveal that these factors had little joint influence beyond their additive impact.

Exhibit 4.12 reports on investments in public schools for companies rated high and low on organization design and commitment to innovation.

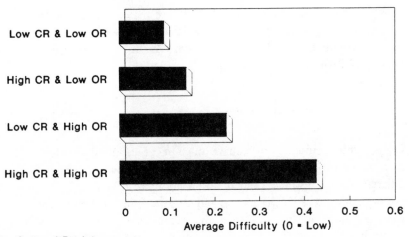

CR ▪ Cultural Resistance
OR ▪ Organizational Redesign

Exhibit 4.11   Difficulty recruiting college graduates by cultural resistance and organization redesign.

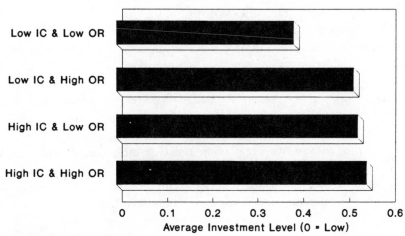

IC ▪ Innovation Commitment
OR ▪ Organizational Redesign

Exhibit 4.12   Investment in public schools by innovation commitment and organizational redesign.

Companies pressed to restructure but whose management takes innovative approaches to human resources are particularly likely to develop working programs with the public school system. Again, however, the effects are largely additive rather than synergistic.

VARIATION WITHIN PRODUCT SECTORS

Firms within an industry often have much in common—similar technologies, markets, even business strategies. We frequently observe, however, radically different human resource strategies even among relatively similar firms within the same industry. This is the case among the firms in the present study as well. We focus on nine industries that represent two-thirds of the sample. Those industries are food and tobacco; paper and printing; chemicals and petroleum; metals and machinery; electronics; wholesale trade; financial services; insurance; and business services.

We concentrate on three issues: problems in recruiting college graduates, frequency of workforce retraining, and whether the company looked favorably on apprenticeship programs. In these areas, variability within each of the nine industries was often as large as, or even larger than, the variability among the population of companies as a whole. In the case of problems in recruiting college graduates, for instance, the standard deviation among the full set of 406 companies is 0.37, while the standard deviation within each of the nine industry categories varied from 0.24 to 0.47.

Since these education and training practices vary within industries as much as in the business community as a whole, much of the variation cannot be due to production technologies, product markets, and other factors that tend to be similar within industries. Management culture, innovation in work design, and organizational redesign, however, vary considerably within industries, and they may account for much of the within-industry variability in education and training.

For this analysis we draw upon the two measures of organizational redesign described earlier, and we consolidate the three aspects of work redesign—changes in work processes, employee involvement, and total quality management—into a single overall measure. Again, for economies of space, we selectively focus on just three areas where, judging from the earlier analysis, maximum impact could be anticipated. Specifically, three effects are expected within the nine industries: (1) Companies that underwent *organizational redesign* are more likely to report problems in recruiting college graduates; (2) companies that undertook *work redesign* are likely to retrain their employees more frequently; and (3), among industries whose workforces are relatively less college educated, organizational redesign is more likely to generate special interest in apprenticeship programs.

In seven of the nine industries, companies that underwent organizational redesign were far more likely than other firms to experience problems in attracting college graduates. Almost regardless of industry, then, firms that had faced the most layoffs, plant closures, and other restructuring actions were at a competitive disadvantage in recruiting college graduates. Similarly, in six of the nine industries, companies that redesigned their workplace were significantly more likely to retrain their employees. Finally, in three of the five industries with large proportions of high school graduates (all manufacturing sectors), companies that had experienced organizational redesign were more likely to be looking to apprenticeship programs.

CONCLUSION

During the late 80s and early 90s, many companies changed their shape, size, and modus operandi.[20] Firms tended to choose either innovative or conservative approaches. Other chapters report that some downsizings were strategically directed, whereas others were more for costcutting. Some companies pursued new human resource directions, whereas others retained conventional personnel practices. Some companies responded to competition by redesigning their work systems and increasing employee involvement; others resisted change and were slow to innovate. This chapter confirms the same for education and training: Some companies sought new approaches, whereas others preferred convention.

The study also affirms that education and training investments are widespread and generally appear to be intensifying among the nation's major companies. Half or more of the surveyed corporations plan remedial or basic skills training for entry level employees; three-fifths retrain their employees in new technologies or production systems; and more than four-fifths expect their investment in job training to expand.

Concern about the quality of future graduates is also widespread. One company in four reports significant difficulties in recruiting new employees. Only half of the high school graduates who reached the recruitment interview are deemed to possess the skills necessary for entry level positions. Some companies are intervening now to avoid problems later: More than half of the firms are extending money, equipment, or employees to assist public schooling. Most companies anticipate even greater involvement in the future.

In light of such problems and actions, a private venue for education appears to be emerging alongside the traditional public venue. Firms invest a significant fraction of their training budget—close to a fifth on average—in engendering skills that public schools could have been expected to provide. For many young people entering employment, the high school diploma is less symbolic of a completed education than a certificate for transferring to a new schoolhouse, one now managed by the corporation.

At the same time, the corporation is also reaching into the public schoolhouse, changing the nature of the school-to-work transition. Rather than passively waiting for its products to arrive, companies are preemptively investing in their development. Employee time, student apprenticeships, company equipment, and cash contributions are going to help schools do what they have been intended but not able to do. Public school functions are moving inside the firm, and company resources are moving inside the schools.

Although the educational foundation of the workforce is a concern shared by all companies, not all companies have responded to that concern in the same way. Large corporations, for example, provide less in the way of remedial and basic skills training than smaller companies, but they place more direct investment in the public education system. Put differently, large companies lean toward moving company resources into the schools, whereas smaller companies lean toward bringing education inside the firm. Similarly, companies with largely blue-collar workforces invest substantially in both areas, whereas white-collar firms do less in either of them. As in most areas of company strategy, education and training policies are divergently shaped by firm structure.

Yet we have also seen that an education and training strategy is shaped by more than company structure. It is also a product of management cultures and corporate change. When senior management creates an innovative climate for human resources practices, the company retrains a larger number of its current workers and invests more in public schooling. When senior management redesigns the architecture of the company's work and restructures it for the sake of productivity, the company invests more in entry level training and ongoing employee development. These factors make a major difference even among companies of similar sizes and workforce compositions operating within similar industries.

If schools are failing to produce the workforce employers require to remain competitive, companies should thus not be viewed largely as passive victims. They can and do intervene, both within their own walls and those of the schoolhouse. And driving those actions is management commitment to innovation and change, to reconfiguration of how they go about running the business.

ACKNOWLEDGMENT

Grateful acknowledgment is extended to the Commonwealth Fund of New York, Louis Harris & Associates, the Conference Board, ICF Incorporated, and National Center on the Educational Quality of the Workforce, University of Pennsylvania, for support and assistance; to Dennis Ross and Constance Gager for technical assistance; and to Peter Cappelli, Harry Katz, Philip Mirvis, and Frits K. Pil for helpful suggestions. Statistical tables from which the chapter's research findings are drawn can be obtained upon request to the author.

NOTES

1. Cooke, W. N., and D. G. Meyer. 1990. Structure and market predictors of corporate labor relations strategies. *Industrial and Labor Relations Review* 43:280–293; Ichniowski, C. 1990. Human resource management systems and the productivity of U.S. manufacturing businesses. Columbia University, Graduate School of Business Administration, New York; Womack, J. P., D. T. Jones, and D. Roos. 1991. *The machine that changed the world: The story of lean production.* New York: Harper Collins; MacDuffie, J. P., and J. Krafcik. 1992. Integrating technology and human resources for high performance manufacturing: Evidence from the international auto industry. In *Transforming organizations,* ed. T. Kochan and M. Useem, New York: Oxford University Press; and Schein, E. H. 1992. The role of the CEO in the management of change: The case of information technology. In *Transforming organizations,* ed. T. Kochan and M. Useem, New York: Oxford University Press.

2. National Education Goals Panel. 1991. *Building a nation of learners.* Washington, D.C.: National Education Goals Panel.

3. Cohen, S. S., and J. Zysman. 1987. *Manufacturing matters: The myth of the post-industrial economy.* New York: Basic Books, p. 228.

4. U.S. Office of Technology Assessment. 1990. *Worker training: Competing in the new international economy.* Washington, D.C.: U.S. Government Printing Office. p. 3.

5. National Academy of Engineering, Committee on Time Horizons and Technology Investments. 1992. *Time horizons and technology investments.* Washington, D.C.: National Academy of Engineering; Competitiveness Policy Council. 1992. *Building a competitive America: First annual report to the president & congress.* Washington, D.C.: Competitiveness Policy Council; and Cappelli, P. 1991a. Summaries of key reports on educational policy. University of Pennsylvania, National Center on the Educational Quality of the Workforce, Philadelphia.

6. Cappelli, P. 1991b. Are skills requirements rising? Evidence from production and clerical jobs. University of Pennsylvania, National Center on Educational Quality of the Workforce, Philadelphia.

7. Bishop, J. 1990. Incentives for learning: Why American high school students compare so poorly to their counterparts overseas. In *Research in labor economics,* ed. L. J. Bassi and D. L. Crawford, Vol. 11, Greenwich, CT: JAI Press; Bishop, J. 1992. Why U.S. students need incentives to learn. *Educational Leadership* 49 (6): 15–18.

8. Committee for Economic Development. 1991. *An assessment of American Education: Views of employers, higher educators, the public, recent students, and their parents.* New York: Louis Harris Associates.

9. Cappelli, P. 1992. Is the 'skills gap' really about attitudes? University of Pennsylvania, Working Paper of the National Center on Educational Quality of the Workforce, Philadelphia.

10. U.S. Office of Technology Assessment, *Worker training;* Brown, C. 1990. Empirical evidence on private training. In *Research in labor economics,* ed. L. J. Bassi and D. L. Crawford, Vol. 11, Greenwich, CT: JAI Press; Womack, et al., Lean production; and Hashimoto, M. 1992. Employment-based training in Japanese firms in Japan and in the United States: Experiences of automobile manufacturers. Ohio State University, Department of Economics, Columbus, OH.

11. Doeringer, P. B., and M. J. Piore. 1971. *Internal labor markets and manpower analysis.* Lexington, MA: D. C. Heath.

12. Jehl, J., and T. W. Payzant. 1992. Philanthropy and public school reform: A view from San Diego. *Teachers College Record* 93:472–487; Bailey, A. L. 1992. RJR Nabisco: A blueprint for school reform. *Chronicle of Philanthropy,* 10.

13. Wartzman, R. 1992. Apprenticeship plans spring up for students not heading to college. *Wall Street Journal,* May 19, 1 ff.

14. U.S. Office of Technology Assessment, *Worker training;* Hamilton, S. F., and M. A. Hamilton. 1992. A progress report on apprenticeships. *Educational Leadership* 49 (March): 44–47.

15. Cook, D. S., and G. R. Ferris. 1986. Strategic human resource management and firm effectiveness in industries experiencing decline. *Human Resource Management* 3:441–458; Napier, N. K. 1989. Mergers and acquisitions, human resource issues and outcomes: A review and suggested typology. *Journal of Management Studies* 26: 271–289; Buono, A. F. and J. L. Bowditch. 1989. *The human side of mergers and acquisitions: Managing collisions between people, cultures, and organizations.* San Francisco: Jossey-Bass; and Doeringer, P. B., K. Christensen, P. M. Flynn, D. T. Hall, H. C. Katz, J. C. Keefe, C. J. Ruhm, A. M. Sum, and M. Useem. 1991. *Turbulence in the American workplace.* New York: Oxford University Press.

16. Nadler, D. A. and M. L. Tushman. 1988. *Strategic organization design.* Glenview, IL: Scott, Foresman.

17. Smith, V. 1990. *Managing in the corporate interest: Control and resistance in an American bank.* Berkeley, CA: University of California Press; Doeringer et al., *Turbulence.*

18. Altonji, J. G., and J. R. Spletzer. 1991. Worker characteristics, job characteristics, and the receipt of on-the-job training. *Industrial and Labor Relations Review* 45: 58–79.

19. Lawler, E. E. 1992. *The ultimate advantage*. Jossey-Bass: San Francisco.
20. Kochan, T. A., R. B. McKersie, and P. Cappelli. 1984. Strategic choice and industrial relations theory. *Industrial Relations* 23:16–39; Kochan, T. A., H. C. Katz, and R. B. McKersie. 1986. *The transformation of American industrial relations*. New York: Basic Books.

5

Workplace Flexibility: Faddish or Fundamental?
Victoria A. Parker and Douglas T. Hall

Warning: Ignoring issues of diversity and of work/family balance can be hazardous to organizational health.

In this period of turbulent change, escalating global competition, and ever-tightening resources, the organizations that survive and thrive will be the ones that most effectively use their full range of resources. The Laborforce 2000 study finds that most firms are restructuring and resizing, many are introducing new technologies, and some are improving work designs and management—all in order to gain competitive advantage. But there is great variability in how companies rate the importance of different human resource issues and in what they deem worthy of attention and investment. In this chapter we consider developments in workplace flexibility: how companies adapt to increasing racial, ethnic, and gender diversity in their workforces and how companies help employees handle the competing demands of their jobs and family, or personal, lives.

Two factors justify the dire warning that begins this chapter; the first concerns the laws of supply and demand. Demographic projections make it plain that most new entrants to the workforce will be different from the majority population in corporations today.[1] There will be more people of color, more immigrants, and more with disabilities and special needs in the years ahead.

Many more women will enter the workforce, as well as more single- or dual-working parents. On the demand side, there will be heightened competition to hire and retain the most qualified workers in a slow-growth labor market. As a result, companies that attract and get the most out of diverse kinds of employees will gain competitive advantage.

Second, many companies do not fully appreciate the significance of the challenges posed by the changing workforce. From our vantage, current programs keyed to work/family and diversity needs are isolated efforts that are initiated at lower levels in the organization and that are rarely connected to strategic goals. Hence, the potential benefits to organizations are largely unrealized, and the benefits to individuals may be unnecessarily constrained. If, by contrast, such programs would be thought of as complementary measures, to achieve overall workplace flexibility, we believe companies could put their work/family and diversity efforts into a broader, more strategically based framework. Doing so would transform "people programs," aimed at segments of the workforce, into broadly based competitive actions that would be worthy of high-level attention.

We begin by defining workplace flexibility, what it means to organizations, and how it compares with traditional models of organizational and human resource management. We find that even though some research has been done on the management of diversity and work/family issues as independent subjects, considering the two issues jointly, under the rubric of flexibility, puts them into a body of theory about organizational adaptability. We analyze data from the 406 human resource executives interviewed in the Laborforce 2000 survey to highlight company practices in these areas, and we compare them with results from other studies. The chapter concludes with an agenda of future research and action.

FLEXIBILITY: PROMOTING PSYCHOLOGICAL AVAILABILITY

Flexibility, for our general purposes, refers to the capacity of an organization to swiftly and smoothly adapt its structures, technologies, work processes, and people to the demands of change. The challenges posed by increased diversity in the workforce and by the complexities of people's work and family lives tax the adaptability of an organization. In this context, the flexible company pays attention to the entirety of an employee's life and adapts itself to enhance the "fit" between different kinds of people and their work and nonwork roles.

The theory here is that a flexible workplace enables employees to bring their "full" selves to work and to be psychologically engaged in the tasks, activities, and relationships that make up their jobs.[2] It rests on three fundamental propositions about people and their work lives.

1. People have personal identities (as women, as Asian-Americans, and so on) and nonwork roles (as caregivers for ill parents, as community volunteers, as partners and parents) beyond those assigned to them by the employer (project manager, data-entry clerk).
2. People "carry" their different identities and nonwork roles into the workplace.
3. People are more fully engaged when such characteristics can be expressed, rather than suppressed, in an organization and work role.

The rationale for corporate action is based in the belief that helping employees to manage transitions between their work and home or to express their full repertoire of ideas and skills serves to increase their psychological availability for the work at hand.[3] But it is important to note that there are individual differences in what helps an employee be fully engaged: For some working parents, it could be full-time work with on-site child care; for others, it could be working from an office at home two days each week. For some employees, it may be help in learning English—for others, a closer affiliation with a peer group. The point is that the flexible workplace can accommodate the individual differences and can translate people's heightened psychological engagement into better performance.

FLEXIBILITY IN TIME, SPACE, AND STYLE

The roster of human resource policies, practices, and programs that seek to extend workplace flexibility is varied. Essentially, companies can increase flexibility with respect to people's work time, space, and style. First, consider options in work time. Organizations can offer flexible work schedules (such as flexible hours and part-time work), accommodate short-term time needs (such as family-related leaves of absence), and provide long-term career options (such as sabbaticals and phased retirement). A distinction is that daily flexibility enables people to balance simultaneously their work and life spheres, whereas short- and long-term arrangements allow them to manage the two spheres sequentially.

Second, there are options in work space. Flexibility gives people the option of working at home (flexplace) or sharing a job with a co-worker. Although not intrinsically slanted toward any one type of worker, these options are particularly attractive to women with school-age children.[4]

Third, there can be flexibility in work style, enabling people to bring a fuller range of their personal characteristics into the workplace rather than conforming to a specific model of corporate behavior and style. Of course, many companies are required to adapt to the needs of employees with disabilities and may choose to accommodate their older workers in redefined work roles. But we include in this category other forms of flexibility that address racial, ethnic, and gender diversity within a firm. For instance, a work role may be expanded to include specialized forms of training, aimed at both majority and minority group members in companies, mentoring programs for women and people of color, and so forth.

FLEXIBILITY VERSUS TRADITION

The idea of increasing workplace flexibility challenges time-honored assumptions about the structure of work and its supervision. Most large work organizations have been modeled on what Morgan describes as the "machine" image.[5] The emphasis is on "fitting man to machine"—in line with Frederick Taylor's principles of scientific management—with workers considered to be extensions of their equipment. The work environment in this mechanistic model is marked by standardization and order. Although few managers espouse Taylor's precepts nowadays, his emphasis still lingers: Consider the popular use of the term *head count* when companies refer to their people.

One legacy of Taylorism has been the separation of people's hands from their brains—so notable in assembly-line work and basic clerical operations. This continues even in the current era of "knowledge work," where many nonphysical jobs require rote repetition and evoke less than full levels of attentiveness. However, such recent innovations as job design, teamwork, and employee involvement begin to eliminate the hands/brain dichotomy. What they do not address is another separation so prominent in American industry: the brain/person dichotomy. Absent a commitment to flexibility, organizations emphasize impersonality and implicitly tell employees to "check" their personal identities and family situations "at the door."

Why? The simplest explanation is that companies would prefer not to deal with people at this most human level. A sampling of opinion from the Conference Board's Work and Family Council illustrates typical reactions to the idea of bringing people's life situations to the business setting: "We should just look for more 'uncomplicated people' to hire." "The company can't solve all these problems, so why start?"[6]

The Case for Flexibility

Although some companies may wish for uncomplicated people and easy-to-solve problems, we are in a time of discontinuous change, as Handy argues, that requires a shake-up in accepted ways of organizing and managing a business.[7] Hence the emphasis is on adapting market plans, product lines, and organizational structures in response to massive and fast-moving changes.[8] Accordingly, companies are moving into more flexible office arrangements; producing with more flexible manufacturing systems; relying on more flexible supply and distribution channels; and getting things done through temporary task forces, project teams, and committees.

All of these changes mean that work is being done in less-mechanistic ways and that adaptability is challenging tradition as a guiding motivation. The human resource department has been influenced by this large-scale transformation in the development of cafeteria-style benefit packages for employees. Yet we suggest that the requirements for flexibility extend beyond the arena of benefits to the basic structure and operations of the business.

Experts in human motivation have argued that firms profit most from "fitting the job to the person" rather than the other way around.[9] We go further and contend that flexible companies need also to take account of and respect the "whole" person. This means *valuing* diversity in the workforce and building flexibility to the point that employees can contribute fully from their varied roster of skills, outlooks, and values.

EQUAL VERSUS IDENTICAL TREATMENT

Another aspect of organizational tradition threatened by flexibility is the belief that equal treatment means the identical treatment of employees. This belief is based in the image of organizations as rule-bound bureaucracies—a close relation to Taylor's machine model—that operate through specified rules and procedures. In this legalistic framework, the emphasis is on establishing precedents and eliminating exceptions to the rules. Needless to say, it is the antithesis of flexibility, which accommodates individual differences.

Yet in this area also, companies are discovering how unadaptive so many work rules can be. Studies show that so-called identical treatment can discriminate against women and minorities, when, for instance, they are being evaluated on criteria and behavioral expectations developed by and for white men. Equal treatment, by comparison, requires flexible assessment procedures, which take account of individual- and group-based differences and encourage a diversity of input for evaluations.

An emphasis on flexibility can, of course, exacerbate tensions over questions of fairness. Conflicts between men and women, between various racial and ethnic groups, and even between parents and nonparents may erupt when companies strive to meet the needs of a diverse employee population. Conflicts may also arise between those who have flexible work hours and those who do not or between those who can work at home and those whose jobs require regular attendance on-site. The point is that questions of equal-versus-identical treatment cannot be ducked in the move toward flexibility.

Advantages of Flexibility

A growing number of case studies confirm that managers and employees can together work out a fair and agreeable approach to addressing individual and group needs. Take the case of Corning, Inc., which in 1986 was losing women professionals at twice the rate of white males, at an annual cost of $3.5–4.0 million.[10] A broadly representative team including men and women, whites and nonwhites, and people from different levels in the company developed objectives and programs aimed at an array of work/family and diversity issues. These efforts reduced the turnover rate of women and reduced the costs of recruiting and training replacements. This case shows that increased flexibility in the workplace offers advantages over standardized policies and practices.

Furthermore, a body of theory suggests that workforce diversity, per se, gives an organization special advantages. The idea is that people from different racial, ethnic, and family backgrounds bring different ideas, perspectives, and worldviews, which in many ways reflect the diversity of human thought and the variability of outlook in the consumer marketplace. Under conditions of psychological inclusion, employees feel free to express their views, and companies gain a richer understanding of problems and opportunities within the workforce and, by extension, in the market. Indeed, studies find that tapping the views of a diverse employee population can enhance creativity and cooperation in work groups.[11]

Corning, Inc.

The commitment and contribution of all employees will determine our success.

Corning, Inc., like a very small number of other corporations, has taken a holistic and strategic approach to the development of workplace flexibility. In 1986, as part of a corporationwide focus on total quality, the problems of retaining and developing talented women and African-Americans were tackled by a quality improvement team. The suggestions developed by this team became part of a top-down, major initiative in which the objective is creating conditions that ensure that "...each employee must have the opportunity to participate fully, to grow professionally, and to develop to his or her highest potential." Meeting diverse employee needs more fully was seen as a way to improve quality. In practical terms, it has meant several kinds of interventions.

- Race and gender awareness training, in which aspects of corporate culture that inhibit flexibility are indentified and addressed. For instance, new employees are no longer encouraged to adopt the dress, style, and social activities of the white male majority.
- Child care services and expanded family care leaves.
- Community intervention to develop services that make the Corning area more attractive to African-American employees.
- Career-planning systems for all, and promotion criteria and processes made more public.
- Management of workplace flexibility is now a dimension of managerial performance ratings and affects raises and bonuses.
- Slowly changing the culture so that the varied styles of employees are seen as a strength, an advantage in relating to the varied styles of customers.

Thus far, the changes seem to be working well for Corning: The recruitment, retention, and advancement of women and African-Americans have all improved, and attention is now being directed to members of other racial groups underrepresented in Corning's workforce. *Based on research by Dana Zackin.*

Some might argue that the sluggish economy and high unemployment rates of the early 90s have reduced the competitive impact of changes in the workforce and have thereby reduced the importance of flexibility. We think otherwise: The move toward increased flexibility requires a radical rethinking of human resource management in companies, and those who have begun it have a strong advantage over their competitors. Moreover, these firms are establishing a reputation as flexible employers and are attracting the very best of the new workforce entrants. Thus, flexible firms are building their future workforce and gaining the experience needed to manage the workplace of the future.

These advantages notwithstanding, there are many barriers to flexibility, including time-honored traditions, projected hassles and legal complications, and concerns as to whether the benefits will truly outweigh the costs. A vision of flexibility and an "individualized" organization can sound wonderful, but it can also evoke resistance. Data from the Laborforce 2000 survey help to illustrate how companies are thinking about and acting on the issues at hand.

FLEXIBILITY IN PRACTICE: TIME AND SPACE

The introductory chapter reported findings from a survey by Louis Harris & Associates showing that a large majority of U.S. office workers place great importance on flexible hours. Media accounts, such as a Mother's Day article in the *Boston Globe*, stress its relevance to working mothers: "If mothers who work outside the home could make a wish list for corporate America this Mother's Day, more flexible work hours would be at the top."[12] Interestingly, men surveyed by Harris placed nearly as much emphasis on flexible hours. As for other flexible options, roughly half of the office workers value child care assistance and the chance to work at home, and one out of every three hope for the chance to work part-time or job share.

The section of the Laborforce 2000 survey covering these subjects started with a list of flexible programs and then asked respondents, "how much demand is there in your company for programs such as these . . . ?" The great majority of human resource officials interviewed reported that there was a great deal (18%) or some (51%) demand for such programs (see Exhibit 5.1). The rest saw little or no interest within their firms.

What is noticeable is the gap between employees' strong desires for flexible options and the perception of modest demand reported by the Laborforce 2000 interviewees. One explanation is that these high-level corporate officials are simply out of touch with employee needs in these areas. Another

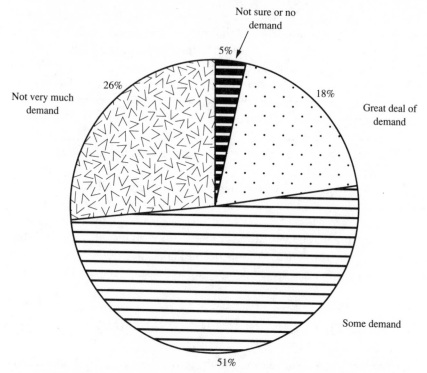

Exhibit 5.1   Perceived demand for flexible work arrangements.

possibility is that they discount the needs in the light of more important ones.

There were, however, some significant differences across companies in ratings of employee desires for flexibility. Firms with a larger percentage of women in their workforce, for instance, perceived more demand for flexibility than those with a larger percentage of men. Firms in the service sector report higher demands for flexibility, too, although this may reflect the relatively large numbers of women in industries such as health care and insurance.[13] Companies with a cutting edge orientation to human resources also see more demand for flexibility than firms that are slower to innovate. In this case, we suggest that these innovative firms may be more attuned to what employees value and need.

Company Practices

Data from the sampled companies show that many flexible options are spreading through industry (see Exhibit 5.2). We asked interviewees whether

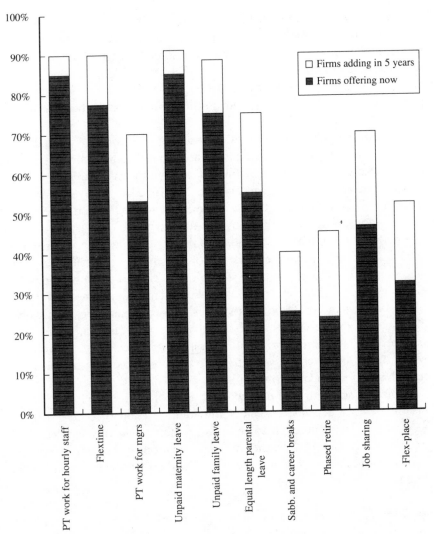

Exhibit 5.2 Flexible work arrangements provided by companies.

or not their companies had one or more of these flexible options today and, if not, whether they planned to introduce them in the mid-90s. Note, however, the percentages reported indicate only that a company offers a flexible option. They do not reflect how many people within a firm can take advantage of specific options or how many presently use them.

Work Schedules. Over three-fourths of the companies in this sample offer flextime options to at least some employees. Exhibit 5.2 shows that even more firms plan to offer flextime by the mid-90s, meaning it will become available in 90% of the sampled companies. In a flextime arrangement, employees work a full week but have some freedom to set their own schedule. Often there is a core number of hours during the middle of the day when everyone is present (say, 10:00 A.M. to 3:00 P.M.), and then employees can vary their starting and quitting times around their particular needs.

Alternatively, there could be different arrangement of days worked. For example, an employee in a university administrative office works Tuesdays through Saturdays, so that her son can be home with a parent for three days instead of two (her husband is home on Saturday); also, Saturday is a quiet day at the university office, a day she uses to catch up on paperwork. Another popular option is the four-day, 40-hour week.

Another form of flexible scheduling is the option to work part-time. The exhibit shows that part-time work options for hourly or nonexempt staff are available in 85% of the firms studied. This enables employees to work either fewer days per week or fewer hours per day. Fewer companies (53%) offer managers and professionals the chance to work part-time, perhaps because such higher-level jobs are less amenable to part-time scheduling. The percentage could increase to 70% if companies implement their projected plans. Again, however, we cannot say how many employees and managers have this option available to them in the sampled firms.

A major issue with part-time work is whether or not employees receive health or other benefits. Usually a minimum fraction of time has to be worked to qualify, although some firms prorate benefit coverage based on hours worked. Significantly, the study finds that one out of four companies plan to employ somewhat more part-time workers who will not qualify for health benefits by the mid-90s.

Short-Term Leaves.   Short-term leaves have also become quite common in industry. For example, 85% of the companies provide unpaid childbirth leave for women beyond the normal disability period. Under such a program, a woman can take an extended amount of time off to care for a new baby and have a job held open for her. (Whether she is guaranteed her old job back varies with the company and with the length of the leave.) Slightly over half of the companies (53%) report offering equal lengths of unpaid parenting leave for men and women. Although men are less likely to utilize this option than women, it seems a popular option and could be available in over three-fourths of the sampled companies in the next years. Many companies (75%) also provide unpaid family leave to care for sick family members. No doubt the number of employers offering these types of leaves will increase with the recent passage of a national "family-leave" bill.

Long-Term Arrangements.   Two forms of longer-term flexibility are available currently in less than one out of four companies studied. Some 24% offer paid sabbaticals and career breaks to at least some employees with another 15% planning to do more in this area in the mid-90s. These options are the most appealing to mid-career employees, who seek a break from job rigors or may need the opportunity to reeducate themselves for future job opportunities. In the light of the widespread restructuring and retraining in industry, this kind of career flexibility may take on greater importance.

The option of phased retirement is offered by 22% of the firms sampled but could be available in over 40% during the mid-90s. Again, company restructuring and downsizing makes it an important career option for older workers, many of whom—absent phased retirement programs—are taking full early retirement.

Work Location.   When it comes to the location of work, flexibility seems to decrease. Job sharing, whereby two employees assume joint responsibility for the same position, is reported by 47% of the firms studied. And flexplace, the option of working in the home or in some other place outside the company plant or office, is found in only 29% of the companies reporting. However, more than one out of five companies that do not offer these options plan to do so.

Even though increases are predicted in the availability of the least-prominent forms of workplace flexibility, it is notable how many firms will *not* offer such options anytime soon: flexplace (35%), sabbaticals and career breaks (52%), and phased retirement (39%). Perhaps because these three practices entail physical separation from the workplace, making supervision and communication more difficult, they are more of a problem for the organization to accommodate. Likewise, part-time work for managers and professionals is apparently unlikely to become universal, either, with 26% of respondents not seeing it in their firms in the near future. It is interesting to note that this ceiling-level percentage is similar to that predicted for job sharing (24%). Job sharing is, most often, a part-time option for managers and professionals. It may be that the responsibilities of certain managerial positions simply require full-time presence on the job. Still, we wonder whether this is a matter of job requirements versus a holdover of organizational tradition.

PROFILE OF FLEXIBLE FIRMS

What kinds of firms are most likely to provide these kinds of flexibility? Similar to other chapter authors, we conducted regression analyses to determine which factors predicted workplace flexibility. The following predictors are notable.

1. *Organizational Structure.* Companies with more flexible options are

   - larger (over $1 billion in sales and over 10,000 employees)
   - multinational (over 20% of the workforce outside the United States)
   - less unionized (less than 30% of employees in a union)

2. *Workforce Composition.* Those with more flexible options have

   - higher percentages of women in the workforce
   - higher percentages of younger employees
   - larger proportion of part-time contingent workers

3. *Company Philosophy.* They are more apt to express a

   - cutting edge or advanced human resource philosophy

Interestingly, a contrasting pattern emerges when we look at the firms that provide sabbaticals and career breaks. These companies are more likely to be smaller, with fewer women, more older employees, and higher levels of education in the workforce. In part, the reason may be that these forms of flexibility originated in academia, and hence are assumed to be applicable solely to more senior, more educated employees. Ironically, of course, precisely these forms of flexibility can enable some individuals to obtain further education. The results also suggest that sabbaticals and career breaks may represent flexibility for men, whereas the other forms offer it for women. And the flexibility for men appears to contain more personal freedom, whereas the other forms (more available to women) provide more freedom to meet family needs. Perhaps in organizations where flexible options are implemented in response to large numbers of women, the need has been defined primarily in terms of work/family balance. Although the *intent* may not be to offer women and men different forms of flexibility, current patterns of availability suggest that this is the result. Moreover, the distinction between meeting family and personal needs is not always clear; whereas a man may take a sabbatical for the public reason of further education, the real reason may be to spend more time with a new child.

RESISTANCE TO FLEXIBILITY

Many sources of resistance to flexible work arrangements were reported by respondents, and they are summarized in Exhibit 5.3. Surprisingly, managerial attitudes (at the top and middle levels) were mentioned by only about one-fourth of the respondents. Effects on quality were cited at about the same rate. The major reason indicated for not implementing flexibility was its impact on work scheduling and supervision (66%). This result could, however, mask resistance by managers, as it may be more socially desirable for managers to report that they are not personally opposed to such programs but are instead opposed to the resultant problems in scheduling and supervision.

To the extent that scheduling and supervision problems are significant barriers to flexibility, they perforce limit the number of people who can avail themselves of flextime and flexplace. They may also be a barrier to leaves and sabbaticals. However, information and communications technologies are making more employees more "available."[14] Hence, reports of scheduling and supervision problems may be grounded less in reality than in prevalent managerial assumptions such as *presence = performance* and *hours = output*.[15] Work/family managers have described this to us as the problem of "facetime"—what counts to many managers is the amount of time an employee shows his or her face at the office. These assumptions are an outgrowth of the mechanistic view of work and are extremely resistant to change.

Exhibit 5.3 Barriers to implementing flexible work arrangements.

Reason for Not Implementing	Percentage of Firms
Impact on scheduling and supervision	66
Attitudes of top managers	27
Reduce quality of product or service	24
Attitudes of middle managers	22
Employees haven't asked	18
Cost	10
Unpopular with nonusers	5
None of the above	8

IMPACT OF FLEXIBLE PRACTICES

The perceived impact of flexible work arrangements is summarized in Exhibit 5.4. What is most interesting here is that the prime benefit of flexibility seems to be an enhanced corporate image. Nine out of ten companies cite it as a major (48%) or minor (40%) benefit of flexible programs. When it comes to other projected benefits of flexibility, however, the results seem rather modest. Roughly one out of three companies cite flexibility as having a major impact on recruiting and on reducing absenteeism and turnover. One out of five credit it with having a major impact on productivity. Otherwise, about half the sample reports that flexibility has only a minor impact on the aspects of company performance just mentioned.

Interestingly, cutting edge (61%) firms were far more likely to cite an enhanced corporate image as a major benefit of flexibility compared to those that describe themselves as "advanced" (54%), "thoughtful" (42%), or "prudent" (35%) in their approach to human resource management. Although there may be a note of self-congratulation in cutting edge firms, it is notable that these companies—much more so than others—see flexibility as having a major impact on recruiting qualified employees (43%), reducing turnover (41%), reducing absenteeism (41%), and increasing productivity (32%).

CHILD CARE AND ELDER CARE BENEFITS

Exhibit 5.5 presents data on the percentage of firms that offer employees specific benefits for child and elder care services. The most prevalent form of assistance is information. Over half (53%) of firms surveyed offer child care information assistance, and over one-fourth (28%) provide information on elder care. Pretax spending accounts (which allow employers to apply nontaxable income to child care) are another prevalent form of child care assistance in half of the firms sampled.

Exhibit 5.4   Impact of flexible work arrangements.

	Major Impact (%)	Minor Impact (%)
Enhancing corporate image	48	40
Recruiting	34	53
Reducing turnover	31	54
Reducing absenteeism	31	56
Increasing productivity	25	54

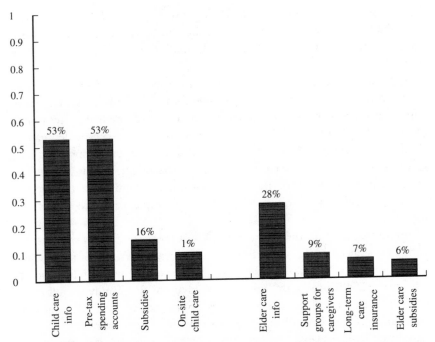

Exhibit 5.5 Child and elder care benefits offered by companies.

Direct financial assistance (vouchers, subsidies, or allowances) for child care (16%) and on-site child care (10%), though receiving much press attention, are still relatively rare in corporate America. Similarly, with elder care, direct support (either financial or social) is quite rare, with support groups for caregivers, long-term care insurance, and elder care subsidies or allowances offered by less than 10% of the firms surveyed.

These data show that most firms are doing very little directly to assist employees with family care responsibilities. The most prevalent form of support is providing information, which, although valuable to employees, can be provided quite inexpensively by the employer. The other most-frequent benefit, pretax spending accounts, accrues only administrative costs to the employer. The more-active (and more expensive) forms of assistance (financial support, on-site care, long-term insurance, support groups) are provided by many fewer employers.

Who is most likely to provide these family assistance benefits? Again, the most frequent providers are larger firms and those with large proportions of women employed. The effects of firm size are more complex in this area, however, than they are in relation to flexible work time options. Not only do the largest firms provide a higher proportion of child care benefits, but the very smallest firms do, as well. In fact, firms grossing $100 million and under had the highest percentage of on-site child care facilities (12% versus 3% for $101–500 million, 5% for $501 million–$1 billion, and 11% for over $1 billion).

The effects of a high proportion of women in the workforce were especially strong in relation to the more-active forms of family assistance. Firms with over 60% women were approximately one and one-half to two times more likely than firms with lower percentages of women to provide financial child care assistance, on-site child care facilities, support groups for caregivers, and long-term elder care assistance. This suggests that as women's numbers in an organization increase, women may be more able to influence the culture and policies in ways that change the organization to better meet their needs.

Additional data on the characteristics and motives of firms that provide family assistance benefits come from the Families and Work Institute, which rates firms on a "Family-Friendly Index." Consistent with findings in the Laborforce 2000 survey, the Institute's study finds that family-friendly firms tend to be larger and to have a public relations motive for addressing work and family issues. In addition, the Institute finds that multisite companies have more family-related benefits. Although this is another indicator of size, it also shows that firms with many decentralized functions and business units can accommodate an employee's family needs.

THE BOTTOM-LINE IMPACT OF FLEXIBLE WORK PROGRAMS

Respondents were asked to assess the overall impact of these flexible work arrangements: "All things considered, do you think the bottom-line impact of flexible work programs (would/will) be very positive, positive, negligible, or negative?" Three-fourths said the impact was either very positive (26%) or positive (49%). The rest saw it as negligible (23%) or negative (3%). As expected, firms with the greatest proportion of *very positive* responses were those with the highest percentage of women employees (31%) and those with cutting edge philosophies (43%).

Surprisingly, smaller and mid-sized firms had more *very positive* responses than did the largest firms, suggesting that, even though the largest firms are more likely to offer the flexible programs, the greatest benefits are seen by the smaller companies. An alternative explanation is that respondents from smaller companies are in closer touch with their employees and thus more aware of positive outcomes.

FLEXIBILITY IN STYLE: WORKFORCE DIVERSITY

Given widespread recognition of demographic trends, many respondents reported that they expect significant increases in the numbers of employees other than white men in their workforces in the mid-90s. In answer to the question, "which groups do you expect to increase significantly as a proportion of your workforce?" firms projected a substantial increase in the number of minority women and men and in white women (see Exhibit 5.6). The most-surprising feature is that 41% of the companies projected *no* substantial change in the composition of their workforce.

Maybe the mid-90s time horizon given was too short to reflect the massive changes expected at the turn of the century. It is also possible that downsizing firms simply cannot project how their workforce will change in the near future. Interestingly, however, half the sample did not project any decrease in the numbers of white males they employ even though the proportion of white men in the U.S. workforce is projected to decline from

Exhibit 5.6 Projected increases in employee groups in the mid-90s.

Employee Group	Percentage of Firms
Minority women	46
Minority men	36
White women	33
Part-time workers	19
Mothers of young children	14
Handicapped workers	13
Workers over age 55	12
Temporary workers	10
New immigrants	10
Workers under age 55	5
Other	4
White men	1
None	41

approximately 43% to 38% from 1990 to 2005.[16] Curiously, respondents seem to have a "head-in-the-sand" outlook on how demographic trends will affect their firms in this regard.

Diversity Programs

Respondents were asked to describe programs they have in place to support the management of diversity. The results are reported in Exhibit 5.7. Almost two-thirds (63%) report having training programs for managers and 50% have statements from top management on the business need for diversity. Fewer have training programs for all employees (39%), task forces on diversity (31%), and minority-mentoring programs (28%).

When asked about plans for the mid-90s to offer such programs, approximately one-sixth to one-quarter of the firms plan to begin programs or implement additional measures. The prevalence of diversity programs was not strongly related to the composition of a firm's workforce. Again, however, cutting edge firms were most likely to have programs of this type.

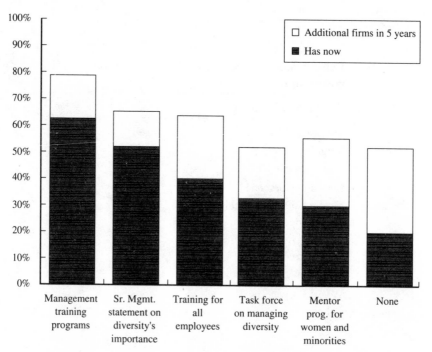

Exhibit 5.7   Programs that support the management of diversity.

Effects of Diversity

Respondents were asked how their top management see the impact of a more diverse workforce on human resources management. Results shown in Exhibit 5.8 indicate that in half of the surveyed companies top management thinks diversity is best handled as "just part of good management." Another third say top managers see it as a major challenge, with a need for new programs and management styles. Fewer companies see it as an affirmative action issue (16%) or as one with no serious impact (15%).

In one out of three companies, top managers see diversity as a competitive opportunity, such that learning to capitalize on diversity will increase the firm's productivity and competitive standing. Top executives most likely to see diversity as a competitive factor are found in companies with *cutting edge* human resource philosophies (55%). Interestingly, these cutting edge firms were least likely to see it handled as "just part of good management."

There seems to be a strong intersection of philosophy and practice in companies. Top executives who see diversity as a competitive opportunity are most apt to issue statements to this effect. And their firms are building flexibility in employee roles to allow for specialized training and mentoring programs. These cutting edge firms are also far more likely to have task forces devoted to the subject. This is the approach taken by Digital Equipment Corporation, which has been a leader in this area.[17] (It is worth noting Digital's severe financial problems and downsizing activities of late 1992, and it will be interesting to see if their diversity activities contribute to long-term corporate adaptability.)

By contrast, firms with a less-progressive and prudent approach to human resources are most likely to see diversity as an affirmative action issue or one

Exhibit 5.8   Impact of more diverse workforce.

Top Management's Attitudes	Percentage of Firms
No serious impact on operations	15
Part of good management—good management automatically deals with diversity issues	49
Affirmative action issue—best approach is to meet equal opportunity requirements	16
Major challenge—new programs and management style needed	34
Opportunity—increased productivity and competitiveness result from learning to capitalize on diversity	34

with no serious impact. Here, too, we find consistency between philosophy and practice as the firms offer much less in the way of diversity programs.

Program Responsibility

As is the case with work/life balance programs, prime responsibility for diversity programs and practices tends to lie in the human resources (HR) area. In the majority of firms, it is either a separate HR function (44%) or a general HR responsibility (11%). In cutting edge firms, the pattern is noticeably different, with the responsibility more likely to reside in training and development (14% versus 8% in the overall population), or more likely to be based in a task force or some other function (14% versus 8% in the overall population).

COMPARATIVE TRENDS AND STUDIES

Data from other surveys suggest that the number of companies offering flexibility in schedules and work location has increased substantially during the past several years (see Exhibit 5.9).[18] Data from Conference Board companies

Exhibit 5.9 Percentages of companies having flexible work arrangements.

	Date of Survey			
Flexible Arrangement	1988[1] (%)	1991[2] (%)	1991[3] (%)	1990[4] (%)
Parental leave beyond disability for mother	60	85	51	49
Regular part-time work	90	85	34	80
Job sharing	22	47	16	24
Flextime	50	77	40	52
Leave for sick family members	67	75	43	NR
Flexplace	7	29	7	15
Sabbatical	24	24	NR	NR
Phase retirement	9	22	NR	NR

[1]1988: Conference Board survey of member companies
[2]1991: Laborforce 2000 survey of conference board companies
[3]1991: Hewitt Associates survey sample of U.S. companies
[4]1990: Survey by International Foundation for Employee Benefits

Valuing Differences as an Approach to Diversity

Organizational productivity depends on how workers deal with the tension and conflict created by the differences among them. Valuing Differences, developed at Digital Equipment Corporation by Barbara Walker, is a philosophy that encourages employees to pay attention to the differences among them—both as unique individuals and as members of groups—in order to capitalize on their differences. The philosophy is anchored in the conviction that the broader the spectrum of differences in the workplace, the richer will be the synergy among the employees and the more excellent the organization's performance.

Valuing Differences is an agenda for *inclusion*. It shifts away from a sole focus on traditional EEO-protected issues and addresses *all* differences. The work is done in a variety of ways.

- EEO-type Multicultural and skill-building workshops that focus on group norms and on behavioral do's and don'ts
- Celebrating Differences events—usually a year-long calendar of cultural and educational events
- Geographic cross-cultural or intercultural workshops, which help participants learn the norms and practices of different countries
- Organizational development activities, which focus on team building and values clarification
- Personal development through small, ongoing dialogues, sometimes called *core groups*

Core groups are discussion groups of seven, eight, or nine people who agree to help one another become serious students of differences. The groups are led by the leader-participant, who has learned how to "keep people safe" and help them stay focused on differences. The focus in the core group is on personal learning, particularly on learning how to learn from people that one regards as different. Participants work on stripping away their stereotypes, listening for the differences in the assumptions of others, raising their levels of empowerment, and building authentic relations with people they regard as different.

From Barbara Walker, founder of the Valuing Differences program at Digital Equipment Corporation. (Ms. Walker is currently doing this work at Silicon Graphics Corporation.)

collected in 1988 compared to Laborforce 2000 results show increases in the number of firms offering leave beyond disability for mothers (from 44% to 85%), and offering job sharing (22% to 47%), flextime (50% to 77%), flexplace (7% to 29%), and phased retirement options (9% to 22%).

However, both the 1988 and current Conference Board samples are skewed to larger companies. Surveys by Hewitt Associates of the benefit plans of salaried employees in over a thousand U.S. employers, and by the International Foundation of Employee Benefit Plans (IFEBP) of 272 benefit plans, find many fewer companies offering flexible options to their employees. Just 51% of the Hewitt and 49% of the IFEBP respondents offer unpaid parental leave (versus 85% in the Laborforce 2000 study). Flextime is reported in only 40% of the Hewitt and 52% of the IFEBP sample companies compared with 77% in Laborforce 2000 study. The number of firms offering job sharing and the chance for employees to work at home is also lower in the Hewitt and IFEBP surveys.

Hence, we caution that, although flexibility seems to be increasing within Conference Board companies, the two other studies show that it may be less widespread than the Laborforce 2000 data suggest. Moreover, in important areas like family leave, even with new legislation U.S. industry lags well behind European firms.[19] We would add that we found no comparable surveys on diversity programs in companies, which may be a telling sign of the lack of interest in issues of race and ethnicity among researchers and HR service providers.[20]

THE MEANING OF FLEXIBILITY FOR ORGANIZATIONS

We have shown that programs to promote work/family flexibility and accommodate workforce diversity form an integral part of the human resource agenda in many companies. But there are many differences in how such programs are positioned with an organization, as described in the following subsections.

Flexibility Can Be a "Benefit" for Employees

Many firms seem to regard flexibility as a benefit that, like health insurance, is made available to all employees. Particular practices are codified into policy and are administered by the HR department. In a related form, flexible options may be treated like compensation, whereby specific options are offered to employees based on circumstances. For instance, a worker might ask for the opportunity to work at home for periods of time or to have a flexible schedule. Some firms extend such options to segments of their workforce: North Carolina National Bank has a "select time" option for professionals, who can negotiate personalized part-time schedules and performance goals.[21] In any case, flexibility is deemed to be something that the company provides for its employees as a part of their employment contract.

The problem with this approach to flexibility is that it focuses attention on the transaction—what companies can be expected to offer employees and to get in return. Family leave policies, for instance, are embroiled in the larger national debate over so-called employee rights and employer responsibilities. And, within firms, such policies are sometimes advanced as "bargaining points," or they are resisted because employees are already getting "too much" in their employment contracts. A fixation on flexibility as an employee-employer *transaction*, in our view, neglects other important benefits of workplace flexibility.

Flexibility Can Be Part of the Corporate Image

Another way of thinking about flexibility concerns its value to the corporate image. It is an implicit part of the employment contract but has the added value of enhancing the company's reputation. Magazines such as *Working Mother* and others regularly feature lists of family-friendly companies, which can help companies recruit employees and project a positive image to customers.[22] The problem involves the inevitable trade-offs. Top company officials, for example, may deem flextime an important recruiting tool and benefit to the company's image. Meanwhile, line supervisors may see it as interfering with their ability to schedule work and may thus prevent certain employees from having it. Whatever favorable publicity the company gains in the public's eye may be offset by discontent in segments of the employee population in these circumstances.

Flexibility Can Be an Aspect of Organizational Design

We have made the case that flexibility can also be seen as integral to an organization's design and can help it adapt to changes in the environment. For instance, companies that employ part-time employees, allow for job sharing, or provide a phased retirement option for older workers have considerably more flexibility than otherwise in staffing for periods of high and low demand and for short-term projects. This type of flexibility is one aspect of what Handy calls the *shamrock* organization, where there are three layers of employees: core professionals, technicians, and managers—who are essential to operations; contract specialists—to do nonessential tasks on a fee-for-service basis; and part-time and temporary workers—whose numbers and hours are adjusted to accommodate fluctuations in workload.[23]

In the same spirit, flextime can increase the number of hours an office or plant is open to serve customers, take deliveries, and ship goods; flexplace can enable an organization to lower its downtown rents and reduce commuting costs; and leaves and sabbaticals can help balance staffing levels. The point made here is that flexibility in time and space provides many options for a company to better serve its needs and those of its employees. But the opportunities can be overlooked if flexibility is cast primarily as an employee benefit or as simply a means of enhancing a company's image.

Flexibility Can Be an Aspect of Corporate Culture

Finally, we think it useful to consider flexibility as part of a corporate culture. Rigid, mechanistic, and bureaucratic forms of organization are most often associated with companies having a monolithic culture dominated by the values and leadership of white males (whose wives assume primary care for children at home). In our view, the movement toward flexible organizational designs will likely necessitate changes in monolithic corporate cultures. This means a shift toward a "multicultural" organization, that is, a culture that accommodates differences in employee's personal identities (including ethnicity, life-style, age, and gender) and the demands of their nonwork roles.

Much has to do with the everyday cultural flexibility of an organization— it shapes the experiences of employees. High-level statements that affirm equal opportunity ring hollow when managers and peers comment that "he's too family-oriented—not ambitious," "she's too feminine—not aggressive enough," or "he acts too black." Multicultural organizations question the assumptions embedded in such statements. Whether an ideal level of cultural flexibility exists is uncertain, but it should be at least flexible enough to acknowledge that different ways of working, and of being at work, may be equally effective in the long run.

In the same way, once an employee's child care arrangements have been made—long after the parental leave is over and after any desired part-time work and benefits have been set up—what counts most is how sensitive and flexible that person's boss is to the employee's everyday crises (an inoperative car, a sitter who doesn't show up, a special event at school, and so forth) and transitions from one world to another. A supportive boss provides leeway to deal with these events and garners loyalty and high effort in return. An unsupportive boss increases the employee's stress level and may elicit a performance problem.

THE MEANING OF FLEXIBILITY
FOR THE INDIVIDUAL

We have shown that flexibility is important to working people. However, as the following paragraphs explain, people differ in how they value flexible work options.

- *Flexibility helps in managing time and place.* Certainly there are clear advantages to flexibility with reference to people's abilities to manage their work time and location. Flextime allows people to work around some family duties or simply arrange a more convenient commuting schedule. Flexplace gives them the chance to work at home, saving travel hassles and costs and intermixing work with home chores and recreation. The key point is that workplace flexibility provides individuals different options for managing the combination of their various roles at work, at home, and in the community. Yet, while this is an important benefit of flexibility for the person, there is another notable advantage to consider.

- *Flexibility helps in managing commitment and psychic energy.* One common notion in behavioral theory is that people typically invest more in one role or another in order to maximize the reward. However, Lobel's research on social identity suggests that work/family conflict can be minimized when people achieve some congruence between their work and nonwork roles or else keep them very separate in time, physical distance, and psychological space.[24] This implies that it is possible to "balance" one's commitment to both spheres. Obviously, workplace flexibility makes the balancing easier.

This research on social identity may also apply to another aspect of flexibility: style. Are women—all women, not just those who have become mothers—confronted with the need to balance their identities as women with their commitment to the organization? It has been suggested that the early stages of women's advancement in organizations were indeed based on such trade-offs and that the highest praise a female manager could get was, "you don't even act like a woman." Similarly, Bell describes the stresses of the bicultural balancing act that career-oriented African-American women perform in order to succeed in predominately white organizations.[25] Flexibility may help eliminate the necessity for members of such groups to downplay their identities (and important differences with the majority culture) in order to demonstrate their commitment. Reducing the necessity for such balancing should reduce stress, freeing energy and ideas for more productive uses.

BENEFITS AND COSTS

An interesting phenomenon seems to have developed around the question of which party derives more benefit from flexibility. Because the purported aim of many work/family programs is to make a company "family-friendly," there is a tendency to assume that *employees* gain the most from flexible work options. However, data suggest that the major beneficiary is the employer. Friedman and Galinsky, in a review of eight studies, find that improved morale was the greatest perceived benefit in the majority of the studies. Reduced absenteeism was the second-highest ranked outcome.[26] In three national surveys, of firms providing child care assistance, improved recruitment and reduced absenteeism were the two greatest perceived benefits. All of these represent cost reductions for companies.

On the employee side, Friedman and Galinsky present six studies of users of employer-sponsored child care centers that affirm that this option is attractive in recruiting and that it reduces absenteeism and turnover. Yet flexible options may limit, rather than increase, people's freedom of choice. For instance, programs that provide for sick and back-up child care not only make it possible, but sometimes even requisite, that employees spend time at work rather than with their families. The option of entering a so-called mommy track may typecast a woman as a "mother first/employee second" in the same way that affirmative-action hiring status can typecast minority employees.[27] Our concern is that some seemingly flexible options may lock people into an undesirable situation. Should, for example, new parents be "expected" to return to work after six weeks of leave because the on-site care center accepts infants at that age? In the long run, this kind of inflexible flexibility may not even be in the organization's interest, as the personal costs of such imbalance become apparent.[28]

The potential bind raises several questions: Is it inherently a good thing to "help" parents spend less time with their children? Or help adults spend less time with older parents? Is it a good thing to provide temporary care for sick children so that the employee can come to work? Who advocates within the corporation for the interests of children and other dependents? What value judgments are implicitly being made about where employees should spend their time? Such questions point to a broader issue—where should the boundary between organization and individual be drawn?

Where to Draw the Line?

A historical perspective makes clear that work and life were not always physically and temporally separated, and it suggests that there are pluses and minuses to welfare capitalism and the idealization of the "organizational family."[29] Plainly, companies are instilling an even deeper level of dependency among employees who rely on their firms to help with child and elder care and to assist in the expression of their individual identities. Doing so could yield blind loyalty and have shattering consequences to employees laid off or fired from such an all-encompassing employer. Further, can organizations use what they learn about personal lives in unfair ways? Does the provision of such programs as sick-child care create the expectation that employees will be able to work no matter how sick their children are? The potential problems of contemporary efforts to reintegrate work and nonwork lives are just beginning to be identified.[30]

On the other side, modern organizations are large, complex systems with multiple interdependencies, which would seem to preclude individual members from coming and going as they please throughout the course of the workday, week, or year. Moreover, some jobs may allow for more flexibility than others; some people, like working parents, may need more flexibility than others; and some groups may profit more from help in social integration at the company than others. It seems that a line must be drawn somewhere, or else organizations run the risk of chaos and conflict.[31] The old paradigm of workers being asked to leave much of their selves outside created a clear boundary between individual and organization. Flexibility raises difficult questions about overstepping boundaries, including the danger of corporate overinvolvement in the personal lives of employees and the danger of people pitted against one another or the corporation in an effort to gain their fair share of flexibility.

IMPLICATIONS FOR RESEARCH

There is no doubt that attention to flexibility represents a significant change in contemporary organizations. But there seems to be a paradox in the impact of work on people's lives: Despite having more options and assistance in managing their work lives, working people are overstressed in both their work and family lives.[32] Naturally, there are many potential contributors to high stress levels, ranging from great personal expectations to heavy demands at work and home. But, in the present context, it is important to determine what role workplace flexibility plays in decreasing, increasing, or mediating the impact of work and life events on people's stress.

We need to get beyond descriptive surveys and see what effects these programs and activities have on working people. Has all of this progress on work/family initiatives actually reduced the stress of the daily transitions of the parents? As Hall and Richter point out, the most stressful parts of the working day for two-earner parents are transitions between home and work.[33] This daily separation-and-reentry process, which requires shifts in both mental and physical activity, is difficult regardless of the kind of child care arrangements made. Are people in fact any better off in these daily transitions as a result of corporate initiatives?

Perhaps the most notable gap in research concerns the impact of diversity programs. The vast majority of current work focuses on the components of programs or on the effects of diversity on work groups.[34] Those are important subjects, but we need more data on the experiences of participants in diversity programs and on the effects of cultural flexibility on the freedom that people have to express their own style in the workplace.

We also need more research on what promotes the psychic energy and what produces psychological engagement at work. Certainly people's sense of psychological safety should increase when they do not have to hide parts of their selves, and their psychic availability should improve when worries about work/life balance are reduced. But it may be that other corporate changes described in this volume and the complexity of family life today simply counterbalance these benefits of flexibility for the employee. Do they, however, serve a benefit for a spouse, children, and companion?

Finally, Friedman points out that much research in the work/family area has focused on managerial and professional employees, and hence we lack research on low-income families, in part because they may have more-difficult needs to serve.[35] Friedman addresses the inequity by suggesting that research should be done on all levels of performers. By extending flexible alternatives only to high performers, organizations ignore the possibility that low performers might be performing below ability solely because of the absence of flexibility.

FLEXIBILITY AND ORGANIZATIONAL CHANGE

A subset of companies—generally, larger firms and those at the cutting edge of human resource management—see flexibility as a competitive issue worthy of continued investment and experimentation. Will other firms follow their lead?

Some external factors pulling organizations in the direction of flexibility have already been alluded to, namely changes in workforce demographics, the need for good public relations, and competition for highly trained employees who demand flexibility. Internal pressures may be the costs of lost productivity, absenteeism, and turnover. But the key to sustained innovation may rest in corporate values and ideology. Some organizations say that it is the "right thing to do" and find that the major benefit of workplace flexibility is a more responsive, adaptive organization.

Friedman and Galinsky find that organizations evolve through three stages in responding to work/family concerns.[36] In the first, one or a few champions take the lead in getting the organization to implement a tentative, programmatic response almost exclusively aimed at women with children. Over time, an integrated approach may evolve, in which a broader spectrum of needs are addressed, in the context of the entire human resources program. In this stage, top-level commitment develops, and policies change as well as programs. A few organizations make it to the third stage, in which cultural change and the mainstreaming of work/family issues occur. Friedman and Galinsky assert that in this third stage, changes permeate not only formal policies and procedures relevant to all employees but also the informal norms and culture of the organization. Their model, we believe, applies to not only work/family but also diversity programs and the broader movement toward corporate flexibility.

In many of the companies in the Laborforce 2000 survey there seems to be an attempt to deliver innovation (flexibility) in traditional forms (programs, coordinators), leading us to wonder how much flexibility will really make its way into the culture and mainstream of organizations. We worry that flexibility in the work/family arena has been too easily accepted in most companies—as merely another benefit. It has become housed in the benefits section of the human resources department, and it is headed by a mid- to low-level coordinator who is anything but an agent of corporate cultural change.

This situation parallels early EEO efforts, which marginalized diversity efforts and led to the conclusion that broadly based cultural change would be necessary in order to get managers beyond conforming merely to the letter of the policy to implementing (and believing) its spirit.[37] Our point is that the traditional forms of implementing flexibility may in fact limit the pervasiveness and staying power of changes.

We see this potential limiting effect as one of the most compelling reasons for grouping diversity and work/life balance together under the rubric of workplace flexibility and for linking flexibility to organizational strategy and culture. This formulation runs the risk of marginalizing both topics—confusing rights with cost/benefit analysis and sidestepping difficult ideological and emotional issues. But it has the advantage of framing the issues in ways such that members of every group are concerned; that moral, social, and economic criteria are all considered; and the critical question of integrating the "full" person and the organization is considered. We see it as a formulation that puts both of these areas (and others) into a broader perspective, which offers new ways to define the organization and laborforce of the future. Finally, it offers a way of thinking about the potential strategic benefits of such change efforts.

What does this formulation mean for implementing flexibility? Proponents of Total Quality Management and other workplace changes aimed at

---

The Work/Family Coordinator

Task forces or employee committees on work/family issues are often followed up by the appointment of a work/family coordinator who is charged with implementing and overseeing the new programs. According to recent Conference Board estimates, over three hundred companies have created such positions.

Many carry out such positions on a part-time basis and/or have additional responsibilities in other areas. Virtually all are located in the human resources function and report either to human resources generalists or to EEO, employee relations, or employee communications managers.

Typical requirements for coordinator positions include a bachelor's degree and three to five years related experience, knowledge of corporate culture and systems, and good communication and interpersonal skills.

Based on information collected by Dana Zackin.

competitiveness stress the need for managers to collaborate with their employees and to get everyone involved in thinking about (and acting on) quality. If employers and employees can collaborate on quality (the content of the work), then why should they not also be able to collaborate on flexibility (the working arrangements)?

"Doing it right" means that top management must reflect on corporate values and the desired relationship between the organization and employees. It also means being very self-conscious about managing the psychological contract between employees and the firm. It means giving employees a voice in stating their needs and in working toward solutions, whether through task forces, surveys, or other means of organizational improvement.[38]

An organization that is providing flexibility in the right way is not just providing a family-friendly work environment or just an employee-friendly environment. Rather, it is experimenting with a new organizational design and a new employment culture. That this will help to attract and retain the most qualified and most engaged workforce is merely one sign of corporate adaptability and vitality in the face of change.

ACKNOWLEDGMENT

We would like to acknowledge the support of the Human Resource Policy Institute and the Executive Roundtable of Boston University. The helpful comments of Kathy Kram, Sharon Lobel, Chuck Wolfe, and Philip Mirvis on earlier drafts of this chapter are gratefully acknowledged. We would also like to acknowledge the research assistance of Stephanie Pryor, Rajeev Sawhney, and Dana Zacklin in various phases of this project. Details on statistical analyses can be obtained by writing to us in care of Boston University.

NOTES

1. Johnston, W. B., and A. H. Packer. 1987. *Workforce 2000*. Indianapolis, IN: Hudson Institute.
2. Kahn, W. A. 1990. Psychological conditions of personal engagement and disengagement at work. *Academy of Management Journal* 33 (4): 692–724.
3. Hall, D. T., and J. Richter. 1988. Balancing work and home life: What can organizations do? *Academy of Management Executive* 2 (3): 213–223.
4. Hall, D. T. 1990. Promoting work/family balance: An organization change approach. *Organizational Dynamics* 18: 5–18.
5. Morgan, G. 1986. *Images of organization*. Beverly Hills, CA: Sage.

6. Friedman, D. E., and A. Johnson. 1991. *Strategies for promoting a work-family agenda*. Conference Board Report #973. New York: Conference Board.

7. Handy, C. 1989. *The age of unreason*. Boston: Harvard Business School Press.

8. DeLuca, J. M., and R. N. McDowell. 1992. Managing diversity: A strategic "grass roots" approach. In *Working through diversity: Human resources initiatives*, ed. S.E. Jackson & Associates, 227–247. New York: Guilford Press.

9. Lawler, E. E. 1974. The individualized organization: Problems and promise. *California Management Review* 17 (2): 31–39.

10. Peters, J. L., B. H. Peters, and F. Caropreso. 1990. *Work & family policies: The new strategic plan*. Conference Board Report #949. New York: Conference Board.

11. Cox, T., S. A. Lobel, and P. L. McLeod. 1991. Effects of ethnic group cultural differences on cooperative and competitive behavior on a group task. *Academy of Management Journal* 34 (4): 827–847; McLeod, P. L., and S. A. Lobel. 1992. The effects of ethnic diversity on idea generation in small groups. To appear in the 1992 *Academy of Management Proceedings*.

12. *Boston Globe*. 1992. Working moms tell companies: Be flexible, May 10, 33.

13. Morgan, H., and F. Milliken. 1992. Keys to action: Understanding differences in organizations' responsiveness to work-and-family issues. Forthcoming in *Human Resources Management*.

14. Hall, "Work/family balance"; Sproull, L., and S. Kiesler. 1991. *Connections: New ways of working in the networked organization*. Cambridge, MA: MIT Press.

15. Friedman, D. E., and E. Galinsky. 1992. Work and family trends. In *Work and family*, ed. S. Zedeck. San Francisco: Jossey-Bass.

16. Fullerton, H. N. 1991. Labor force projections: The baby boom moves on. *Monthly Labor Review*, November: 31–44.

17. Walker, B. A., and W. C. Hanson. 1992. Valuing differences at Digital Equipment Corporation. In *Working through diversity: human resources initiatives*, ed. S. E. Jackson & Associates, 119–137. New York: Guilford Press.

18. Christensen, K. 1989. Flexible staffing and scheduling in U.S. corporations. *Conference Board Bulletin*, Research Bulletin No. 240. New York: Conference Board; Googins, B. K. 1991. *Work/family conflicts*. New York: Auburn House; and Hewitt Associates. 1991. Work and family benefits provided by major U.S. employers in 1991: Based on practices of 1006 employers. Hewitt Associates.

19. Googins, *Work/family conflicts*.

20. Cox, T., and S. M. Nkomo. 1990. Invisible men and women: A status report on race as a variable in organizational behavior research. *Journal of Organizational Behavior* 11 (6): 419–431.

21. Galinsky, E., D. E. Friedman, and C. A. Hernandez. 1991. *The corporate reference guide to work-family programs*. New York: Families and Work Institute.

22. *Working Mother*. 1991. 85 best companies for working mothers. October.

23. Handy, *The age of unreason*.

24. Lobel, S. A. 1991. Allocation of investment in work and family roles: alternative theories and implications for research. *Academy of Management Review* 16 (3): 507–521.

25. Bell, E. L. 1990. The bicultural life experience of career-oriented black women. *Journal of Organizational Behavior* 11 (6): 459–477.

26. Friedman and Galinsky, Work and family trends.

27. Schwartz, F. 1989. Management women and the new facts of life. *Harvard Business Review* 67 (1): 65–76.

28. Kofodimos, J. 1990. Why executives lose their balance. *Organizational Dynamics*, 19 (1): 58–73.

29. Googins, *Work/family conflicts*; Orthner, D. K., G. L. Bowen, and V. G. Beare. 1990. The organization family: A question of work and family boundaries. *Marriage and Family Review* 15 (3-4): 15–36.

30. Guzzo, R. A., G. L. Nelson, and K. A. Noonan. 1992. Commitment and employer involvement in employees' non-work lives. In *Work and family*, ed. S. Zedeck. San Francisco: Jossey-Bass.

31. Zedeck, S. 1992. *Work, families, and organizations.* San Francisco: Jossey-Bass.

32. Harris, Louis. 1987. Stress: A singular mark of modern life. *Inside America*. New York: Vintage.

33. Hall and Richter, Balancing work and home life.

34. Cox, T. 1991. The multicultural organization. *Executive* 5 (2): 34–47; McLeod and Lobel, "Effects of ethnic diversity."

35. Friedman, D. E., 1991. *Linking work-family issues to the bottom line*. Conference Board Report #962. New York: Conference Board.

36. Friedman and Galinsky, Work and family trends.

37. Thomas, R. R. 1990. From affirmative action to affirming diversity. *Harvard Business Review* 68 (2): 107–17.

38. Hall, Work/family balance.

6

Corporations and the Aging Workforce

Michael C. Barth,
William McNaught,
and Philip Rizzi

Market

One of the strongest demographic trends affecting the United States today is the aging of its population. In the last decade, companies increasingly focused on older Americans as worthy of their own special products and marketing efforts. The workforce within many companies is also graying, but it seems that American businesses have not responded to older workers with the same effort and ingenuity as they have to older customers.

Indeed, based on data from the 406 companies sampled in the Laborforce 2000 study, our conclusions showed workers over age 55 leaving firms en masse via downsizing and early retirement programs, deprived of training monies spent on underprepared entry workers, and threatened by cutbacks in their health benefits. At the same time, many businesses are experiencing skill shortages in technical and blue-collar areas and gravitating toward more flexible work arrangements, including new types of career paths and more part-time employment options. This presents new opportunites for many older workers who are primed for retraining and eager for more flexible or part-time employment opportunities. The question at hand is whether or not employers will capitalize on these vital human resources.

In this chapter we look at demographic trends and management attitudes and practices pertaining to older workers. Then we will hone in on the barriers to hiring, retraining, and redeploying older workers as identified by the

156

human resource officials interviewed in this study. Finally, we will report on the current plans and future intentions of companies in this area and how they compare with needs and opportunities. Our conclusion is that more attention is needed and more concerted action would prove beneficial for companies and older workers alike.

THE AGING OF THE LABORFORCE

The demographic trends are clear: Over the next three decades, the number of Americans age 55 and older will increase dramatically. By the year 2020, nearly 32% of the American population will be age 55 or over, up from 13% in 1990. This will directly affect the labor market. Take the current situation as a baseline, and project ahead: In 1990 persons age 55 and older composed some 27.1% of the working-age population in the U.S. (defined as those age 16 and older). By 2005, those 55 and older are projected to number 29.3% of the working age population and by 2020, a staggering 39.1% (see Exhibit 6.1). In actual numbers, this translates into an increase from 51.0 million persons 55 and older in 1990 to more than 93.2 million in 2020. This means that, over the next thirty years, the number of older Americans will grow by 83%, while the population age 16 to 54 increases a scant 6%.[1]

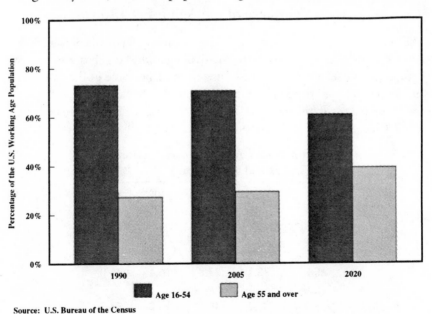

Source: U.S. Bureau of the Census

Exhibit 6.1 Change in working age population, 1990–2020.

The participation rate of older men declined steadily between 1962 and 1987 as increases in real income, the structure of pension plans, and the personal preferences of workers made retirement more attractive.[2] More recently, the laborforce participation rate for older men has leveled off, and the U.S. Bureau of Labor Statistics expects that the laborforce participation rates of older workers will increase somewhat between now and 2005, which is as far in the future as the Bureau has forecast (see Exhibit 6.2).[3] The laborforce participation rate for older women is projected to continue rising, reflecting the aging of those women who entered the laborforce over the last thirty years as opportunities increased for women in paid employment.

As a result of these changes in the age of the population and age-based participation rates, we project that the proportion of the laborforce that is age 55 or over will grow from 12.3% today to over 20% by 2020 (as shown in Exhibit 6.3). This projection is a base estimate derived by extrapolating current demographic projections and laborforce participation rates. For a number of reasons discussed in detail later on, we believe that more baby boomers will continue to work after age 55 than one might predict from demographic projections alone, which would further increase the percentage of the laborforce that is age 55 and older.

The Importance of the Aging Laborforce

The aging of the laborforce is significant because older workers have different needs, priorities, and concerns than younger workers. For instance, the baby boom generation of workers entered the laborforce in the 60s, when employees expected to spend their entire career at one company and American industrial predominance was largely unchallenged. That world no longer exists. Changes in the U.S. economy such as increasing foreign competition,

Exhibit 6.2 Laborforce participation rates by sex and age cohort.

	1960 (%)	1975 (%)	1990 (%)	2005 (%)
Male				
55–64	86.8	75.6	67.7	67.9
65+	33.1	21.8	16.4	16.0
Female				
55–64	37.2	40.9	45.3	54.3
65+	10.8	8.2	8.7	8.8

Source: Bureau of Labor statistics.

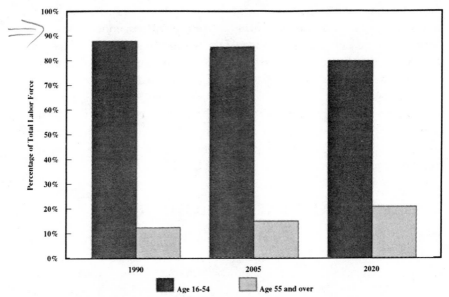

Source: Author's projections based on Bureau of the Census and Bureau of Labor Statistics data

Exhibit 6.3 Age composition of the U.S. laborforce, 1990–2020.

downsizing, outsourcing, and the relative decline of heavy manufacturing have eroded the job security that many of these workers once knew. The implicit contract between employer and worker is being transformed to reflect this new world of uncertainty. Companies looking simultaneously to control skyrocketing health care costs, shed unneeded workers, and eliminate managerial deadwood have focused retrenchment efforts on older workers, as evidenced by the prevalence of early retirement incentive programs offered to this segment of the laborforce in the 80s.

At the same time, longer life expectancy and increased opportunities for productive engagement have led many older Americans to reconsider their views about work and retirement. Many now desire to ease gradually into retirement through continued work on a reduced basis either in their current occupation or in a part-time second career. The desire to continue employment is reinforced by concerns about the quality of retired life. Baby boomers face retirement in an uncertain world where the long-term viability of the Social Security system in its current form is questionable and rising health care costs can overwhelm even the well off.

A company's workforce—its human capital—is often its largest investment, and more and more companies recognize that the quality of their workforce is crucial to remaining competitive in a global economy. Yet the emerging desire of the baby boom generation for continued, flexible, productive employment stands at odds with competing pressures and priorities confronting many businesses, including the need to train underskilled entry workers, integrate increasing numbers of women and minorities into the workforce, and control costs aggressively. The tensions between what older workers want and where corporate America believes it needs to go are likely to mount over time. How companies can balance these competing priorities may not be clear at present, but it would be dangerous to ignore demographic trends simply because the change is gradual and inevitable, and such neglect would have significant negative implications for U.S. competitiveness and the standard of living for society overall.

OLDER WORKERS IN U.S. INDUSTRY

At this point, U.S. companies are more and less affected by the aging of their workforces. The percentage of workers age 50 and over within individual companies in the survey varied considerably, from a low of no older workers to a high of 80%. Older workers were more prominent in particular industries and types of companies, a finding that has notable implications for human resource management practices.

Older Workers Are Concentrated in Mature and Declining Industries

As shown in Exhibit 6.4, on average, about every fifth worker is age 50 or over in companies that reported the age distribution of their workforce (210 of

Exhibit 6.4   Mean percentage of older workers employed by companies in study.[a]

Age Group	All Companies[b] (%)	Manufacturing Companies (%)	Companies with at Least 30% of the Workforce Unionized (%)	Companies with 25% or Less College Graduates (%)
50–59	14.9	17.7	18.4	17.6
60 and over	5.1	6.6	6.0	6.6
Total 50 and over	20.0	24.3	24.4	24.2

[a] Data presented are means; medians do not differ in any material way.

[b] Data for the 210 companies that provided this information.

the 406 surveyed companies). But, among manufacturing companies, those with substantial unionization, and those with relatively less educated workforces, roughly one worker in four is age 50 or older. And compared with the entire survey, companies with 30% or more workers age 50 or over are:

- Nearly twice as likely to have male-dominated workforces
- Twice as likely to be substantially unionized
- One-third more likely to be in manufacturing
- Fifty percent more likely to have more than ten thousand employees
- One-third more likely to have laid off substantial numbers of workers

We found a high correlation among these characteristics, which leads to the conclusion that a higher proportion of older workers are to be found in mature companies in industries that have experienced little, no, or negative growth over the last two decades. Because these companies have not been hiring younger workers at the same pace as other firms, the average age of their workforces has steadily grown and now is noticeably higher than the age of workforces of other companies in the survey. Having a relatively older workforce appears not to be the result of conscious choice as much as the result of other forces, such as the rate of corporate growth.

The nonrandom distribution of older workers has implications for how older workers are treated now and in the future. Because of competitive pressures in their industries, companies with relatively high percentages of older workers face the most immediate or severe cost and productivity problems and have experienced wrenching retrenchments. Their current crisis undoubtedly has a bearing on their treatment of older workers and their human resource policies overall.

Older Workers Are Concentrated in Companies without an Innovative Human Resource Management Orientation

Exhibit 6.5 compares all companies in the survey with those with 30% or more older workers in their workforces in terms of their industry and human resource orientation. As noted in other chapters, *cutting edge* companies are those that describe themselves at the forefront of adopting new human resource policies. They are typically the first to focus on emerging human resource issues, develop the pioneering programs, and spread their results to other companies. *Prudent* companies, at the other extreme, adopt policies only after they have proven effective in other companies. *Advanced* and *thoughtful* companies fall in between.

Exhibit 6.5 Percentage of older workers by industry group and company human resources philosophy.

Category	All Companies (%)	Companies with 30% or More of Workforce Age 50 and Over (%)
Sector		
Manufacturing	35	48
Finance/Insurance/ Real Estate	27	17
Other services	27	21
Human resource orientation		
Cutting edge	11	2
Advanced	39	43
Thoughtful	37	36
Prudent	11	19
Not sure	3	—

As indicated in the lower panel of Exhibit 6.5, companies with relatively more older workers are rarely on the cutting edge in developing new human resource policies (2% versus 11% for the entire sample) and are nearly twice as likely to be prudent about adopting new policies. Therefore, by orientation and competitive circumstances, the companies with relatively older workforces are less likely than average to make special efforts or implement new policies to deal with emerging laborforce issues, such as those posed by older workers.

CURRENT MANAGEMENT ATTITUDES TOWARD OLDER WORKERS

In the light of the changes rippling through corporate America in the continuous effort to remain competitive, the survey asked about management's assessment of older workers. Are older workers considered an important asset because of their accumulated experience and knowledge, or are they viewed as outdated, expensive, and expendable? Current attitudes not only bear on company decisions to retain, retrain, and redeploy older workers in this time of restructuring and downsizing but they are also a leading indicator of the future response to the aging of the laborforce.

Management attitudes toward the performance of older workers are best characterized as ambivalent (although, as we point out later, policies and practices may not coincide with attitudes). The human resource executives surveyed cited both advantages and disadvantages of older workers (as shown in Exhibit 6.6) without indicating a strong overall opinion. In specific, older workers were consistently rated as having more positive attitudes, being more reliable, and possessing better skills than the average worker. Executives from companies with a higher percentage of older workers in their workforce held views comparable to the rest of the sample on these counts.

Ratings of the superior skills of older workers are explained partly by their accumulated experience and partly by the dissatisfaction of companies with the intellectual and technical skills of more recent graduates of the American educational system. The advantages that older workers possess in terms of their work attitudes, and lower rates of turnover and absenteeism, may result from the lingering loyalty of this generation whose childhood included recent memory of the Great Depression and World War II and whose early career decisions were premised on the idea of a lifetime career with one employer. These survey findings about management attitudes corroborate those of an earlier study by the American Association of Retired Persons, which found that human resource executives gave very good or excellent ratings to older workers with respect to reliable performance (87%), solid experience (78%), commitment to quality (89%), loyalty (86%), and attendance/punctuality (91%).[4]

Survey respondents also noted the disadvantages of older workers, seeing them as incurring higher health care costs than the average worker and being

Exhibit 6.6 Areas where older workers are reported as better/worse than average workers.

Better—	All Companies (%)	Companies with 30% or More of Workforce Age 50 or Over (%)
Work attitudes	57	64
Turnover	76	74
Absenteeism	66	60
Job skills	48	45
Worse—		
Health care costs	64	79
Flexibility in accepting new assignments	57	62
Suitability for training	37	50

Days Inns of America

Days Inns of America is the third-largest hotel chain in the country, nearly all of whose properties are franchises. Aside from the Days Inns name, the primary service the corporation provides to its franchisees is access to a 24-hour national toll-free reservation system, In 1986, Days Inns faced a serious problem in fulfilling this vital service: The corporation had a difficult time finding enough workers to staff its Atlanta reservations center.

An obvious solution would have been to increase wages, because entry wage rates for reservation agents were no higher than those paid at local fast food restaurants. But Days Inns executives did not believe that modest wage increases would significantly increase job applications or reduce the rate of turnover. Instead, Days Inns selected a new recruiting strategy focusing on older workers. Days Inns realized that its new strategy was risky because the reservation agent job required skills not typically associated with older workers. A reservation agent must simultaneously engage in a conversation with the prospective client, query the reservation system for information, report on room availability, price, and location data appearing on the computer screen, and obtain local amenity and environment information from an accompanying five-inch thick binder. Calls come one after another allowing little idle time. The job requires working quickly, executing multiple tasks simultaneously, and working directly with sophisticated computer and telecommunications equipment. It was by no means obvious that older workers would be successful in these positions.

In the eyes of Days Inns's management, older workers' performance in training for the position would be a useful indicator of the likely success or failure of their new strategy. Initially, older workers took a few extra days to adjust to the computer equipment. The primary obstacle, however, was older workers' fear that they would not be able to learn the system. Once Days Inns's instructors learned how to better train older workers and older workers felt relaxed and confident, they typically learned as rapidly as younger workers.

On other performance measures including annual employment cost and productivity, older workers proved at least as good as younger workers. Older workers tended to have higher talk times (longer conversations with prospective customers) than younger workers but also had higher booking rates (percentage of calls resulting in a reservation).

In some areas, such as turnover, older workers were clearly superior. One year after completing training, fewer than 30% of younger workers remained at the job, but more than 87% of the older workers were still at work. More than one-half of the older workers were still employed after three years, compared to about one younger worker in ten. Factoring in the costs of recruiting and training, direct wages, and benefits, the net cost of older workers is nearly identical to that of younger workers.

The value of older workers was not lost on the management of Days Inns. By 1990, more than one-quarter of the reservation agents in Atlanta were age 50 or older, including four over age 70.

---

less flexible in taking on new assignments and less suitable for training. The reasons behind these assessments seem straightforward, but other factors may influence into managers' judgments in these areas. For instance, the cost of health care insurance naturally increases with a worker's age. Yet, nearly all companies (93%) stated that health care costs were not a major factor in their retention of older employees. Perhaps it is heightened concern over the total corporate health care bill that makes the cost of older workers more salient.

The perception that older workers are less flexible in taking on new assignments and less suitable for training than the average worker reflects the adage that old dogs cannot learn new tricks. Yet only one in three firms surveyed found older workers to be uncomfortable in learning new skills and technologies. Furthermore, our studies of companies that hired and trained older workers challenge stereotypes about their flexibility, interests in learning, and productivity.

The broader point is that negative ratings of older workers' flexibility and suitability for training may have less to do with these workers, per se, and more to do with managers' calculations of the immediate costs and return-on-investment of retraining and redeploying them. The rationalization is that because older workers have fewer remaining years of employment, the benefits of retraining and redeployment may not be recouped before their retirement.

It is notable that companies with relatively older workforces share these negative perceptions of older workers. But these firms are more concerned about the competitive impact of their health care costs overall and more focused on cutting costs and improving profitability. Here, again, the broader economics of corporate survival may be influencing judgments of older workers as much as direct experience.

Overall, companies seem to put a high value on the experience workers gain over their careers. On this subject, human resource executives were asked to describe the typical worker's contributions over the course of his or her career at their corporation. As shown in Exhibit 6.7, 28% of the sample see a worker's value to the company as increasing, making an "upward slope" throughout a career. Another 28% reported that an employee's value increases during the early stages of the career and then remains constant, resulting in a "plateau" pattern. The most frequent response, at 37%, was labelled "training dependent," meaning that the employee's value depends on whether he or she maintains skills. These three career contribution patterns—upward sloping, training dependent, and plateauing—support the value of older employees. Only a few (4%) of the respondents stated that the inverted U pattern, in which the worker's value to the corporation increases during the early stages of the career, remains constant for a period, and then declines sharply after a certain age, was the typical one. Companies with relatively older workforces replied in virtually the same proportion as the overall survey.

If companies' management of their employees were consistent with these views, two-thirds of the firms studied would put a premium on retaining

Exhibit 6.7   Perceived value of employees over their career.

	All Companies (%)	Companies with 30% or More of Workforce Age 50 and Over (%)
Upward sloping pattern: Value to the corporation tends to increase through the worker's entire career.	28	29
Training dependent pattern: Value of the corporation depends on whether workers maintain their skills	37	36
Plateau pattern: Value to the corporation increases during the early states of the career, then remains constant for the rest of the career	28	26
Inverted "U" pattern: Value to the corporation increases during the early stages of the career, remains constant for a period, then declines sharply after a certain age	4	7

valued older workers or providing them with additional training. Even at a company where the managers believe in a plateau-shaped career contribution pattern, the older worker should be on par with other workers and superior to new hires. When it comes to companies putting these attitudes into practice, however, the opposite seems true.

CURRENT MANAGEMENT PRACTICES TOWARD OLDER WORKERS

The distinction between attitudes and actions is critical because the continued productivity of older workers depends on their opportunities to contribute in the workplace. In many cases, for these opportunities to exist, companies will have to overcome prejudices about older workers as being less fit physically and mentally for demanding tasks or unwilling to acquire new skills. Older workers also need retraining and programs that assist them in managing their careers. Some may wish to alter their work patterns to accommodate their changing preferences for challenge and responsibility and the company's changing needs. Finally, the continued productivity of older workers is premised on companies desiring to retain them—an assumption that is, in many instances, highly questionable amidst the avalanche of early retirement programs being offered to thin the workforce.

Training and Retraining

In many companies, maintaining and upgrading skills through training is the key to job security and advancement with over 70% of the firms surveyed stating that retraining employees to keep their skills current is a somewhat or very serious human resource issue for their companies. Yet, there is evidence in the survey that older workers are not treated comparably to younger workers in gaining access to training. For instance, only 17% of companies spend "a lot of money" training workers 51 and over, compared to 29% that spend a lot training workers 35 and under (see Exhibit 6.8). In addition, 34% of managers stated that their companies spend very little money training older workers, compared to only 21% who spend very little on training workers 35 and under. Interestingly, spending levels across age groups for companies with 30% or more older workers were not significantly different than in other firms. Despite having more older workers, these companies are no more inclined to spend money training them.

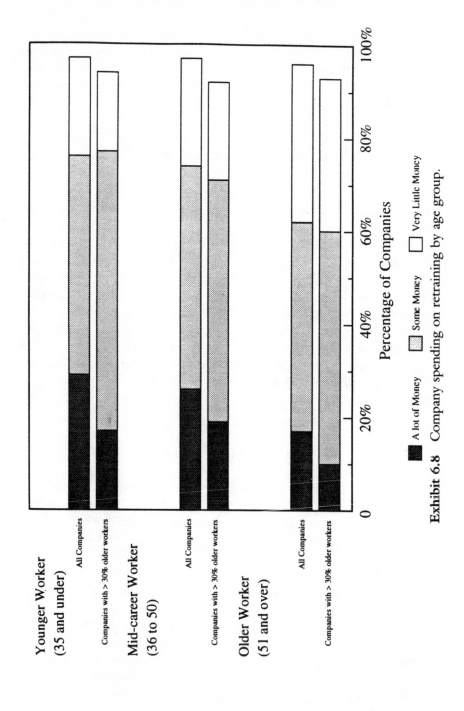

Younger Worker (35 and under)

All Companies

Companies with > 30% older workers

Mid-career Worker (36 to 50)

All Companies

Companies with > 30% older workers

Older Worker (51 and over)

All Companies

Companies with > 30% older workers

0   20%   40%   60%   80%   100%

Percentage of Companies

■ A lot of Money   ▨ Some Money   □ Very Little Money

Exhibit 6.8 Company spending on retraining by age group.

Do companies expend monies on training consistent with their view of an employee's value over his or her career? As seen in Exhibit 6.9, firms that subscribe to a training-dependent view of employee development are most likely to devote more resources to the training of all workers, whereas those that see an employee's value decline over a career spend less overall and much less on the training of older workers. However, equally noticeable, all four categories of companies, no matter what their view of employee's career value, report spending less resources on older workers than younger ones.

These data reveal a systematic *bias* against investing in older workers. Granted some 78% of the companies surveyed stated they encourage training and education to promote the continued employment of their older employees. But encouraging training may mean that the employee, not the company, pays the cost. And, when it comes to in-house training, the great majority (83%) of companies surveyed do not vary training methods to allow for the different age levels of the employees being trained, thus making no adjustments for the learning styles of older employees who have been out of classrooms for many years.

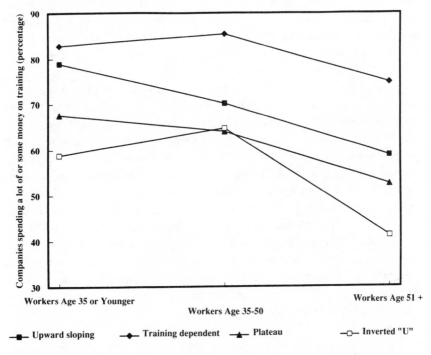

Exhibit 6.9 Training expenditures according to value of employees over their careers.

Career Management

Another area where practices are out of sync with older worker's needs concerns programs and assistance in career management. Exhibit 6.10 shows that only three types of support programs (programs that encourage training, hire retirees back as consultants or seasonal employees, or provide preretirement counseling) are offered by the majority of companies in this study, and none of these necessarily help to extend older workers' careers or enhance their productivity in the later stages of their careers.

We have just shown that companies' efforts to encourage training for older workers are to some extent undermined by their failure to provide older workers with equal access to training. In turn, preretirement and employment counseling is geared to help workers when they leave the company. And hiring back retirees as consultants or seasonal employees may extend careers but not necessarily at the level of effort, responsibility, and salary desired by the older worker.

A smaller number of companies are taking active steps to retain older workers and accommodate their career needs. Just over one-third of the firms sampled provide opportunities for workers over age 55 to transfer to jobs with reduced pay and responsibilities. As valuable as this might be, demand far exceeds supply: A 1989 survey estimated that nearly three million workers aged 50–64 would work longer than they planned to if they were offered a job with fewer hours and responsibilities and somewhat lower pay.[5] Alternative career tracks, which provide promotion and career pathways outside of the traditional managerial ladder, are available at about one of four companies, and phased retirement is offered by one in five. Such programs may take different forms: Some offer older employees a change in position and responsibility to one that is less demanding; others scale back their work hours in their current position. In some cases, these options entice older workers to stay on beyond normal retirement; in other cases, they provide a gradual transition to full retirement but at the normal age.

Significantly, Exhibit 6.10 shows that companies with a larger percentage of older workers are no more likely to offer these career management programs than firms with fewer older workers. There is also evidence that programs for older workers are the most likely to be scaled back or dropped when resources are squeezed by economic downturns or business slowdowns.[6]

Finally, we find that firms with a larger proportion of older workers are more likely than other companies to have career management policies that are, at best, indifferent to the knowledge and experience accumulated by older workers. Overall, 65% of the companies surveyed describe their

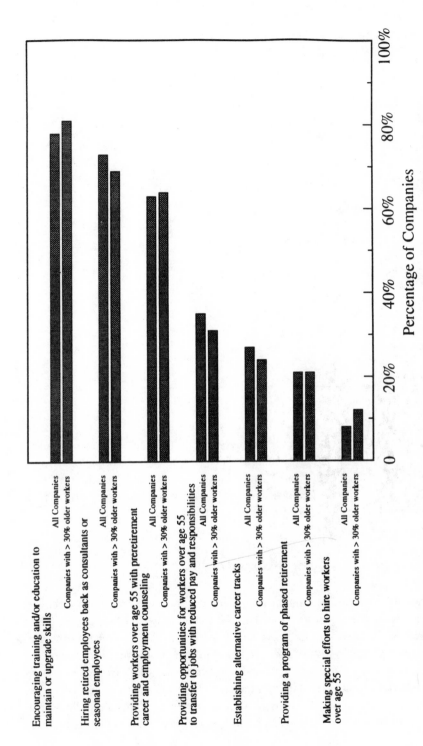

Exhibit 6.10 Current company programs to promote the continued employment of older employees.

171

Exhibit 6.11 How companies manage the career length of employees.

	All Companies (%)	Companies with 30% or More Older Workers in Workforce (%)
Experience-oriented: Attempt to retain all productive employees for as many years as possible	65	52
Market-driven: Allow usual career length to fluctuate according to market conditions	19	24
Fixed career-oriented: Encourage employees to work up to a standard retirement age and then retire to make way for younger workers	8	12
Promotion-oriented: Expect all employees to continuously compete aggressively for promotions, those who are not promoted are expected to seek other jobs	7	10

corporate policy on career length as experience-oriented, meaning that their company attempts to retain all productive employees for as long as possible (see Exhibit 6.11). By comparison, fewer (52%) of the firms employing a large percentage of older workers subscribe to this policy. They are somewhat more inclined than other firms to allow careers to fluctuate with market dynamics or to encourage retirement at a fixed age.

Early Retirement Programs

Although firms are lagging in providing training and career management programs for older workers, they have been aggressive in offering them early retirement incentive programs (ERIPs). As the earlier chapter on downsizing reported, some 40% of the companies in this sample that had downsized made use of ERIPs to eliminate staff, and more than half of the companies with a larger number of older workers had offered such programs. There are, of course, many ways to downsize, including closing plants and selling business units, that have more or less impact on different working age groups. In this study, 36% of the companies said they lost a disproportionate number of older workers to downsizing, but another one-third said they lost fewer older workers, and the rest reported no age-related differences in their loss of people due to downsizing.

Still, there are notable examples in which downsizing has been targeted at older workers, as evidenced by the increasing number of age discrimination suits being filed against companies that downsize, such as IBM, R. H. Macy & Co., and Merrill Lynch & Co.[7] The targeted impact of downsizing on older workers is, of course, pronounced in the frequent use of ERIPs.

An ERIP typically offers workers an enhanced pension, and possibly other benefits, if he or she retires earlier than usually permitted by the company's pension plan. In companies choosing to downsize with ERIPs, 40% of the managers stated that the major reason they used this method to reduce their laborforce was that ERIPs were a "regularly used and an accepted management practice" (see Exhibit 6.12). Fewer than 20% of the managers reported that the major reason they used ERIPs was to eliminate either the most expensive workers (15%) or the least productive ones (18%). In other words, managers are choosing ERIPs not as part of a targeted, coherent bottom-line strategy to eliminate cost-inefficient workers, but more or less because "that is what everyone else does." ERIPs are chosen because they are a conventional, predictable, and safe way to cut the size of a workforce in a short time.

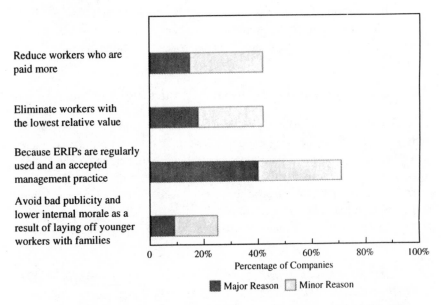

Exhibit 6.12   Why companies offer older workers early retirement.

ATTITUDES VERSUS PRACTICES: A VICIOUS CYCLE

Ambivalent managerial attitudes toward older employees, the general dearth of training and career management programs to promote their continued productivity and employment, and the prevalence of human resource policies and practices that negatively impact older employees all reinforce one another and contribute to a vicious cycle.

For instance, we have seen that managers in many companies find that older workers are more difficult to train and that training them is less valuable to the company. Given such an opinion, they would logically be disinclined to spend as many resources attempting to train older workers as they do to train younger workers, which the study documents. The lack of access to training for older workers, in turn, results in a gradual erosion of their value to the company relative to younger workers and encourages management to believe that older workers are most expendable during corporate cutbacks. To compound their problems, their failure to maintain and enhance their job skills because of a lack of training prevents older workers from switching jobs and companies, and reentering the laborforce after retirement. This is a complex and vicious cycle.

In the same way, if older workers believe that there is an age-based ceiling on their advancement in a company, then the perceived ceiling can become a self-fulfilling prophecy. Older workers would reduce their effort and commitment to seeking promotions on the basis that such efforts would be futile anyway. In addition, if older workers believe that their careers have reached a plateau, all else equal, they would be more likely to accept the benefits of an early retirement incentive program. This, too, is a vicious cycle.

Explaining the Gap between Attitudes and Practices

To break out of these vicious cycles, it is necessary to understand what fuels them. Consider, first, the apparent gap between attitudes and practice. Here we have seen that most companies profess to believe that an employee's value to the company rises over time or is dependent on training and that their general policy is to retain all productive employees as long as possible, but their actions indicate otherwise. We would offer the following explanations for this gap between management attitudes and corporate policies toward older workers:

1. Negative Attitudes and Stereotypes about Older Workers Are More Significant than Reported.   One hypothesis worth considering is that although business executives report favorable beliefs about their older workers, they may unconsciously hold negative opinions about them. Research on prejudice is replete with evidence that people have negative stereotypes about older persons that they may not be aware of or cannot articulate.[8] There is also a body of literature on how such stereotypes play out in organizations. As an example, one study found that supervisors' ratings of older workers, when compared with objective data, were consistently more negative.[9] Other studies find that biases in organizations were expressed in performance evaluations, feedback, and promotion decisions.[10]

But stereotyping alone cannot account fully for the gap between the way older workers are perceived and treated in the studied companies. Moreover, negative biases aside, replies to other questions suggest that management's overall attitude toward older workers is very favorable. For example, 55% of the respondents agreed that employees who have worked for the firm for more than 20 years deserve special treatment. And among companies with relatively older workforces, the number was 74%—signaling a high level of paternalism and concern. In addition, fewer than one in seven companies believed that most workers over age 55 want to retire as soon as they are eligible for pension benefits, contradicting the idea that companies view older workers as superannuated employees. These findings suggest that attitudes alone may matter little in the face of other priorities and concerns.

2. Older Workers Lack the Clout of Other Employee Populations.

A second hypothesis to consider is that older workers, as a group, are simply a less visible and vocal population within organizations. Part of the explanation for this may be that older workers are a relatively small proportion of the workforce at most companies in the survey. Recall that workers over age 50 represent, on average, approximately 20% of the workforce of the companies surveyed. Based on this, it is not surprising that companies are relatively unfocused on their older workers and have not made greater efforts to develop and implement programs to promote their continued employment.

Furthermore, although many human resource executives project significant increases in the numbers of women and minorities in their companies over the next few years, only 12% expect a significant increase in the number of their employees over 55. They are correct in this regard, for the large increase in older workers will not occur until the turn of the century, when the baby boomers reaches this age.

We suspect, however, that numbers alone do not account for corporations relative neglect of the needs of their older workers. The employment needs of women and minorities, by comparison, receive constant attention in the media and in publications on human resource management. In many instances, too, women and minorities have committees in companies that elevate their agendas and lobby for needed programs. In addition, companies typically have training and development programs that aim at entry workers and those in early stages of their careers. While retirees surely have political clout, older workers within companies simply do not have as much common group identity nor have they been traditionally served by aggressive training and career programs. Thus, when human resource initiatives and programs are losing out to cost cutting, the weakest workforce constituency (older workers) are likely to feel the effects first and to a greater extent than other groups.

3. Older Workers Are the Scapegoats of Corporate Cost Containment.

As a third hypothesis, we must consider whether or not older workers are being scapegoated in corporate efforts to cut costs and reduce staff. We have seen that American corporations currently do not place a high value on their older employees and, indeed, that managers appear to be treating their older employees as less important than other segments of their workforce. In this context, prejudices and stereotypes about the deficiencies of older workers serve the function of justifying decisions that adversely affect them.

It is possible, as noted, to rationalize spending less on the training of older workers because they might retire before a company recoups its full investment. But the views that older workers are less suitable for training, less flexible in taking new assignments, and have a harder time learning is added justification for spending less on them. The notion here is that although executives may generally hold positive attitudes toward older workers, the pressures they face to cut costs, reduce the number of employees, and thus eliminate their costliest workers all tend to fuel negative opinions of older workers—notably about their flexibility, adaptability, and aggressive spirit. Holding on to these stereotypes, however unjustified, reduces the dissonance associated with depriving them of training monies and shedding them in downsizing decisions.

This survey does not allow for any direct testing of these hypotheses, which we acknowledge are speculative. In this light, however, it is important to look closer at the practical and attitudinal barriers within companies to responding to the needs of older workers. A comparison of perceptions with facts and figures shows that companies may be seriously misestimating both the costs and benefits of the ways they currently manage their older workers.

BARRIERS TO RESPONDING
TO THE AGING WORKFORCE

To get a better fix on specific factors that influence company practices toward older workers, company interviewees were asked to rate the importance of health benefit costs, training costs, the physical and mental demands of work, and other factors in decisions about hiring or retaining older workers. Responses to these questions, coupled with other survey data, show that there are strong barriers to the employment and retention of older workers in American industry.

Health Care Costs

We noted earlier that two-thirds of the companies surveyed rate older workers as worse than the average worker in their health care costs. Further, nearly all companies (94%) cited increasing health care costs as a competitive concern and human resource priority in coming years. In answer to a specific questions, over one-third of the respondents (36%) said that high health care costs influenced their decisions about hiring and retaining older workers.

At the same time, most managers in this study believe that the forces increasing the costs of health care are too strong to be controlled by changes in their company's health plan and two-thirds say that some form of government-designated cost-containment plan will eventually be necessary. One factor that increasingly threatens the viability of the current health care system is the tendency of insurers to abandon rates based on the medical experience of the whole community, and instead to base each company's rates on the experience of their employees. For small companies, this means that one medical emergency or major illness—a premature birth or cancer, for example—among their employees or employees' dependents will cause a huge rate increase the next year. This rating system is pricing small businesses out of the health insurance market and contributing to the tremendous growth in the size of the uninsured working population. It also is causing the costs of health insurance for companies with more older employees—who are more likely to be struck with a costly medical emergency—to be higher than those with more younger workers.

It is likely that any reform of the system of financing health care will attempt to allocate costs equally across much larger groups, with the costs of older people averaged into the cost of younger people. If this is done, the relatively high health costs of older workers, which now appear as a deterrent to hiring and retaining them, could disappear. Of course, if a national health care system resembling Britain's or Canada's were implemented in the United States, the higher health costs of older workers would cease to be an employment-related consideration. For now, however, the high costs of health insurance are a competitive issue in companies, and the extra costs associated with older workers could be a subtle factor in decisions about their employment and retention.

Competitive Pressures to Reduce Costs

More prominent a factor is the perceived cost savings associated with having higher-paid older workers leave the company through downsizing. As noted, over 80% of the companies in this study downsized in the latter 80s. Moreover, two-thirds expect to downsize further in the 90s. At the same time, the earlier chapter on downsizing reported that firms that reduced staff for reasons of cost-containment incurred higher than expected severance and retiree health benefit costs, lost the wrong kind of people, and suffered from a greater loss in morale.

Interestingly, those that used ERIPs as a downsizing tactic had these same kinds of post-downsizing problems. Indeed, more than one-half of the companies using ERIPs reported increased retiree health care costs, as compared to less than one-third of all companies that downsized. Among the other problems with ERIPs are the following:

- Employee expectations of "generosity" change so that each subsequent ERIP must be more lucrative than the last.
- The best employees may leave because they are most likely to think they can find work elsewhere.
- The risk of age discrimination lawsuits may increase.
- Unions resist ERIPs.
- Morale declines among remaining employees.
- Company reputation and ability to recruit declines.

Managers recognize that ERIPs disproportionately affect their older workers. Of the companies that offered ERIPs in downsizing, 60% stated that older workers were much or somewhat more likely to have left the company. Yet a recent study concluded that the costs associated with the use of ERIPs in downsizing are as much as 41% greater than the costs of reductions focused on younger workers.[11] The comparatively higher costs of retiring early older workers result from the expensive pension benefits that must be offered to induce them to retire and the fact that older retirees continue to incur escalating health costs as if they were active employees. A younger employee leaving the firm will often have no, or very minimal, vested pension benefits and no long-term continuation of health benefits.

The more-general conclusion is that many companies who downsize primarily for cost savings may be overestimating the gains that come from targeting their higher-paid, older workers. Now it seems that human resource managers are at least becoming more aware of the downside of ERIPs. In a recent survey, 45% of the respondents stated that they believe that early retirement programs no longer make good business sense. Another 35% were neutral, while only 30% continued to favor ERIPs.[12] A study conducted by the American Management Association also found ERIPs losing favor in practice.[13] Just 28% of the AMA's 1991 sample of companies offered early retirement plans, compared to 44% in 1988, 37% in 1989, and 32% in 1990.

Still, competitive pressures to reduce costs make older workers an easy target for supposed savings. While more data on the costs of shaving payroll in this way may influence company practice, as in the case of ERIPs, it is also important that companies learn more about the benefits that come from retaining and retraining their older workers.

Management Attitudes

As we described above, managerial attitudes about older workers are ambivalent, but they indicate lingering prejudices and stereotypes that work against older employees. Firms cited high training costs (16%), the physical demands of the work (40%), and the mental demands of the work (25%) as factors affecting decisions about hiring or retaining workers over age 55, despite evidence from case studies we have performed, that these factors are not significant in determining the job performance of older workers.[14]

There were also the aforementioned concerns that older workers are less suitable for training and less flexible in taking new assignments. To counter these barriers to retraining and redeploying older workers requires action on two fronts. First, there is the matter of perception. Although some managers may believe that older workers are not interested in training, a 1989 survey of men 55 to 64 and women 50 to 59, conducted by Louis Harris and Associates, contradicts this view, finding that 3.5 million workers in these age ranges would accept training for a new job with different responsibilities but the same hours and pay in order to extend their working careers.[15] A more recent survey found that 4.6 million workers age 55–64 would consider taking classes to improve their employment opportunities or job skills.[16]

Second, there is the matter of not only providing more company funded training but also age-appropriate instruction methods and materials. Merely encouraging older workers to take some courses and pay for them with their own money is not sufficient. A better alternative is to offer in-house training where co-workers study common subjects together and apply them to existing or relevant work problems. In addition, it is important to tailor teaching methods to the learning styles of older workers who may be more concerned with poor performance and out of touch with the demands of formal education.[17] Research has shown that older workers do not learn less well; they just learn differently.

Plainly, there is a set of companies in this sample that has made such a commitment to retraining older workers. Those firms that retrain most of the main-line workers every year make sure that older workers receive a fairer share of training monies. Some 37% of these (versus 17% overall) state that they spend a lot of money retraining older workers, and only 15% (versus 34% overall) spend very little on older workers. What differentiates the firms that retrain a majority of their main-line workers from others that do not is that they have a human resource philosophy that sees retaining and retraining older workers as increasing productivity and advancing their business strategy.

Structural Barriers

There are structural and legal barriers to retaining older workers. For instance, a longstanding policy of many companies, particularly old-line U.S. manufacturing companies, has been to offer employees defined-benefit pension plans. Such plans are usually structured so that after worker reaches a certain age, typically the late fifties, his or her additional accrual of pension benefits is increasingly offset by the pension payments forfeited because he or she is still working. This pension structure provides an incentive for workers to cease working at the time of maximum pension value. Although much of the drive for defined-benefit pensions has come from labor unions interested in securing a guaranteed retirement income for their members, the structure of these pensions may now be at odds with the work preferences of older workers. We believe that such a pension structure is not in the best interests of all workers since it encourages earlier retirement than they might otherwise select. Employers can provide equal-value pensions through other plans (such as defined contribution) that provide no disincentive for continued work.

A further problem for corporations might be that establishing programs especially to retain older workers (or to recruit and hire them) may risk violating the Age Discrimination in Employment Act (ADEA), by establishing a discriminatory labor practice. Because the legal boundaries of the ADEA are not clear under such circumstances, companies may be reluctant to risk such a violation with any form of targeted program. Of course, the most straightforward way to avoid running afoul of ADEA is to offer all employees equal access to all services, irrespective of age.

Understanding the Importance of the Issue

Equally important, compared to other considerations, this study found that most companies do not think that the aging of the laborforce will affect their ability to compete in the 90s, as shown in Exhibit 6.13. Aging ranks far below health care costs, the poor quality of education of entry workers, and the family responsibilities of employees as a competitive consideration.

Exhibit 6.13 Aging of workforce not expected to affect companies' ability to compete in the next five years.

Laborforce Factor	Will Affect Ability to Compete a Great Deal (%)
Increasing cost of health benefits	64
Poor quality of education among new job applicants	47
Poor work attitudes of entry-level job applicants	25
Family responsibilities of workers	23
Higher cost of U.S. workers relative to those in other countries	16
Growing proportion of African-Americans and Hispanics in the labor force	15
Aging of the laborforce	12

Furthermore, executives in companies with older workforces are only slightly more concerned than others that the aging of the laborforce will affect their company's ability to compete (see Exhibit 6.14).

Even cutting edge companies, those who are most tuned in to the competitive impact of education, family needs, and the growing proportion of African-Americans and Hispanics in the workforce, are out of touch on this issue. But these firms, which are most progressive in adopting new human resource policies, perhaps because they employ a smaller percentage of older workers than other companies, expect to be less affected by the aging of the workforce than prudent companies. As a result, it may be left to firms that are typically more cautious in adopting new human resource policies to develop innovative programs to ensure the continued productivity and employment of their older employees.

Because a one-time survey can only present a single snapshot in time, it is not possible to measure the durability of the opinions expressed by managers nor how quickly their views may change as the aging of the laborforce is felt more strongly in the coming decade. Still, the survey suggests that overall corporate attitudes to older workers may be changing in a positive direction, albeit on a limited basis. For example, 27% of the companies reported that management's attitude toward older workers was "substantially" or "somewhat" more favorable than it was in the mid-80s. In contrast, only six percent of the companies reported a less favorable attitude. However, the majority of the companies (64%) reported no change in attitudes toward older workers. Based on management's current assessment of the magnitude and significance of this trend, we cannot predict when managers' focus will shift more squarely to the aging of their workforce or even if it will. However, given the inevitable time required to design, develop, and implement programs to recruit and retain select constituencies within the laborforce, we believe that it is a high-risk decision to wait until the issue is fully upon us before acting.

ARE CORPORATIONS PREPARED FOR THE AGING WORKFORCE?

At present, the aging of the laborforce has not captured the attention and energy of human resource executives in a meaningful way. Addressing the issue more comprehensively has lost out to competing financial and human resource priorities, nagging prejudices and stereotypes, and doubts about the competitive implications of an aging workforce. This section examines what specific corporate policies and programs are planned in the mid-90s.

Exhibit 6.14 Competitive impact of an older workforce: Key comparisons.

	All Respondents (%)	Percentage of Workers Age 50 and Over			Cutting Edge Companies (%)	Prudent Companies (%)
		10% or More	20% or More	30% or More		
Percent of companies that believe aging of the laborforce will affect their ability to compete over the next five years a *great deal*	23	25	27	33	14	30
Percent of companies that believe aging of the laborforce will affect their ability to compete over the next five years *somewhat*	77	75	73	67	86	70
Total	100	100	100	100	100	100

Note: Survey question included additional possible responses of "not very much," "not at all," and "not sure." Data reported in table have been adjusted to present percent distribution only for responses included in the table.

Base: Companies that rate the aging of the workforce as a competitive issue.

The Present as Prologue

In contrast to corporate programs addressing family issues important to working parents (e.g., flextime, unpaid childbirth leave), and those dealing with workforce diversity or skills shortages issues, programs for older workers are much less common among American corporations. This finding confirms the results of other surveys that report that programs (existing and planned) for dealing with an aging workforce are less than half as prevalent as programs addressing skills shortages, cultural diversity, changing worker values, or women in the workforce.[18] It appears that corporations have come to recognize the value of programs that help women and minority employees in whom they have made a substantial investment, but that comparable recognition regarding older workers is still largely missing.

Still, many so-called work-family programs—such as flextime, job sharing, and flexplace—might be just as popular with the older worker as they are with a working parent attempting to balance a career and family. The 1989 Harris survey mentioned previously found that 18% of men working full-time would prefer part-time work, as would 33% of women working full-time.[19] There are, however, no available data indicating whether or not older employees can or have taken advantage of the flexible work opportunities set up to facilitate the lives of working parents. Because of the widespread prevalence of these programs, they may represent useful models that, with only minor modification, could adequately address the needs of older employees.

The Planned Response to the Aging Laborforce

There are indications that companies plan to do more with programs that are specifically targeted at older workers in the near future. As shown in Exhibit 6.15, the greatest growth is planned in programs aimed at recruiting older workers. Although they exist in fewer than one in ten companies today, the number of such programs is expected to triple by the mid-90s when they should be in place in nearly every fourth company. Underlying this trend undoubtedly is the finding that more than three-quarters of the companies reported that their top management and midlevel supervisors were supportive of efforts to hire workers over age 55.

Human resource executives also expect to offer more phased retirement options to older employees. If plans translate into programs, this will double the number of firms offering such programs (from 21% to 42%). The problem here is that although many workers say they want phased

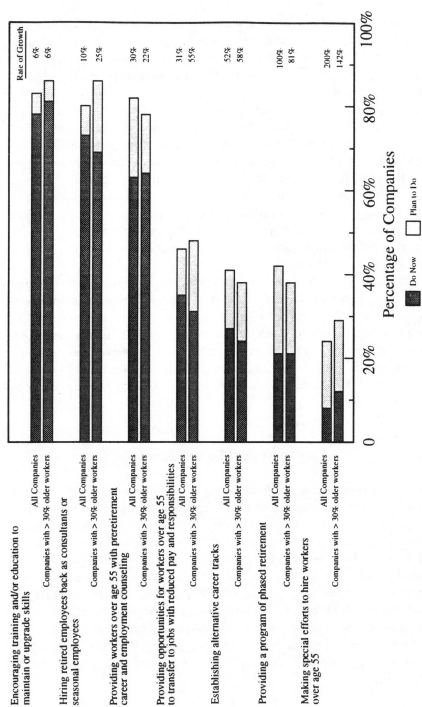

Exhibit 6.15 Planned changes in programs to promote the continued employment of older employees.

retirement, few take it when it is offered, suggesting a gap between the desires of older workers and the options offered by current programs. At Corning, Inc. for example, a phased retirement option has been virtually ignored by production workers and white-collar workers outside of the human resource function.

The percentage of firms offering alternative career tracks for older workers is expected to increase from 27% to 41% by the mid-90s. The survey results also suggest an increase in the percentage of companies (from 35% to 46%) that plan to provide opportunities for workers over age 55 to transfer to jobs with reduced pay and responsibilities. Both of these programs offer more options for older workers to satisfy their changing preferences for work, pay, and responsibility. One reason they appeal to companies is that they induce their skilled, experienced workers to extend their careers at a reduced number of hours per week; companies can benefit from their continued employment and still lower payroll costs.

The future plans of companies with 30% or more older workers in their workforce are not significantly different from other companies except in one respect. These firms expect to hire back retirees as consultants or seasonal workers more aggressively than other companies. This enables these companies to capture the valuable experience of older workers at lesser expense. It may also facilitate further downsizing by allowing companies to reduce the number of full-time workers they employ, and increase the number of contingent workers.

Assessing the Planned Response

Only one-quarter of the companies in the survey have specific plans to begin or add to programs targeted at the aging of the workforce in the next few years. And, given corporations' lack of current experience with programs to retain and ensure the continued productivity of older employees, the success of these measures is far from assured. It takes time to design new programs, to test their effectiveness and attractiveness to older employees, and to make corrective changes as called for. When we take this into account, we find that it is not clear whether companies will be ready to respond when the aging of the laborforce becomes significant beginning early in the next century. Moreover, as discussed below, the extent of the aging of the laborforce may be greater than expected, and current plans could prove woefully insufficient.

PROJECTED WORK PREFERENCES
OF THE BABY BOOMER GENERATION

We have shown that the number of older Americans will grow rapidly in the next few decades as the baby boomers, the largest generation in American history, reach middle age and beyond. We see from the statistics presented at the beginning of this chapter that the percentage of the laborforce that is between 55 and 64 is expected to increase from 10% today to 16% by 2020, while the percentage of those 65 and over would increase from 2.8% today to 4.1% in 2020. But, if more baby boomers decide to continue working beyond what is now considered normal retirement age, 62–65, the aging of the laborforce will occur even more rapidly.

There are several reasons to think baby boomers may choose to work longer. From the 1960s through the mid-1980s, American men sought earlier and earlier retirement. Since the late 1980s, however, laborforce participation rates have stabilized at about 67% for men ages 55 to 64 and 16% for men ages 65 and over. Although it is still too early to identify the exact causes for this stabilization, it may be that older men's preferences for early retirement have peaked and that instead they desire continued work. In contrast, laborforce participation rates for older women have generally been rising since 1950. Elsewhere, we have reported that 5.4 million older retired people are willing and able to return to work. In addition, another 1.1 million workers in their 50s and early 60s expect to retire before they would really like to. Over 40% of these people would like to stay employed for another three to five years, and well over a third said, in essence, that they wanted to work forever.[20]

The retirement environment facing members of the baby boom generation in the twenty-first century will be decidedly less attractive than today's, which could influence them to extend their working careers:

- *Prospective retirees will be supporting a larger number of dependents.* Many members of the baby boom generation delayed their childbearing into their thirties, so they will be more likely to have children still at home or in college during their late fifties and early sixties. In addition, baby boomers may simultaneously face the burden of caring for their elderly parents—at a time when elderly people are likely to be living longer and health care is costing more. The financial burden created by these two pressures could encourage boomers to extend their working careers.

- *Prospective retirees may have a smaller level of housing wealth.* Baby boomers are not likely to benefit from large increases in housing prices over the course of their lives as did their parents, who bought housing in the 50s when such assets were relatively cheap and profited from the substantial run up in real housing prices of the decades of the 60s through the 80s. In contrast, boomers have experienced more difficulty purchasing a home as the growth in real incomes has lagged behind the increase in housing prices and as those who could afford a home are much less likely to reap substantial increases in the value of their real estate investments.[21] Housing is not the only asset determining future levels of wealth, but it has traditionally been a significant percentage of the wealth of older people. Whether overall saving and wealth accumulation will be lower for boomers will depend very much on the rate of growth of the U.S. economy.[22]

- *Older Americans are enjoying better health.* With the rapid improvements in medical technology, the vast majority of elderly people in their younger retirement years are relatively healthy and are not limited in their activities.[23] Consequently, the percentage of older workers retiring for health reasons is lower than formerly. Furthermore, older people will enjoy their health for a longer period of time than people have in the past. As the average life expectancy increases, it is reasonable to speculate that baby boomers may wish to delay their retirement either because they do not wish to be retired for such a long period of their lives or because they believe that they will need to earn and save more money to support themselves during the extra years they will be alive.

- *Prospective retirees face rising health care costs.* Baby boomers are generally in better health than previous generations. But this does not ensure that they will escape the rising cost of health care. Increases in health care costs continue to outpace those of other goods and services, with scant prospects for effective cost control in the near term. Persons age 65 and over, 12% of the population, account for over one-third of the country's total personal health care expenditures. Between 1980 and 1990, the health care component of the consumer price index (CPI) rose by 8.8% per annum; during the same period, the overall CPI rose by 4.8% per annum. In addition, many companies surveyed plan to cut back health benefits for future retirees or make their future retirees share more costs.

- *Older Americans' satisfaction with life and desire to work.* There is considerable evidence correlating purposeful work and life satisfaction among older Americans. In the 1991 Harris survey of older Americans, 67% of the respondents who worked reported being very satisfied with life.[24] In contrast, 29% of those not working who wished to work were very satisfied. The positive correlation between working and life satisfaction is a benefit above and beyond the benefits of employment generated by higher income.[25] For example, women in this generation are more likely to have completed an entire working career and attained positions of significant responsibility and prestige, making further work for them more attractive.

Collectively, these factors could well result in a greater desire on the part of baby boomers to extend their working careers either in their current jobs or elsewhere. If so, the American laborforce would change not only as a result of the inexorable aging of the baby boom generation, but also because more and more baby boomers will stay in the laborforce for a longer time.

Another Twist: A Possible Skill Shortage

A more immediate factor that could propel corporate America to reconsider its position toward older workers would be the emergence of a skills shortage. American employers, including those surveyed for this book, continue to evidence great dissatisfaction with the skills of their workers.[26] However, companies do not appear to realize the potential of using older workers to compensate for a shortage of skilled younger workers. When asked about plans if unable to recruit qualified employees, only 14% of the companies intended to adopt measures to increase productivity of existing workers, and just 9% would retain existing workers longer. Since older workers are consistently rated highly on their job skills, they should be an obvious target of corporate recruiting and hiring. Indeed, companies that have taken such steps have reaped substantial benefits. Each older worker could also be paired with a younger worker to act as a mentor and to provide direct supervision, guidance, and transfer of skills and knowledge to compensate for the low level of technical and educational qualifications of high school graduates.

WHAT MANAGERS NEED TO DO

Surely it would be to companies' advantage to think more systematically about and plan for the programs that may be needed before the turn of the century in order to manage and extend the productive work lives of

B&Q, p.l.c.

B&Q operates a chain of 280 housewares stores in the United Kingdom that produce annual revenues in excess of $1.6 billion. B&Q's stores are primarily large supercenters open 12 hours a day that offer goods ranging from plumbing supplies to gardening equipment to furniture. Annual sales per store average between $2.0 and $2.3 million. Because of a general shift in consumer shopping habits to large out-of-town shopping centers, B&Q grew rapidly in the 80s. At the same time, the average annual labor turnover at the company exceeded 48%, and the company was experiencing difficulty in meeting recruiting targets to staff its continuing expansion.

To address both problems, B&Q's senior management adopted a strategy of broadening its recruiting efforts to include older workers and women returning to work after child rearing. Among the qualities identified in older workers was the fact that many were home owners with a lifetime of experience carrying out repairs around their homes. Thus, they had an invaluable base of product knowledge grounded in actual experience, which could be leveraged to provide superior customer service.

Putting its strategy into practice, in October 1989 B&Q opened a store in Macclesfield, a market town in the county of Cheshire in northwest England, entirely staffed by persons over age 50. Reflecting its view about the potential benefits of older salespersons, B&Q's recruiting advertisement stated, "we appreciate how much mature staff can bring to B&Q in the way of practical skills and experience . . . they can pass on the benefits of this experience to our customers." Over six hundred applications were received for the 55 openings at the Macclesfield store.

At the same time, B&Q's management remained concerned whether older workers could carry out the work and whether absenteeism because of sickness would be unbearably high. Many of the reasons why older workers might not prove suitable for the jobs did not arise. Although the application form asked detailed questions about the candidate's health and previous serious illness, the applicants were not asked to take a medical examination, and the health issue has not proved to be a problem. As in the case of Days Inns, among older persons, the healthy tend to be the ones preferring to work so that the health care costs for newly recruited older workers are not out of line with those for younger staff. Physical ability was not an issue because any item in the company's product line could be safely lifted by two persons.

Management had also been concerned initially that older workers would require a longer training period, so eight weeks of training were provided rather than the usual four. This turned out to be excessive, and when a second store opened that was entirely staffed by older persons, the training period was cut back to four to six weeks. Older workers were apprehensive about using new technology such as the electronic point-of-sale terminals and asked many probing questions during training, but B&Q now requires no special content or duration for training older workers.

Comparing the Macclesfield store to similar B&Q stores elsewhere, staffed primarily by new entrants to the job market, reflects favorably on the value of older workers:

- The other stores had labor turnover rates three to six times higher than that of the Macclesfield store.

- Older persons at the Macclesfield store were just as flexible in taking new assignments and working extra hours as younger staff in other stores, as measured by the amount of overtime worked.

- Absenteeism at the Macclesfield store was less than two-thirds that of the five-store comparison group and 19% less than the companywide average. The low rate of absenteeism was attributed in part to the general good health of the older workers and in part to the high degree of caution they demonstrated, which reduced the number of work-related accidents.

- Shrinkage (pilferage, and goods destroyed or damaged) at the Macclesfield store was only 40% of the average for the five-store comparison group, which management believes was due to the high levels of attention that older workers gave to all shoppers, thereby reducing the opportunity for shoplifting.

Overall, the Macclesfield store was 18% more profitable than the comparison group and 9% more profitable than the companywide average, although the level of profitability cannot be directly attributed to the presence of older workers. However, many of the measures on which older workers were superior, such as shrinkage and absenteeism, directly reduce costs and contribute to an improved bottom line.

B&Q has judged its experiment with the Macclesfield store "an overwhelming success," and the company has set a target of soon having 10% of its workforce composed of workers over age 50.

their older employees. In this section, we discuss the potential benefits from planning for an increase in the proportion of older employees and the types of programs that we believe will be most useful to corporations. Such planning is a prudent response to the demographic challenge ahead. The hopeful part of our message is that careful planning can enable corporations to transcend the aging issue and capitalize on the potential of an older workforce.

The Importance of the Workforce

First, we briefly look at some possible consequences of not planning. Managers who do not plan for the demographic and social environment of the twenty-first century risk endangering the performance of their corporations by not being positioned to respond to the changing realities of their workforces and the pool of available labor. The following considerations are worth repeating.

- Without a doubt, tomorrow's workforce will be older. If companies do not provide for the needs and legitimate aspirations of older workers (such as training, flexibility, and phased retirement), they will face a future of reduced workforce morale and reduced productivity.

- With competition at home and abroad becoming more and more intense, the importance to the bottom line of using all workers more effectively will grow. As the ratio of older to younger employees rises, ignoring the concerns and needs of older workers will increasingly hurt a company's competitive position.

- The need for a high-quality, trainable, flexible workforce is increasing. Older workers have these characteristics, often in greater measure than younger entrants, if a myriad of studies are to be believed.[27]

The focus in the coming decades will be on increasing labor productivity and real wage growth to maintain both America's competitive position in a world economy and its standard of living. In an economy that continues to shift from brawn work to brain work, the search for means of boosting productivity will center around skills training and upgrading. It is interesting to note that the benefits of technological innovations designed to boost labor productivity in white-collar occupations, such as personal computers and facsimile machines, are difficult to discern in current measures of productivity. Although this may have much to do with the difficulty of measuring white-collar productivity, it is possible that greater gains in productivity are possible from investments in training and education than in new technology alone, or that the two are complementary.

The Potential of Older Workers

If American companies increasingly focus on employee training as a key to competitive success in the future, a logical focus of this attention is the older worker. There are several reasons why companies could enjoy substantial benefits by upgrading the skills of older workers, who are already in the company's workforce and are growing in numbers. First, the companies surveyed have directed, on average, fewer resources toward training older employees than they have toward younger ones, so the opportunity for improvement in job performance as a result of training may be greatest for older workers. As we noted earlier, significant research indicates that managerial fears that older workers are slower or less able learners and thus do not benefit as much as other workers from training appear to be unfounded. Moreover, companies have expressed widespread disappointment in the quality of entry level workers, especially in their basic reading and computational skills, which limit their ability to take advantage of higher-level job training. In contrast, older workers typically have a solid base of existing job skills and experience on which to base advanced training. Thus, older workers are a good bet for productivity gains based on skills upgrading if companies would make the same retraining investment in them that they make in younger workers.

Older workers also may be tremendous resources for those manufacturing corporations that adopt employee involvement and total quality production methods. These arrangements emphasize training employees in multiple skills, monitoring quality at each stage of the production process, and increasing the participation of employees in problem solving and decision making. It is sometimes suggested that older workers frequently resist change. We believe that this resistance, to the extent that it is real, is in most cases not a resistance to organizational change itself. Rather, it usually represents an anxiety about being trained in new skills. These worries can easily be overcome if management properly prepares older workers for the training they will receive. For example, our study of Days Inns of America's reservation center found that if older workers had one-half day of computer familiarization training to overcome their initial anxiety about a computer, they learned the center's sophisticated computer system as easily as other trainees. Once older employees learn that they will receive substantial training support, observe their peers successfully learning new skills, and realize that these changes enhance their own job security, they become supporters of the management initiatives.[28] In addition, our conversations with managers suggest to us that older employees also tend to be more concerned about the quality of their work effort and are even more supportive of team-oriented production styles than younger employees.

The continued shift away from production-oriented tasks into service-oriented tasks also puts older employees at a competitive advantage. Most service-oriented jobs depend heavily on the effectiveness of employees' contacts with customers. Our research suggests that older people are friendlier, more patient and understanding in their relations with customers, and better at communicating, perhaps due to their lifetime of experience. Case studies of Days Inns and B&Q in this chapter suggest that corporations wishing to improve customer service ought to consider increasing their reliance on older employees.

Beginning to Plan for the Aging of the Laborforce

What corporations need to do now is to recognize the potential significance of the changing workforce and its relationship to other structural changes in the economy. Having recognized that, they can take relatively simple and inexpensive steps to stay ahead of these trends. Among the steps that can be taken immediately are the following:

- Evaluate current policies toward training to ensure that current older employees have an equal opportunity to maintain their value to the company.

- Design training that responds to the different ways in which older workers learn. Our research shows that older workers can be trained and welcome an opportunity to learn new technologies. Nonetheless, effective training programs for older workers must recognize that older workers learn differently than younger workers, so new training methods may have to be developed.[29] It is particularly important to acquaint new trainers with the special factors they will encounter when they teach persons who have not been in a classroom environment in a few decades. Experience has shown that the differences in learning techniques are readily and inexpensively dealt with.

- Examine current performance measurement and evaluation methods to remove biases against older workers that may creep in as a result of managerial beliefs about the relative disadvantages of older workers.

- Evaluate benefit packages to determine which elements reduce incentives for working beyond normal retirement age and what kinds of compensatory benefits could be offered to lessen these disincentives.

- Market to older workers the flexible work arrangements that were established for working parents. Job sharing, part-time work, and work at home, (which is increasingly facilitated by new communications technology such as faxes and modems) are already in place in many corporations. Since these programs were created for working parents, however, it is likely that few corporations have thought about their relevance to older workers who wish to cut back their hours while remaining productively employed; marketing them aggressively to older employees makes sense.

- Reassess the training and experience requirements of current company jobs and the jobs that the company expects to have in the future to determine whether older persons could fill these jobs.

These recommendations highlight immediate changes that would increase the productivity of the company's current older workers, would help to recruit additional older employees, and would provide a basis for estimating the changes that may be necessary in the future. A number of planning questions logically flow from undertaking such an assessment. For example, what types of approaches are needed to retain or recruit older people? Are there nontraditional means of recruiting older people? Merely running newspaper advertisements and listing jobs with employment agencies may not attract older people who would be interested in the job because they may not believe the ads, or they may be so discouraged in their job search that they have stopped looking. Days Inns discovered that fliers at senior centers and senior housing complexes produced much better results. Once they had hired a number of older people, word of mouth about job openings also helped recruit qualified older workers.

In addition to planning and positioning, companies may wish to consider instituting specific programs to attract or retain older workers, such as phased retirement or other type of career extension program.[30] (See "Travelers' Retiree Job Bank" on pages 196–197.) Consideration of such programs means thinking about whether they might make sense for the company's particular workforce, what type of program is most appropriate, and what resources and lead time are necessary to develop and implement such a program. All of these tasks involve a limited commitment of resources immediately—mostly in the form of rigorous thinking and analysis. The

Travelers' Retiree Job Bank

The Travelers Corporation, headquartered in Hartford, Connecticut, is the third-largest financial services company in the United States. Like many insurance companies, it has a reputation for progressive human resource policies. In the late 70s, the company started a customer service hotline and needed employees who were familiar with company operations and procedures to staff it. Rather than shifting permanent staff from their current positions, which would have disrupted the operations of other departments, the Travelers decided to hire back some of its retirees part-time to answer the calls.

The effort proved so successful that the company sought other roles for its retirees. Following a 1980 survey of its older employees that indicated that many of them wanted to continue working past retirement, the company saw the potential to gain a flexible, knowledgeable corps of temporary staff with a proven performance record and, at the same time, offer employees the prospect of an even longer-term relationship with the company to ease the transition into retirement. In 1981 the company established the Travelers' Retiree Job Bank, a centralized office that registered retirees and processed all requests from company managers for temporary help. Interest was sufficiently high among retirees that little formal recruitment was necessary. Wages were negotiated on an individual basis based on each employee's qualifications. No benefits were provided because they were judged superfluous given the retirement benefits package already offered by the company.

By 1985 the demand for retirees to perform tasks ranging from letter stuffing to computer programming was more than double the available supply, and the Travelers decided to expand the job bank to include retirees from other insurance companies. Through a publicity campaign and word of mouth from Travelers retirees, finding qualified retirees in the Hartford area, a locus of insurance companies, was not difficult. Compensation was similar to that for Travelers retirees. Non-Travelers retirees were given an initiation period to learn about the company's procedures, but soon performed at the levels of the company's own retirees.

In January 1990, facing still more demand for temporary workers, the Travelers formed its own in-house temporary agency, called TravTemps, to replace the outside agencies that had been used. Trav-

Temps enlarged the pool of available temporary labor to include younger workers, who were recruited by traditional methods such as help-wanted ads and job fairs. Two other changes also occurred. The program instituted a benefits program. If a temporary employee worked more than 500 hours over a six-month period, he or she became eligible for holiday pay and modest health insurance benefits. The program also standardized its wage setting system so that pay was determined by specific job requirements.

By 1991, on any given week, the Travelers was likely to employee over 400 temps (more than 60% of whom were Travelers retirees). Each retiree temp worked an average of 516 hours each year, whereas nonretirees were employed an average of 608 hours. In analyzing the program, Travelers found that using its retirees could prove quite valuable; for example, the company:

- Saved money by eliminating the fees paid to an outside temporary agency, including cutting direct costs for temps by more than $1 million in 1989. Even factoring the costs of operating the job bank, the savings exceeded $800,000. There were other indirect savings as well. If a temp is hired permanently, an outside agency typically receives a finder's fee of up to 7% of the employee's annual salary. Employees hired permanently from TravTemps pay no finder's fee.

- Lowered recruiting costs because prospective temps are easily identified among future retirees.

- Saved on health benefit costs because retirees have their insurance paid through their pension plans.

- Lowered rates of absenteeism for temps, which frequently had been as high as 15%. Retirees have much lower rates of absenteeism, which may be attributed to either loyalty to the company or the greater reliability generally exhibited by older workers.

- Increased efficiency because employees require little initial training; they already are familiar with the company and its practices and naturally feel comfortable in the work environment.

More important, Travelers' managers—the internal customers—have reported high levels of satisfaction with the retiree job bank.

much larger costs of actually changing policies or initiating new programs can be deferred until a greater proportion of a company's employees are in their late forties or early fifties.

CONCLUSION

The current lack of a corporate focus on older employees is reflected both in the general absence of programs to retain and retrain them and in managers' reported widespread belief that the aging of the laborforce in the coming decades is not worth particular attention now or in the immediate future.

Our assessment of the importance of this demographic trend is different. We believe that current views about the productive potential of older workers may be inaccurate and that appreciation of the importance of the aging of the laborforce is inadequate. Furthermore, we think that, because of likely changes in the desire of older persons to work, the number of older people in the laborforce could be even higher than currently projected, which, in turn, would have greater competitive implications for companies than currently envisioned.

Simply suggesting that the future holds many changes is not sufficient to prove the need for planning for these changes. Successful companies, however, are those that anticipate change in their competitive environment and position themselves to respond effectively to that change or even harness it in their favor. Beginning to plan today for the inevitable aging of the laborforce early in the next century represents the kind of strategic thinking that could turn a potential problem into an opportunity for many companies.

The proactive human resource manager should, in our view, begin to develop a plan to ensure the continued productive employment of current older employees, as well as the inevitable increase in the proportion of older employees in his or her company—especially since much of the planning can be undertaken at modest initial cost. At a minimum, the human resource manager should project the future demographic makeup of the workforce available to his or her company and contrast that with the company's needs for workers with various skills, educational levels, and work experiences. From this assessment, a manager should be able to see the various options available for retaining current older workers or recruiting new ones.

The gap between stated attitudes and actual practices that we have found in this study may represent a lag in time between a change in attitude and change in practice. Certainly it has taken time for companies to recognize the strategic and competitive implications of having more women and minorities in their workforces, and to grasp the problems associated with having so many underprepared young people join their ranks. However, both attitudes about these issues and practices that relate to them have changed. In our estimation, companies that scan the human resource environment and that have a strong inclination toward strategic planning and positioning will go further than others and extract whatever competitive advantage they can by increasing use of older workers. In our judgment, this could be considerable and would set an example for the rest of American industry.

NOTES

1. U.S. Bureau of the Census. 1988. Projections of the population, by age, sex, and race, for the United States: 1988 to 2080. *Current population reports,* ser. P-25, no. 1018. Washington, D.C.: Census.

2. Barth, M. C., and W. McNaught. 1991. The impact of future demographic shifts on the employment of older workers. *Human Resource Management* 30 (1): 420–434.

3. U.S. Bureau of Labor Statistics. 1992. *Outlook: 1990–2005.* Washington, D.C.: BLS, Office of Employment Projections, April.

4. American Association of Retired Persons. 1989. *Business and older workers: Current perceptions and new directions for the 1990's.* Washington, D.C.: AARP.

5. Quinn, J. F. and R. V. Burkhauser. 1990. *Retirement preferences and plans of older American workers.* Americans Over 55 At Work Program Background Paper #4. New York: The Commonwealth Fund.

6. Towers Perrin. 1992. *Workforce 2000 today: A bottom-line concern. Revisiting corporate views on workforce change.* New York: Towers, Perrin.

7. Anand, V. 1992. Older workers bear brunt of corporate cutbacks. *Investors Business Daily,* January 29, 10.

8. Branco, K. J., and J. B. Williamson. 1982. Stereotyping and the life cycle: Views of aging and the aged. In *In the eye of the beholder: Contemporary issues in stereotyping,* ed. A. G. Miller, New York: Praeger.

9. Waldman, D. A. and B. J. Aviolo. 1986. A meta-analysis of age differences in job performance. *Journal of Applied Psychology* 71: 33–38.

10. Rosen, B., and T. H. Jerdee. 1977. Too Old or Not Too Old. *Harvard Business Review.* November–December, 97–106.

11. Morrison, M. H. 1990. *A new look at corporate costs for early retirement: Retaining vs. retiring older workers.* Washington, D.C.: National Foundation for Occupational and Environmental Health.

12. Towers Perrin, *Workforce 2000 today.*

13. American Management Association. 1990. *Responsible reductions in force—An AMA research report on downsizings and outplacement.* New York: AMA Briefings and Surveys.

14. Hogarth, T., and M. C. Barth. 1991. Costs and benefits of hiring older workers: A case study of B&Q. *International Journal of Manpower* 12 (8): 5–17;

McNaught, W., and M. C. Barth. 1992. Are older workers "good buys"?—A case study of Days Inn of America. *Sloan Management Review* 33: Spring, 53–63.

15. Louis Harris & Associates. 1989. *Older Americans: The untapped labor source*. Study No. 884030. New York: Harris; Quinn and Burkhauser, Retirement preferences and plans.

16. Louis Harris & Associates. 1991. *Productive aging: A survey of Americans age 55 and over*. Study No. 902061. New York: Harris.

17. Bass, S. A., and M. C. Barth. (forthcoming). *The next educational opportunity: Career training for older adults*. Americans Over 55 At Work Program Background Paper. New York: The Commonwealth Fund.

18. Galinsky, E., D. E. Friedman, and C. A. Hernandez. 1991. *The corporate reference guide to work-family programs*. New York: Families and Work Institute; Towers Perrin, *Workforce 2000 today*.

19. Louis Harris and Associates, *Older Americans*; Quinn and Burkhauser, Retirement preferences and plans.

20. Louis Harris and Associates, *Productive aging*; Quinn and Burkhauser, "Retirement preferences and plans;" and Louis Harris and Associates, *Older Americans*.

21. Hendershott, P. H. 1991. Are real house prices likely to decline by 47%? *Regional Science and Urban Economics* 21: 553–563; Mankiw, N. G., and D. N. Weil. 1989. The baby boom, the baby bust, and the housing market. *Regional Science and Urban Economics* 19: 235–258.

22. Advisory Council on Social Security. 1991. *Future financial resources of the elderly. A view of pensions, savings, social security, and earnings in the 21st century*. Washington, D.C.: ACSS.

23. U.S. Congress. Senate. Special Committee on Aging. 1990. *Aging America: Projections and trends*. 101st Cong., 2d sess., S. Rept. 101–80; Yelin, E. (forthcoming). *Disability and the displaced worker*. Rutgers, N.J.: Rutgers University Press.

24. Louis Harris and Associates, *Productive aging*.

25. Davis, K. 1991. *Life satisfaction and older adults*. Americans Over 55 At Work Program Background Paper No. 6. New York: The Commonwealth Fund.

26. Barnow, B. S., and D. L. Bawden. 1990. *Urban Institute policy memorandum: Skill gaps in the year 2000: A review of the literature*. Washington, D.C.: The Urban Institute; Johnston, W. B., and A. Packer. 1987. *Workforce 2000: Work and workers for the twenty-first century*. Indianapolis, IN: Hudson Institute; and Mishel, L., and R. A. Teixeira. 1991. *The myth of the coming labor shortage: Jobs, skills, and incomes of America's workforce 2000*. Washington, D.C.: The Economic Policy Institute.

27. AARP, Business and older workers; Hogarth and Barth, Hiring older workers; and McNaught and Barth, Older workers . . . Days Inn.

28. McNaught and Barth, Older workers . . . Days Inn.

29. Bass and Barth, *Career training for older adults*.

30. McNaught, W., and M. C. Barth. 1991. *Using retirees to fill temporary labor needs: The Travellers experience*. Americans Over 55 At Work Program Background Paper No. 5. New York: The Commonwealth Fund.

7

The Changing Nature of Employee Health Benefits

Karen Davis

The United States has evolved a system of health insurance coverage tied to the workplace. Approximately two-thirds of all working age Americans receive health insurance through their place of employment.[1] Employers paid $137 billion for health insurance premiums in 1989, up from $6 billion in 1965.[2]

The dramatic increase in health costs has led to serious strains on private industry. In addition to health insurance premiums for workers and their dependents, businesses contribute to Medicare, workers' compensation, and temporary disability insurance. In total, costs paid by privately owned businesses for health were $173 billion in 1989.[3] As a share of total health spending, private business contributions increased from 17% in 1965 to 30% in 1989.

Employer health spending represented 4.2% of the gross private domestic product in 1989, up from 1.0% in 1965. As a percentage of wages and salaries, employer health spending increased from 2.2% in 1965 to 7.0% in 1989. Most startling, health spending increased from 14% of corporate after-tax profits in 1965 to 100% in 1989.

The policy of tying health insurance coverage to the place of employment makes coverage extremely sensitive to economic conditions. Recessions and rising unemployment create not only a loss of employment but also a loss of health insurance coverage. Less well recognized is the fact that structural changes in the economy and in the economic circumstances of individual firms affect health benefits of workers—even when the nation is not experiencing a recession. For example, international competition has led to a major reduction in employment for some industries and firms. Corporate downsizing in response to changing market conditions also affects employment and insurance. Other trends in the laborforce, such as a greater reliance on contingent or temporary workers, have had the effect of increasing the number of uninsured workers. In 1990 65.2% of Americans were covered by their own job or a family member's job, down from 66.9% in 1989.[4]

Even those workers with insurance, however, have had to face major changes in coverage as businesses have tried to combat rising health care costs at a time of increased economic pressure. Companies have asked workers to shoulder an increasing share of the cost of health care.[5] For example, in 1980 85% of employees of mid- to large-size firms had deductibles of $100 or less. By 1989 more than half had deductibles greater than $100. In addition, in 1980 72% of all employees with individual policies and 51% of employees with family coverage had premiums completely paid by employers; in 1989 only 48% of employees with individual policies and 31% of employees with family coverage had premiums completely paid by employers.[6]

The 90s are likely to bring an acceleration of such changes in employment and health benefits. To ascertain the likely nature of future changes, this chapter reports findings from the Laborforce 2000 survey and summarizes recent trends in health benefits. It highlights the containment of health care costs through increased employee cost sharing, managed care, and the reduction of retiree health benefits. The chapter assesses the prospect that a stronger role for government in controlling health costs will be required and how it might be viewed by industry.

CHANGES IN HEALTH BENEFITS

The rapid rise in health care costs in the 80s has led to major changes in employee health benefit plans.[7] Employers have contained their cost of providing health benefits to workers through such strategies as shifting costs to employees directly through higher employee premium contributions and indirectly through increased deductibles or copayments for health services. Employers have also turned very dramatically in the 80s to managed care plans, including health maintenance organizations, preferred provider organizations, and utilization review.[8]

These trends are also documented by the Laborforce 2000 survey findings. Virtually all of the companies surveyed changed their plans a great deal (56%) or somewhat (32%) in the latter 80s in order to contain health care cost inflation. In the eyes of the interviewees, employees seem for the most part to have accepted the changes in health benefits. Only 10% rate the changes as not very acceptable to employees and 1% as not acceptable at all. By contrast, one-third believe the changes are very acceptable, and the remaining 56% say somewhat acceptable to employees.

The Laborforce 2000 survey did not differentiate what types of changes in plans that employees found acceptable. However, another Harris survey found that, even though a majority of American workers (71%) are satisfied with the health insurance benefits provided by their employers, a large minority (45%) are dissatisfied with their out-of-pocket costs.

How U.S. Workers View Health Care Plans

Ron Bass

Harris surveys find that nearly nine-tenths of working Americans say that the health benefits offered are very (67%) or somewhat (21%) important to them in deciding to change jobs or work for a particular employer.

The Laborforce 2000 surveys finds that most employers believe that changes in the health plans during the late 80s have been either very or at least somewhat acceptable to employees. Most employers believe that changes were acceptable to employees. Only 10% say they were unacceptable. Other Harris surveys, of 1,250 adults, paint a less favorable picture of current attitudes:

	Satisfied (%)	Dissatisfied (%)
Health insurance benefits	71	17
Out-of-pocket costs	54	45

Source: Survey of Health Consumers. Louis Harris and Associates, 1990.

Predictors of Change

Who made the most changes in their health plans? Firms with sales in excess of $1 billion were more likely to have changed their plans a great deal (66%) when compared to smaller firms (see Exhibit 7.1). In part this may reflect the fact that larger firms have a broader array of realistic options for altering their health benefit plans. Managed care options, for example, are much more common in larger firms. Such firms are also more likely to have an array of fringe benefits against which trade-offs can be made. However, this survey result should not be interpreted as implying that health care costs are of greater concern to larger firms. In fact, employer-paid premiums and administrative expenses associated with health benefits are proportionately higher in smaller firms.[9]

Manufacturing companies and publicly owned firms were also more likely to have changed their plans a great deal (61%), which may reflect not only their larger size but also heightened pressures to contain costs and increase earnings. The survey finds that unionization is a factor: Heavily unionized firms—although typically larger, in manufacturing, and publicly owned—were somewhat less likely to have implemented a great deal of change (52%) and were more likely to have instituted no changes at all. This situation suggests that unions comprise a force that resists employer attempts to shift a greater share of the cost of employee health benefits on to workers.

The impact of unionization is also seen in two other findings: Firms with a larger proportion of older workers, typically larger but more unionized, were somewhat less likely to have changed plans a great deal in the late 80s. By comparison, companies with a larger proportion of contingent workers, typically less unionized, were somewhat more likely to have changed their plans.

Statistical analyses were conducted to determine the independent effects of company structure and workforce composition on changes in health plans. Multiple logistic regression analysis confirms that companies with more than ten thousand employees were significantly more likely to have changed health care plans a great deal. And unionized firms were least likely to have changed health care plans a great deal.

When it comes to the impact of changes (see Exhibit 7.2), somewhat fewer large and publicly owned companies saw the changes as being *very* acceptable to employees. Acceptance was even more problematic in selected firms having a larger share of unionized and older workers, who were more apt to see the changes as not very or not at all acceptable (17% versus 11% overall). Multiple regression analyses confirm that employees of larger and publicly owned firms were less likely to find changes very acceptable.

Exhibit 7.1 How much companies changed their health care plans to contain costs in the late 80s and early 90s.

Response	All Companies (%)	Company Size				Industry			Ownership		Workforce Composition		
		$100 m and Less (%)	$101 m to $500 m (%)	$501 m to $1 b (%)	$1 b and More (%)	Mfg. (%)	Fin. Svcs. (%)	Other Svcs. (%)	Pub. (%)	Prvt. (%)	30% + Union (%)	10% + Contg. (%)	20% + 50 & Older (%)
A great deal	56	51	51	51	66	61	57	54	61	44	52	59	52
Somewhat	32	33	38	40	26	29	33	30	29	41	37	31	35
Not much	7	11	10	2	5	6	4	12	5	10	5	5	8
Not at all	4	4	2	7	3	4	6	2	4	5	6	4	4

Note: Figures may not add up to 100% because of companies that are "not sure."

Exhibit 7.2 Acceptability of changes in health care plans to employees: Company perspective.

Acceptable?	All Companies (%)	Company Size				Industry			Ownership		Workforce Composition		
		$100 m and Less (%)	$101 m to $500 m (%)	$501 m to $1 b (%)	$1 b and More (%)	Mfg. (%)	Fin. Svcs. (%)	Other Svcs. (%)	Pub. (%)	Prvt. (%)	30% + Union (%)	10% + Contg. (%)	20% + 50 & Older (%)
Very	33	37	42	28	27	29	37	30	26	45	30	37	29
Somewhat	56	48	50	65	60	56	54	58	61	45	53	54	56
Not very	10	15	7	5	13	14	8	10	13	9	16	8	14
Not at all	1	—	2	—	1	—	1	2	1	2	1	1	1

Note: Figures may not add up to 100% because of companies that are "not sure."

EXPECTED INCREASES IN
EMPLOYEE COST SHARING

The rising cost of health benefits is a major concern to human resources executives. Most feel that it will have a great impact on the company's ability to compete during the mid-90s. One response to the concern is to shift a greater portion of costs onto workers.[10] The attractiveness of increasing deductibles or employee-paid premiums or other cost-sharing provisions is the certainty that they will reduce the cost to the employer.

The trend toward greater employee cost sharing is documented in a Foster Higgins survey of 2,409 employers in 1991. This survey found that the median medical plan deductible for individual coverage increased from $150 in 1990 to $200 in 1991.[11] The median out-of-pocket cost for workers increased to $1,050 from $1,000 in 1990. Even with these increased costs borne by workers, the cost to employers increased by 13%, to an average cost per employee of $3,573 in 1991.

The Laborforce 2000 survey finds that most companies expect to require employees to pay for an even greater share of premiums or health care costs directly. Nine out of ten human resources executives interviewed anticipate that employees will be paying much more (30%) or a little more (58%) in out-of-pocket health care expense.

Neither size, sector, nor workforce composition seem to be related to company decisions to increase employee cost sharing. Interestingly, however, a firm's orientation to human resource management is a significant predictor. Multiple logistic regression analysis shows that companies with a "prudent" (44%) approach to innovation are more likely to have employees pay much more in the next few years than firms that have an "advanced" (26%) or "cutting edge" (29%) philosophy. Prudent firms, as noted throughout this book, offer less training to employees and less flexibility on their jobs. In this realm, too, they seem to be taking the least imaginative approach to controlling health care plan costs. By contrast, firms with a more forward-looking philosophy plan to adopt other cost containment measures, such as an emphasis on managed care programs, which restrict an employee's choice in health care provider.

Neither measure, however, is agreeable to a large segment of the work-force. But an increase in cost sharing is least acceptable and could lead to greater conflict between management and labor. Reductions in health benefits have become a major cause of employee strikes.[12] Attempts to shift more costs directly to workers are particularly likely to intensify this pattern.

TRADE-OFFS BETWEEN HEALTH AND
OTHER BENEFITS OR COMPENSATION

At a time when companies are under greater pressure to reduce health benefit costs, one option is to permit employees to select among an array of fringe benefits those that are most important to their individual needs. Workers who do not desire certain benefits, such as dental benefits, can drop such coverage, or they can keep health benefits while cutting back on life insurance or other fringe benefits. These arrangements, often called *cafeteria* plans because they let employees choose among a variety of benefits, have been growing in popularity since the 80s. In some plans, companies even permit employees to take benefit dollars in cash income if they do not want comprehensive benefits.

The Laborforce 2000 survey examined how companies plan to approach questions of benefit flexibility in the future. The key questions considered are (1) whether or not employees will be offered more flexibility in the choice of health benefits; (2) whether increases in flexibility will offer employees a chance to trade off health care benefits against salary or other benefits; and (3) whether the company considers increases in health insurance premiums or other costs a trade-off for additional salary increases.

Each of the three questions has important policy implications. When people choose among different types of health benefits, for instance, there are many potential undesirable consequences. As an example, individuals who anticipate dental care needs would likely select dental coverage, whereas those with chronic health problems would opt for prescription drug coverage. Such flexibility could well increase costs, not reduce them. By contrast, if individuals encounter health care needs that they had not selected in cafeteria coverage, their satisfaction with their plan and employer might drop sharply.

The form of the flexibility has tax consequences. Employer contributions to health care are a form of in-kind income, which does not count as taxable income to workers. If employers permit individuals to trade off health benefits for direct salary compensation, tax revenues would increase as workers receive more of their compensation in the form of taxable wages.

The third issue—whether employers view health benefits and salary increases as perfect substitutes—is also important. Distributional analyses that describe the impact of changes in the way in which health care is financed must make some assumption about who currently pays for health care—workers, taxpayers, consumers, or owners of capital. Economists typically assume a backward shifting of health costs; that is, if employers pay health premiums, they reduce employee wages dollar for dollar. However, there is little empirical evidence on which to base that assumption.

Flexibility in Choice of Health Care Benefits

The Laborforce 2000 survey found that 79% of firms anticipate that they will give employees either a lot more (38%) or a little more (41%) choice among types of health care benefits by the mid-90s. Again, neither size, sector, nor composition of the workforce in general are related to company plans in this area. Interestingly, human resource philosophy is also not a predictor of a movement toward more flexibility in benefits—one indication of how widespread the practice has become.

Multiple logistic regression analysis reveals, however, that those firms that expect to offer employees a lot more choice in benefits have a higher percentage of contingent workers and have laid off more workers in the past. It could be that, in addition to possible cost savings, the greater provision of flexible benefits is considered valuable in employee recruiting and retention. It could also be that these firms did not do as much in the past in this area and are, in effect, catching up to competitors.

Employee Trade-offs between Health Benefits and Salary

Most firms restrict trade-offs to choosing among fringe benefits rather than between salary and benefits. Only 22% of those companies anticipating changes in flexibility expect to permit trade-offs between benefits and salary. Interestingly, firms with a higher proportion of women workers are more likely to foresee letting employees make trade-offs between health benefits and salary. Perhaps firms with a predominantly female workforce feel that workers can receive health insurance through a husband's employer. Yet employers are increasingly declining to contribute toward the health insurance coverage of working spouses because they believe it to be an unfair form of cost shifting.

Employer Trade-off of Health Premium Increases and Salary Increases

Finally, most companies do not view increases in health insurance premiums as a trade-off against salary increases. Only 17% of companies say they explicitly trade off health insurance increases for salary, whereas three-fourths say they consider salary increases and health care cost increases separately. This is contrary to the assumption made by most economists that the burden of health benefit costs are shifted back to workers in the form of lower wages. Although the perception of human resources executives may not reflect more subtle forces shaping management decisions, the very low proportion of human resources executives who perceive a trade-off between salary and health benefits does cast some doubt on the traditional economic assumption.

THE CHANGING NATURE OF THE LABORFORCE AND HEALTH BENEFITS

One trend that has eroded the health insurance coverage of workers in the 80s is the increasing tendency to rely on temporary or contingent workers. Such workers typically do not qualify for health benefits. The Laborforce 2000 survey indicates, however, that this trend may not significantly increase through the 90s. Only one-fourth (26%) of employers think they will be using more contingent workers who do not qualify for health benefits (Exhibit 7.3). And 56% indicate that they will use about the same number of such workers.

Nonetheless, a greater reliance on contingent workers is an element in some companies' efforts to control labor costs and increase flexibility. More than one-third (36%) of the firms that already make heavy use of contingent workers anticipate increasing their reliance on such workers. Manufacturing and financial service companies, which have traditionally relied on full-time staff covered by full benefit packages, also plan to do more hiring of uninsured temporary workers.

Retiree Health Benefits

Another trend in reduced coverage concerns retirees. At the present time, not only do most businesses provide health insurance to active workers, they also provide health benefits for retirees. As shown in Exhibit 7.4, 78% of all companies in this survey provide health insurance benefits to retirees. For retirees under age 65, employer-provided coverage is likely to be the primary if not the sole source of coverage. For employees age 65 and over, employer-provided health benefits tend to supplement Medicare coverage.

Exhibit 7.3 Whether companies will employ more workers who do not qualify for health benefits.

Will Employ?	All Companies (%)	Company Size					Industry			Ownership		Workforce Composition		
		$100 m and Less (%)	$101 m to $500 m (%)	$501 m to $1 b (%)	$1 b and More (%)		Mfg. (%)	Fin. Svcs. (%)	Other Svcs. (%)	Pub. (%)	Prvt. (%)	30% + Union (%)	10% + Contg. (%)	20% + 50 & Older (%)
More	26	21	23	28	31		33	34	19	31	23	19	36	26
About same	56	60	57	49	55		50	51	62	53	60	64	52	62
Fewer	11	7	10	14	11		9	7	14	10	8	7	5	10

Note: Figures may not add up to 100% because of companies that are "not sure."

Exhibit 7.4 Whether companies provide health insurance benefits to retirees.

Provide?	All Companies (%)	Company Size				Industry			Ownership		Workforce Composition		
		$100 m and Less (%)	$101 m to $500 m (%)	$501 m to $1 b (%)	$1 b and More (%)	Mfg. (%)	Fin. Svcs. (%)	Other Svcs. (%)	Pub. (%)	Prvt. (%)	30% + Union (%)	10% + Contg. (%)	20% + 50 & Older (%)
Yes	78	61	66	79	88	82	81	73	78	78	89	72	83
No	20	37	34	21	11	16	19	26	20	21	11	25	17

Note: Figures may not add up to 100% because of companies that are "not sure."

212

Retiree health benefits are much more common among larger firms: nine out of ten (88%) firms with sales in excess of $1 billion provide retiree health benefits, compared with 61% of firms with less than $100 million in sales. Retiree health benefits are also somewhat more typical in manufacturing than in service firms. As in other areas of health plan coverage, firms with a larger proportion of unionized employees (89%) and a larger proportion of older workers (83%) offer retiree benefits. By contrast, only 72% of firms that are heavy users of contingent workers provide retiree health benefits.

However, the requirement of the Financial Accounting Standards Board that—having begun in January 1993—companies must report their obligations to future retirees is leading many firms to reassess their retiree health benefit policies. A Foster Higgins survey found that 78% of companies intend to make future retirees pay more of their own medical bills.[13] Only 1%, however, are eliminating all retiree health coverage. Similar findings are reflected in the Laborforce 2000 survey.

Looking ahead, many human resources executives interviewed in the Laborforce 2000 study anticipate substantial cutbacks in retiree health benefits. Three-fourths anticipate increasing retiree cost sharing, and over half anticipate reducing their benefits. Less than one-fourth, however, expect to reduce retiree health benefits for current retirees. In this connection, larger firms are the most likely to reduce retiree health benefits, whereas 88% of firms with a disproportionate share of older workers anticipate increasing retiree cost sharing. These results suggest that as the workforce ages firms may become more sensitive to the economic burden of generous retiree health benefits.

MANAGED CARE

One of the most important trends that developed over the 80s in employee health benefit plans has been the tremendous growth in managed care plans.[14] They offer employees the choice of enrolling in health maintenance organizations (HMOs), or giving employees an incentive to select from a preferred list of physician and hospital providers (PPOs), whose costs are lower.

Managed care has been promoted as a major solution to rising health care costs.[15] The argument is that if an employer provides employees with a choice of systems of health care delivery and gives them appropriate financial incentives to enroll in lower-cost plans, then costs will automatically be controlled. Employees are in turn expected to reject those plans that do not succeed in controlling costs. As a result, insurers, HMOs, and PPOs have an incentive to use physicians and hospitals charging lower rates and practicing care more efficiently. Still, despite its advocates, critics point to the absence of conclusive evidence that savings can be obtained from a wide variety of managed care approaches.[16]

This mixed evidence on the effectiveness of managed care plans may be a factor in the Laborforce 2000 survey finding that only about 22% of all companies *actively* encourage employees to join plans such as HMOs (see Exhibit 7.5). Another 65% give employees a managed care option, but do not actively encourage it. This neutral stance may reflect the tentativeness with which business executives hold managed care as a solution to rising costs.

Managed care is much more available and much more actively encouraged in larger firms. In firms with sales in excess of $1 billion, 31% actively encourage the HMO option, compared with 11% of firms with less than $100 million in sales. Over one-fourth of small firms, in fact, do not have a managed care option, compared with only 6% of the larger firms. Public companies and firms with a larger segment of unionized workers are also more likely to actively encourage employees to join HMOs.

Interestingly, cutting edge companies (34%) are far more likely than prudent firms (12%) to emphasize HMO enrollment. Indeed, some one in three of the cutting edge companies report that they push employees "very hard" to join such plans. Here a contradiction in philosophy emerges: Although these progressive firms lead the way in providing flexible work hours and other options that accommodate individual differences among employees, they are pushing HMOs at the expense of other health care options perhaps more suited to individual needs.

SUPPORT FOR A GOVERNMENTAL ROLE IN CONTROLLING HEALTH CARE COSTS

The frustration of business executives owing to their inability to stem rapid increases in health benefit costs has led to a greater openness for the idea that government intervention could significantly control costs. While over half of the executives surveyed believe that the cost-containment strategies they are pursuing are somewhat effective, the majority feel that a much-stronger role for government will be required to contain overall health care costs. Indeed, over two-thirds of those surveyed in this study believe that some form of government-designated cost-containment plan will eventually be necessary.

Exhibit 7.5 Whether company actively encourages employees to join tightly managed health care plans.

	All Companies	Company Size				Industry			Ownership		Workforce Composition		
		$100 m and Less (%)	$101 m to $500 m (%)	$501 m to $1 b (%)	$1 b and More (%)	Mfg. (%)	Fin. Svcs. (%)	Other Svcs. (%)	Pub. (%)	Prvt. (%)	30% + Union (%)	10% + Contg. (%)	20% + 50 & Older (%)
Actively encourages	22	11	11	28	31	26	20	23	27	19	31	35	25
Gives them option	65	63	70	67	61	66	66	61	65	63	57	64	65
No HMO option	11	26	15	5	6	9	10	15	7	16	11	9	8

Note: Figures may not add up to 100% because of companies that are "not sure."

However, most firms do not believe that waiting for government action is the most prudent strategy. Indeed, three-fourths of firms plan to offer employees a managed care plan or require them to pay substantially more of their health care costs themselves. Plainly, the working public feels that the health care system in the United States is broken and anticipates some increase in out-of-pocket expenditure. At this point, however, there is scant acceptance of many of the implications of managed care and cost sharing arrangements. It remains to be seen whether managed care will contain costs and be accepted by the American workforce.

SUMMARY AND CONCLUSIONS

The Laborforce 2000 survey sheds important light on the changing nature of employee health benefits. Employers' concern with the rapid increase in employee health benefit costs is continuing and will lead to intensified efforts in cost containment. Employers anticipate making significant changes in plans, primarily in the form of increased employee cost sharing and greater reliance on managed care. In addition, employers anticipate reducing retiree health benefits for future retirees. Despite these planned changes, firms are not optimistic that they can succeed in controlling costs without major governmental intervention.

The findings have important policy considerations. The strategy of shifting more costs to workers may intensify labor-management conflict, including labor strikes over management-proposed reductions in health benefits. Such strikes are obviously costly to the economy in terms of lost output and economic growth. On the human side, they may weaken employee loyalty, undermining good morale and productivity.

Future changes in employee health benefits may also have an adverse consequence for access to health care. If employers cut back on contributions to dependent coverage, more workers may elect to drop dependent coverage and thereby increase the number of people without health insurance. If deductibles are significantly increased, workers and their families may face serious financial barriers to obtaining preventive or needed care.

Anticipated cutbacks in retiree health benefits also have important policy implications. Pressure may be increased on government to expand benefits under Medicare in order to compensate. In addition, Medicare may be pressured to lower the age of eligibility to age 60—a move already endorsed by the AFL-CIO and by auto and steel manufacturing firms, which have large numbers of retired workers under age 65.

Future Directions in Health Coverage

Ron Bass

Harris surveys find that over half of the American public are dissatisfied with the total costs of health care, including both what they and their insurance pay. And most (68%) think that total health care costs could be signficantly reduced without a sacrifice in quality.

The Laborforce 2000 study finds that companies are taking or planning to take steps to control health care coverage costs. A comparison between corporate actions and the attitudes of U.S. workers shows that, even though some of the following changes are understood and accepted, others are seen as unacceptable.

1. The Laborforce 2000 survey finds that 30% of the companies expect that employees will be paying a much larger share of health care costs. Some 58% say a little more of costs.

1a. Other Harris surveys find that 91% of the American public expect that people will be paying more out of pocket.

2. The Laborforce 2000 survey finds that 79% of the firms expect that employees will have more flexibility in choosing their benefits. Few expect that employees will have to make trade-offs between health and other benefits.

2a. Harris surveys find that 76% of the public would find it acceptable for an employer to cap the level of money that it contributes and for the employees to pick the benefits they want to pay for.

3. The Laborforce 2000 survey shows that three-fourths of the companies intend to offer employees the option of either joining a company-approved health care plan or paying substantially more themselves.

3a. Harris surveys of the American public suggest the cautions listed in the following table.

	Acceptable (%)	Not Acceptable (%)
Required to see authorized doctor before specialist	65	35
Choice of GP restricted	28	70
Choice of specialist restricted	24	75
Copayment increased $10	31	58
Deductible increased $200	24	75

Source: Survey of Health Consumers. Louis Harris and Associates, 1990.

The Laborforce 2000 survey suggests that the trend toward managed care will be accelerated in the 90s. Reliance on traditional fee-for-service care may become increasingly rare over the decade. Solo practice by physicians is likely to ebb, as group-practice or network arrangements become the dominant organizational form in health delivery.

Perhaps most interesting is the pessimism widely held by business executives that managed care will in itself be effective in controlling health care costs. The perception is widespread that a more-active role for government will be required in negotiating or establishing hospital and physician payment rates. To date, business has been relatively lukewarm or outright opposed to comprehensive health care reform with a major role for government. As the impact of high health care costs continues to be felt, however, business may increasingly shift toward explicit support of a stronger role for government.

NOTES

1. Ways and Means, U.S. Congress Committee on, 1992. *Green Book 1992,* Washington, D.C.: Government Printing Office.
2. Levit, K. R., and C. A. Cowan. 1990. The burden of health care costs: Business, households, and governments, *Health Care Financing Review* 12 (2).
3. Levit and Cowan, Burden of health care costs.
4. Levit and Cowan, Burden of health care costs.
5. David, K., G. Anderson, D. Rowland, and E. Steinberg. 1990. *Health care cost containment,* Baltimore, MD: Johns Hopkins University Press; Foster Higgins, 1992. Medical plan costs top $3500 per employee in 1991, *Newsbreak,* January 27; and Health Insurance Association of America (HIAA), 1991b. *Source book of health insurance data, 1991,* Washington, D.C.: HIAA.
6. Levit and Cowan, Burden of health care costs.
7. Gabel, J., C. Jajich-Toth, G. deLissovoy, et al. 1988. The changing world of group health insurance, *Health Affairs* 7(3): 48–65; Gold, M. 1991. HMOs and managed care, *Health Affairs* 10 (4): 189–206; Davis, Anderson, Rowland, and Stienberg, *Health care cost containment*; and Hoy, E., R. E. Curtis, and T. Rice. 1991. Change and growth in managed care, *Health Affairs* 10 (4): 18–36.
8. Health Insurance Association of America (HIAA), 1991a. *The fundamentals of managed care,* Washington, D.C.: HIAA; Gabel, Jajich-Toth, deLissovoy, et al., *Group health insurance;* Gold, HMOs; HIAA, *Health insurance data;* Short, P. F. 1988. Trends in employee health insurance benefits, *Health Affairs* 7 (3): 186–196; and Hoy, Curtis, and Rice, Managed care.
9. Congressional Research Service. 1991. *Health resources chart book.* Washington, D.C.: Government Printing Office.

10. Jensen, G. A., M. A. Morrisey, and J. W. Marcus. 1987. Cost sharing and the changing pattern of employer-sponsored health benefits, *The Milbank Quarterly* 65 (4): 521–550.

11. Foster Higgins, Medical plan costs per employee.

12. Service Employees International Union (SEIU), 1990. *Labor and management: On a collision course over health care*, Washington, D.C.: AFL-CIO, February.

13. Freudenheim, M. 1991. Paying the tab for retirees, *New York Times*, December 24.

14. Gold, HMOs; Hoy, Curtis, and Rice, Managed care.

15. Enthoven, A. C. 1988. Managed competition: An agenda for action, *Health Affairs* 7(3): 25–47; Enthoven, A. C. 1991. Universal health insurance through incentives reform, *Journal of the American Medical Association* 265 (19): 2532–2536.

16. Congressional Budget Office. 1991. *Rising health care costs: Causes, implications, and strategies*, Washington, D.C.: Government Printing Office, April; Ginzberg, E. 1992. Managed care hasn't lived up to its promises, *New York Times*, February 20; and Hadley, J. P., and K. Langweil. 1991. Managed care in the United States: Promises, evidence to date and future direction, *Health Policy* 19: 91–118.

8

The Findings and Their Implications

Philip H. Mirvis

The most upbeat conclusion of this Laborforce 2000 study of 406 companies is that American industry recognizes an urgent need to build a more competitive workforce. The importance of this point should be stressed. From the late 60s through the early 80s, U.S. corporations tended to pooh-pooh the relationship between innovative human resource management and productivity. Meanwhile, many executives were unreceptive, even hostile, to the heightened aspirations and nonconformist values of massive numbers of baby boomers then entering their companies and were at a loss to respond to the demands for equal opportunity and upward mobility expressed by women and minorities. Furthermore, the nascent threat posed by Japanese auto, tool, and electronics manufacturers was largely discounted, and Pacific-Rim and European competitors were scarcely blips on the strategic screen.

This study, by comparison, finds industry having a keen awareness of foreign and domestic competition and striving to increase productivity, enhance quality, improve service, and control costs. Companies now understand that many people want to apply their knowledge and skills at work, thrive with more freedom and flexibility on their jobs, and have much to contribute to work decisions. They also recognize that new entrants to their workforce require extensive training to catch up to foreign counterparts and that employees at all levels have to be retrained regularly to keep pace with rapid change and the challenge of high-technology jobs.

A second encouraging finding is that select firms know how to capitalize on and further develop the talents and motivation of their employees. Companies who are at the *cutting edge* or an *advanced* stage of human resource management, roughly half of the sample, invest heavily in innovative work redesign, employee involvement, and total quality management programs. They train and retrain their people to boost their bank of human capital and ensure that they turn out better products and services. They have flextime and flexplace programs that help there employees to balance the stressful demands of their jobs and family lives, and they have policies and programs to respond to increased racial, ethnic, and gender diversity in their workforce.

Does this mean, in turn, that the new ideas and human resource management practices of these pacesetting companies will inevitably spread to heretofore less progressive and imaginative organizations? Alas, the final conclusion of this study is cautionary: Building a world-class workforce and putting it to effective use will take considerably more investment, innovation, and perseverance than many companies, even some leaders, have mustered to this point. Heightened competition can drain, as well as energize, and this study shows plainly that current economic conditions and the need for constant cost-cutting have fixed many firms solely on short-term survival. Regular restructuring and downsizing have shaken corporate confidence, and the threat of takeover, the demand for increased earnings, and the high cost of health insurance further deflect attention from investment in human resources and long-range productivity. Neglect of the nation's infrastructure and lower social spending, relative to competitor nations, only adds to worries about the future.

Will American industry make the necessary investments in human capital to compete in the 90s? This is the question taken up from several angles by authors of each chapter in this volume. Here we return to the issues raised in the introduction to summarize what the Laborforce 2000 study finds about corporate practices and directions.

Q. Is Human Resource Management a Top Priority of Senior Executives?

To this most fundamental question there is no definitive answer in these data, and that is an important finding in its own right. It depends on the company and the human resource issue in question. Certainly training and development command more attention in many firms today. But when it comes to changing traditional patterns of work and decision making, responding to the differing needs of entry-level and older workers, proactively managing workforce diversity, or assisting people with their work/family concerns, there are sharp differences in the ways companies see and handle these labor-force issues. Some companies see these issues in competitive terms; others express modest interest and give them some attention; still others turn to more immediate and pressing matters.

This is a kind of Rorschach inkblot test of what is in the corporate mind of the varied companies in this sample. What differentiates "cutting edge" and "advanced" firms, those that take the lead in innovating, is the way that they project human resource management into nearly every facet of the competitive picture. *These firms are imbued with the cultural presumption that investing in people is essential to their success.* They have no fewer competing and costly pressures than other firms in this study and have had to face just as much painful change, including downsizing and cost cutting. Yet their emphasis in recent years has been on rebuilding and retraining their workforces, and their plans for the period from 1993 to 1997 are to spend and do more to capitalize on people.

Most of the companies studied here made substantial investments in computer technology in the latter 80s. Cutting edge and advanced firms have, in addition, put a premium on recruiting and retaining engineers and technicians as well as skilled blue-collar workers—those whose talents are needed to develop, operate, and add value to new technologies. These pacesetting firms have spent more than other companies to redesign work processes, develop total quality programs, and involve employees in work planning and decisions. They have also put more into training and motivating their employees, who have to work smarter to master today's work demands and communicate more effectively in new team-based management systems. Their track record of investing in people is not a matter of fad or philanthropy: What makes investing in human resources a top priority in these leading companies is its perceived connection to business needs.

Early in this volume we made the point that corporate culture can be a boon or bane to innovative human resource management. The Labor-force 2000 study shows, in support of this, that top executives in cutting edge and advanced companies are stronger and more consistent backers of human resource innovation than their counterparts in less progressive firms. Furthermore, the study finds that middle managers and employees in leading firms are more supportive of change and that unions are more apt to cooperate in its implementation. Finally, these companies seem to be constantly on the lookout for new ideas and management practices that might improve the capability of their workforces and keep them ahead of the competition.

In sampled companies where human resource innovation is less of a priority, by comparison, top management does not really make the connection between people and productivity. Perhaps because executives are seen as giving lip service to human resource issues, middle managers, employees, and unions are also more apt to resist change. Various competing crises and cost pressures dominate the agenda in these less progressive companies, and their corporate culture is rated as inhospitable to new ideas. Not surprisingly, these firms spend less on work redesign and employee involvement and have had a harder time coping with the pressing laborforce issues examined throughout this volume.

Q. What Is the Role of the HR Department in Company Competitiveness?

One of the most worrisome findings in this study is how few human resource (HR) departments put themselves at the forefront of developing human capital in their firms—no matter how progressive they say their companies are. When asked about the two highest priorities of their department, for example, only three out of every ten human resource officials give top priority to improving the quality of their company's workforce or rate employee training and management development as central thrusts of their function. More broadly, Edward Lawler, Susan Cohen, and Lei Chang show that there is a significant gap between top management's emphasis on improving productivity, quality, and customer service and the HR departments' primary concerns: managing benefits and holding the line on insurance costs. Note, too, that one-fourth of HR functions reported that either they have *no* major responsibility for meeting their company's strategic objectives, or they simply are not sure where they fit in. The authors conclude, therefore, that very few human resource departments are true partners with line managers in running the business.

One reason that this partnership does not exist is that meeting business objectives has not traditionally been the responsibility of the personnel function. Despite all the talk about *strategic* human resource management, this study finds that most human resource departments are stuck in their *administrative* role processing people and paperwork. Second, a job in human resources remains a second class position in many companies, and many human resource executives and staffers are themselves careerists who never held a line management job. Overall, this study finds that the department lacks clout in many companies and does not advance the competitive agenda of the business.

Other forces that work to disempower the HR function are worth noting: Many line managers, for instance, do not invite or welcome HR's assistance when setting and executing their business strategies. The increasing complexities of human resource duties also work against the HR department having a partnership relationship with managers. Recruiting, compensation and benefits, training and counseling, and the legal aspects of human resource work have become specialties in their own right. The department's specialization has, in turn, precluded its involvement in the general management of the business. Finally, it is hard for human resource employees to think about innovative programs in the midst of corporate cutbacks and downsizing. The HR department itself has been shrunk in many companies and charged with planning staff reductions and guiding outplacement. This has had serious consequences for morale in human resource departments and has dampened its reputation in many firms.

One heartening finding from the Laborforce 2000 study, however, is that 70% of those surveyed say that their top management is becoming more interested in and attentive to human resource management. Does this mean that the HR department will gain in stature and influence? Much depends on the priorities of top executives. The survey finds these executives more and less preoccupied with profitability and cost control, quality and customer service, and improving the caliber of their workforces. Thus it remains to be seen what form their increased interest in human resources will take. Current economic conditions, along with restructuring, acquisitions, and global expansion, will likely focus the attention of senior managers in some companies primarily on labor costs and the immediate savings associated with reducing the number of employees. In others, by contrast, those same forces could stimulate vigorous top-level human resource leadership and a flowering of innovative practice, ultimately giving the HR department a stronger strategic thrust. An example of this is the transformation of Jack Welch at General Electric. Welch earned the title "Neutron Jack" in his first years as CEO of industrial giant GE because after he visited a plant, it was said, the buildings were left standing but the people were gone! Now, 10 years later, HR specialists lead GE managers through periodic "workout" programs to redesign work processes and reduce bureaucracy, and Welch has become a public champion of HR innovation and is leading GE through a massive culture change.[1]

Q. Will Downsizing Continue? Will Companies Be Better or Worse for It?

Eight out of every ten companies in this study restructured and downsized in the latter 80s and more than seven out of ten plan to do more of this through the mid-90s. It has reached the point that a full half of the HR executives interviewed believe that periodic downsizing is essential to competitiveness. It is safe to say, then, that downsizing will continue into the near future.

What has this meant for the firms in this sample? Over 60% downsized by combining operating units, and half sold off businesses. These moves reflect the impact of mergers and a refocusing of corporate strategies and resources. Some 38% removed layers of management or significantly reduced corporate staff. Here the emphasis has been on "trimming the fat" to reduce overhead and bring mid-level executives closer to operations and the customer. Finally, nearly half of the firms in this sample have laid off a substantial number of workers with one out of every six firms that downsized getting rid of 20% or more of its employees.

Overall, this is more than twice the number of jobs lost during the re-structuring of the late 50s and 60s when the great conglomerates—unrelated businesses combined into a holding company structure—were formed. But then, unlike now, the nation's economy was robust, and displaced workers could find good jobs at good pay rates. Moreover, most of the job loss at that time was borne by blue-collar workers. Managers, professionals, and office workers are just as likely to see their jobs eliminated today.

Mitchell Marks comes to some interesting conclusions about what is favor-able and unfavorable about downsizing today when he looks at companies' motivations. He divides the sample into two categories: firms that down-sized for financial reasons (cost containment or profitability) and those that downsized for strategic reasons (productivity, competitiveness, or new busi-ness directions). Those firms that downsized for financial reasons were far more likely to incur higher than expected severance costs, to increase their use of costly overtime and consultants, and to lose more of the "wrong kind of people" when compared with firms that reduced staff with strategic in-tent. In addition, firms that downsized for financial reasons had more morale problems among their remaining workforce.

This leaves us with two different depictions of the consequences of corpo-rate downsizing. In the case of financially driven cutbacks, Marks feels that manangement may be operating too reactively. Indeed, some of these firms could find themselves in a downward spiral, unable to cut costs enough to make up for lost revenue and missing the skills and motivation needed to retain market share and stay competitive. By contrast, firms that downsized for strategic reasons seem to have a more proactive outlook. They have their own post-downsizing problems, but, they have retrained a far larger proportion of their remaining workforce than firms that cut back for financial reasons. The result of this strategic outlook, Marks concludes, is that firms that have both cut back *and* reinvested in people will likely have better competitive prospects in the future.

Q. How Big Is the "Skills Gap" and Can It Be Closed?

Another interesting finding of the Laborforce 2000 study is that, given all the downsizing, labor shortages per se are not a major issue for companies in this sample. But a skills gap pervades industries of all types and sizes. Three-fourths of the executives interviewed anticipate problems in recruiting scientists and technologists over the next few years and over half foresee problems getting high-skill blue-collar workers. Futhermore, there is some concern about the availability of well-qualified top managers, professionals, and office workers.

The Department of Labor/Hudson Institute's report *Workforce 2000* lays out the mismatch between the increasing numbers of highly skilled professional and technical jobs in the United States and the declining numbers of qualified job applicants.[2] As an example, the National Science Foundation estimates that there could be a shortfall of 400,000 science and engineering graduates by the end of the decade. Here we have concentrated on the supply of more generally qualified college and high school graduates. What do employers say about them? More than 50% of the entry level job applicants that these companies interview lack the skills to be hired.

This is not a problem in Japan, where high school students score two to three years ahead of their American counterparts on standardized tests. What, then, will American businesses do to close the skills gap? Many firms plan to improve recruiting, in hopes of getting a larger share of the qualified job applicants, and roughly half will offer a mix of remedial education and basic skill training to new hires, in effect doing the work of the nation's high schools. In addition, businesses are taking steps to become more involved in public education. Already, over half of the companies in this study encourage their employees to work in public schools and make substantial donations of money and equipment. More activism is projected in the future. This might take forms ranging from "adopt a school" programs, in which employers provide training and part-time work for high school students and a job after graduation, to community efforts like The Boston Compact, a consortium of Boston-based companies that create summer jobs for three thousand high school students and hire a thousand interns annually.

Michael Useem finds some notable differences in what companies are doing in response to the educational deficiencies of entry workers. Smaller firms, he finds, emphasize in-house remedial and basic training for new hires. Their needs may be more immediate, and their resources more limited. One good example is Peavy Electronic, which adapted a computer program developed by the U.S. Army to teach new hires the mathematics needed to operate numeric-control machinery.[3] By contrast, larger firms are more apt to involve themselves in public schools. Still, it is notable that only one out of every ten employers today give employees leaves of absence to teach in public schools. Moreover, firms with a higher proportion of college graduates, and those that employ more engineers and technicians, are less likely to concern themselves with the public school system. Although this may be rational in terms of the firm-specific benefits of such investments, it will deprive students of the chance to learn from the best and brightest employed in industry.

How will industries meet their need for more technicians and craftspeople? The Laborforce 2000 survey finds companies taking an interest in European-style apprenticeship programs, such as those that have worked so successfully in Germany and Sweden. One out of every three firms surveyed. say it is very likely that it will institute such programs in the next few years. Still, the success of the European apprenticeship programs has been highly dependent on cooperation among regional industry groups and multiple trade unions—lacking in the United States—and has not proved an antidote to the shortage of scientifically trained talent on the continent.[4] The implication, then, is that nothing short of a sweeping overhaul of the eduational system in this country may be required to truly close the skills gap.

To complicate matters, the need for entry level training is more than matched by the requirement to retrain current employees. Four-fifths of the firm in this study expect to do more in the way of retraining in the future. Which companies lead in this area? Those that restructured in an effort to increase productivity are retraining more of their workforce. In addition, Useem finds that companies that have redesigned their work processes do considerably more retraining than others. The same is true of firms with employee involvement and total quality management programs. The point is that leading firms are not investing in education and training for its own sake. Rather, they combine training with other innovations in the workplace to ensure a favorable return on their investments in human capital. In these cases, there is technical knowledge that employees must master. Useem notes, as well, that leading companies put a heavy emphasis on teaching communication, problem-solving, and human relations skills—"soft" skills needed in this era of "hard" competition.

Q. Are Companies Prepared to Deal with Diversity and Work/Family Issues?

Most companies in this sample are experiencing changes in the makeup of their workforce and are cognizant of future demographic trends. Many are sensitive to the conflicting demands of work and family life that their employees encounter. Yet these laborforce issues are rated as far less urgent than the training needs of entry workers and current employees. Victoria Parker and Tim Hall contend that this is because most firms see programs aimed at diversity and work/family needs as benefits for employees rather than core investments in the organization.

The great majority of companies in this study are either now offering a variety of flexible work options to employees, including flextime, part-time work options, and extended childbirth and family leave, or are planning to do so in the near future. And, by 1997, two-thirds expect to offer job sharing opportunities, and over half expect to give people the chance to work at home—what has come to be called flexplace. It is apparent, however, that not all company employees will have access to these flexible options. Moreover, even the seemingly "family-friendly" firms in this sample offer little to employees in the way of direct child or elder care assistance.

The authors make the case that these kinds of innovations create a more flexible workplace. Flexibility in work time and space, they contend, allows people to better balance their work and life spheres and, in turn, enables a firm to adapt to changes in the composition and needs of its workforce. Firms are investing in flexible technology and office spaces, and setting up more flexible arrangements with suppliers and distributors. Why not more flexible staffing and scheduling? Hence, they view workplace flexibility as a feature of organization design. Up to the time of the Laborforce 2000 survey, however, only one out of every three companies has seen flexibility as having a major impact on recruiting, turnover, and productivity. Indeed, it seems that its primary benefit is an enhanced company image. As a consequence, the authors conclude, companies are missing the real benefits of flexibility and are self-limiting what they might otherwise offer to their employees.

In an area where U.S. industry faces unique challenges, the Laborforce 2000 survey finds that nearly four out of every five companies either offer now or will offer training to managers on managing a diverse workforce. Fewer currently offer diversity training to employees or a mentoring program for women and minorities, although these are expected to increase by the mid-90s. What is most interesting is how firms with a cutting edge human resource philosophy translate this into a competitive issue. Until recent years, the employment needs of women and minorities were seen in terms of equal opportunity or affirmative action. In most instances, the personnel function was charged with "policing" employment practices and ensuring that managers followed the letter and spirit of the law, and, in many cases, there was hue and cry over fairness and reverse discrimination.

This is where things still stand in some companies, whereas many others see workforce diversity as something that managers can handle as a matter of course. Cutting edge companies, by comparison, subscribe to what Parker and Hall call flexibility in work style. At base, this means taking proactive measures to acknowledge and respect differences in the temperament, needs, and style of women, African-Americans, Hispanics, and other minorities rather than forcing them to conform to the prevailing white, male corporate mold. This corporate commitment is not a matter of social work or political correctness. On the contrary, the underlying thinking is that people are simply more productive when they bring their whole selves to work. As a result, leading firms socialize managers and employees to *value diversity* and believe that a multicultural work environment has special advantages over a more homogenous one. Experts on this subject point to importance of variability in gene pools and biodiversity in natural ecology as signs that nature favors diversity and depends on it. Closer to home, there is also a body of evidence that racial and gender diversity in work groups enhances creativity and promotes cooperation. The point is that strong arguments are being marshalled in favor of valuing diversity and gaining currency in cutting edge companies. Plainly, many firms see increased diversity as something that is far off—a problem of the year 2000 or later. Hence their knowledge and attitudes have not had to rise to the occasion. Cutting edge firms are instead preparing themselves with the latest in thinking and practice.

Q. Will Older Workers Become "Deadwood" or a Source of Skill and Service?

Michael Barth, William McNaught, and Philip Rizzi make the point that most firms have not faced squarely the long-term implications of the aging of the laborforce. The age group 50 years old and older is the fastest-growing age segment in the workforce today, and it will become substantially larger as baby boomers mature and life spans increase. The authors contend, further, that many more older workers will delay full retirement in the future and will desire to work in part-time jobs or jobs with scaled-down responsibilities. Indeed, many may have to work in order to provide for themselves and cover the costs of health care.

What are companies doing to assist older workers? Only one out of every five firms provide workers the option of a phased retirement program such that they can work part-time prior to their full retirement from a company. And just one out of three provides opportunities for mature employees to transfer to jobs with reduced pay and responsibilities. The Laborforce 2000 data show clearly that companies are far more likely to provide flexible options for working parents than for older members of their workforce. In addition, companies spend less on retraining older workers than they do on training and retraining younger ones, and few adapt their training to the learning styles and needs of older people. Here, the authors suggest, is a subtle bias in favor of younger workers.

On the not-so-subtle side, this study shows many companies (41%) using early retirement incentive programs (ERIPs) to eliminate higher-paid, older employees from their payroll. Indeed, older workers are getting a "double whammy" in the ongoing wave of corporate downsizing. First, companies with a larger proportion of employees over age 50—chiefly large manufacturers with more unionized employees—have eliminated many more jobs and a larger percentage of their workforce than employers with a younger workforce. To compound matters, many of these firms got rid of a disproportionate number of their older workers through ERIPs and job elimination.

The core issue here, as the authors see it, is the gap between attitudes and practices. The human resource executives interviewed profess to see older workers as having better work attitudes and job skills than younger workers and being less prone to absenteeism and turnover. In practice, however, the majority of firms are not accommodating their older workers' needs for flexible work arrangements, are investing less in their retraining, and are more likely to urge or shove them out the door when downsizing. Perhaps, as the authors suggest, the larger implications of an aging laborforce are simply too far away on the corporate horizon to register attention. But current practice, they contend, sets a bad precedent for the year 2000 when baby boomers reach age 55 and will have to face such stark treatment.

Does this mean, at least in the interim, that older workers will be seen as deadwood rather than as vital human resources in many firms? Two factors suggest otherwise. First, older workers may help to fill the skills gap currently experienced and projected to expand over the rest of the decade. This would, of course, require massive retraining and substantial corporate and public investment. But we find that three out of four companies say that problems in recruiting qualified, skilled people would cause them to reassess their current programs or start new ones to hire and use more older workers. Second, older workers may fill new and expanding roles in the service sector. The cases of Day's Inn and B&Q p.l.c. summarized in Chapter 6 give only a hint of how service companies can capitalize on the interpersonal skills and work ethic of older people.

Q. Can Companies Cope with Skyrocketing Health Care Costs?

Nearly all the human resource executives interviewed see the increasing costs of health benefits as having a great deal (67%) or some (23%) impact on their company's ability to compete. And they make it a top priority of their department to control these costs. What are companies doing? Most have changed their health plans since 1987—shifting costs to employees in the form of higher deductibles and out-of-pockets expenses and moving to managed care arrangements. What will the future bring? Most companies will offer employees more flexibility in their choice of benefits through cafeteria style plans. Still, nine of ten say that employees will be paying much more (30%) or a little more (58%) for their health insurance. And most say they will either require or strongly encourage employees to join a managed care program or else pay more out-of-pocket.

Karen Davis, detailing the soaring costs of health care coverage, makes the point that planned approaches to managing costs will not likely prove sufficient. First, most insurance plans do not especially reward preventative medicine or effectively curb the use of expensive diagnostic tests and treatments. Second, she notes that although the majority of companies find that employees have at least grudgingly accepted changes in health plans to date, further limits on choice and increases in expenses are likely to yield widespread resistance. Finally, plans to increase cost-sharing of current retirees and reduce the benefits of future retirees are likely to place an unacceptable burden on older citizens and Medicare. Problems in meeting their health needs, not to mention the needs of the millions of citizens who are not covered by corporate health plans, means that government intervention is likely. Only a minority of companies surveyed believe that their company's health plans can bring health care costs under control. By contrast, over two-thirds say that government-designated cost-containment plans will be necessary. Needless to say, corporate America joins the nation in concluding that our current health insurance system is "broke."

PATTERNS IN HUMAN RESOURCE MANAGEMENT

In each of the chapters in this volume, authors have discovered factors that predict whether or not companies see laborforce issues in competitive terms and are apt to invest in new programs and innovations to address them.

Size Factors

Bigger is not necessarily better when it comes to human resource management. Larger firms, by definition, have more resources and more people and thus typically do more training, are more involved in public schools, and offer more flexible work options to their employees. But, in almost every case, factors other than size influence the human resource investments of large firms. For example, there is in this sample a constellation of large manufacturing firms that employ a larger proportion of males and older workers and that are more highly unionized. These old-line industrials are most affected by short-term crises and most sensitive to the costs of human resource investments. However, each of these companies takes one of two sharply differing approaches to the future.

Roughly half these firms have cut back on staff and expect to make additional cuts in the next few years. They have not invested much in worker retraining and are having more trouble attracting qualified high school and college graduates. By contrast, the other large manufacturers, which have also downsized, have instead chosen to invest heavily in worker retraining and have an active involvement in public schools. These firms also offer more flexible employment options for people and are more apt to have diversity training programs. What differentiates between manufacturers that are spiraling down from those that are making a comeback? Just this: Companies that are making future-oriented investments have the strong support of top management, middle managers, employees, and unions. Many are not necessarily cutting edge firms, but they see human resource issues in competitive terms and are fast followers when it comes to innovative practices. By contrast, those that are not investing in people lack top-level commitment to change and have a corporate culture that devalues human resource innovation. In summary, it is leadership and corporate values, rather than size and assets, that stimulate innovation in human resource management.

Industry Sector

Industry sector makes a difference in human resource practices. Firms in the manufacturing sector, large and small, have taken the lead in total quality management and employee involvement programs. Manufacturers have, of course, been most affected by international competition and are most attentive to best practice around the world. Furthermore, their human resource departments are also more focused on company competitiveness. Interestingly, smaller manufacturers spend more, as a percentage of sales, on entry level training and retraining of employees. They are also more apt to provide vouchers or have child care facilities for their workers. Perhaps they can see a more immediate payoff from these laborforce investments than larger companies.

Financial and nonfinancial service companies also emphasize flexible hours and practices reflecting, perhaps, the disproportionate size of their female workforce. However, financial service firms do much more in the way of employee training and retraining than other companies in the service sector and invest more in technology and quality programs. Looking ahead, the entire service sector is expected to go through massive restructuring in the 90s. We have to wonder if nonfinancial service firms will be able to make required gains in productivity and quality in the decade ahead. Furthermore, it is doubtful that many will be able to rebuild through the throes of downsizing. This is worrisome outlook in the nation's increasingly service-based economy.

Multinational Presence

Whether or not companies have a multinational presence also figures into their approach to human resource management although here, too, motives make a difference. Those multinational companies (firms with over 20% of their workforce overseas) that have expanded primarily to reach new markets and compete with other businesses rate themselves as human resource innovators. They have made very substantial investments in employee development, workplace flexibility, and productivity and quality improvement, in both their U.S. and overseas organizations.

By contrast, multinational firms that are most troubled by the high cost of U.S. labor are far less innovative, do not do as much in the way of work redesign or quality improvement, and spend less on their domestic workforces. Granted, these firms are having more trouble attracting quality high school and college grads than other companies are, but this may reflect as much on their management practices and wage rates as it does on the available labor pool. As things stand, these companies have been able to underinvest in domestic human capital while exploiting comparatively cheap offshore labor. One worry is that this option could become even more attractive as the skills of the U.S. workforce erode and those of overseas labor increase. The cost of this option, as Lester Thurow notes, is the further depreciation of human capital in the United States.[5]

Employees as Stakeholders

Several chapters lend support to the idea that employee groups represent key "stakeholders" for human resource programs in organizations. Firms that have a larger proportion of women workers, for instance, are more apt to offer employees the options of flextime, leaves to care for children and sick family members, and the chance to work part-time or at home. These firms plainly see the competitive value of work/family programs for attracting, motivating, and retaining a large bloc of their employees. In the same vein, firms employing a larger proportion of African-Americans and Hispanics assign more importance to this laborforce issue and are somewhat more likely to have diversity programs.

But there are also some complex cross-currents having to do with age cohorts in the workforce. On the one hand, Useem suggests that problems in the public education of new hires are forcing companies to spend more on entry level training at the expense of retraining and ongoing employee development. By contrast, Davis finds that the increased health insurance costs of older workers contribute to the increased costs of coverage throughout a firm's workforce. In a sense, then, younger workers are consuming a disproportionate share of training monies while older workers are consuming a disproportionate share of health insurance dollars.

This illustrates, in microcosm, conflicts between the interests of younger and older workers that are likely to be exacerbated in the future. The data show, however, that older workers are more at risk of job loss and more likely to find their health insurance cut back considerably in the case of retirement. It is tempting to conclude that sheer numbers determine the relative strength of employee groups when it comes to human resource programs. Plainly older workers are in the minority relative to women and workers under age 55. However, Barth, McNaught, and Rizzi have made the case that prejudices and stereotypes also play a role in how companies invest their human capital.

Corporate Culture and Philosophy

Finally, corporate culture and philosophy make a crucial difference in human resource management. We have seen clear differences between the practices of firms that describe themselves as having a cutting edge (11%) or advanced (39%) approach to human resource innovation as compared to those that describe themselves as having a more thoughtful (37%) or prudent (11%) orientation. Specifically, cutting edge and advanced firms are

- More likely to redesign work, promote employee involvement, and operate a total quality program.
- Less likely to perceive top management's attitudes and corporate culture as barriers to change.
- More likely to combine downsizing with retraining of their workforce.
- More likely to be active in public schools.
- More likely to have work/family programs.
- More likely to view diversity as a competitive opportunity.
- More likely to actively encourage employees to join tightly managed health care programs.
- No more or less likely to have favorable attitudes toward older workers, but more likely to offer alternative career tracks and phased retirement.

It is worth remembering, too, that human resource departments in cutting edge companies pay closer attention to the actions of competitors and to trends in the marketplace. This means that department executives and staff in these firms are constantly scanning for opportunities and problems and are quick to innovate when the need arises. No doubt this is what keeps these firms at the cutting edge.

FROM IDEAS TO PRACTICE

The premise behind our exploration of a company's philosophy about human resource management is that ideas make their way into practice along an innovation diffusion curve with early adopters being the first to experiment with new thinking, followers picking up on proven practices, and laggards waiting for widespread adoption by their peers.[6] Indeed, many of the so-called modern practices found today in cutting edge and advanced companies come from theories and research up to three decades ago.[7] For instance, industry has known about the importance of the "human factor" in productivity since the time of the Hawthorne studies.[8] But the breakthrough came with publication of McGregor's 1960 publication on Theory X and Y models of management, which was followed by a gradual change in managerial opinion about the value of people in organizations.[9]

Theories on the motivating potential of job enrichment and team-based production were developed during the 60s and tested during the 70s when research on participatory management and group problem solving made its way into management literature.[10] Studies also documented that more "organic" organizations, with larger spans of control, a less rigid chain of command, and fewer rules and regulations, were more adaptive to change than traditionally organized "mechanistic" companies.[11] These ideas were the forebears of the work redesigns, employee involvement programs, and productive restructuring we find in leading businesses today. Furthermore, there were important studies on the changing work values and aspirations of young people and consciousness-raising about the issues facing women and minorities on the job.[12]

As timely as these ideas seem to be in retrospect, they were largely dismissed as idealistic, ivory-towerish, or just plain irrelevant to mainstream corporate America through the 70s. Business was consumed by new techniques of systems analysis and managing "by the numbers." Large industrial and financial service companies, which had the resources to invest in people, gave low priority to new ideas about human resource management. Success had seemingly bred arrogance and complacency. Smaller firms were not conversant with the latest thinking. Of course, a few notable innovators, such as Polaroid, Digital Equipment, Bank of America, and some smaller companies, like Graphic Controls Corporation and Herman Miller, experimented with new work forms in the 70s and instituted programs to increase employee motivation. But it has been estimated that fewer than 15% of companies employing 100 or more persons had innovative human resource programs in place by 1980.[13]

HUMAN RESOURCE MANAGEMENT WINS OUT

Today, in this Laborforce 2000 study, we find many more firms innovating in this area. Ideas about integrating people and the organization now imply valuing the whole person. The precepts of scientific management are being abandoned in favor of work designs that require high-level skills, responsibility, and teamwork. Indeed, it is not unusual to see a self-managing work team producing an entire finished product, or providing every aspect of a service. Participatory management is being accepted as best practice, and leading firms use employee involvement in decision making as a matter of course. Big, bloated bureaucracies are being supplanted by lean structures and nonhierarchical forms of organization. Even job descriptions, fixed work schedules, and standard operating procedures are giving way to flexible arrangements that accommodate customer demand and meet the needs of employees.

It took ten to fifteen years for many of the ideas and theories developed in the 60s to first make their way into industry. Now they are spreading through the broad base of companies. Cutting edge firms have taken the lead in most aspects of human resource management investigated in this study. Self-described advanced and thoughtful companies have adopted some proven new practices, as the diffusion curve would predict. Prudent firms, those who wait for new methods to be adopted by peer companies, clearly lag, but one hopeful prediction is that progressive human resource management practices will eventually find their way into these firms.

Certainly the demonstrable success of Japanese companies, along with interest in Japanese-style management practices, has helped to speed some types of innovations through American industry. For instance, quality specialist W. Edwards Deming, so influential in Japanese industry, has finally become a prophet in his own land. Interestingly, some of the ideas behind work redesign were first developed in Europe and pioneered in firms like Volvo. Europe has also provided an example on work/family programs. The global market has further increased the diffusion of new practices in industry.

Receptivity is another factor. Who could have imagined General Motors, once in the vanguard of American corporations, losing a substantial chunk of market share, lampooned in film documentaries, shaken up by a coup led by its Board of Directors, and now short of capital needed to fund further development of the top new car in its line? How the mighty have fallen. This object lesson has not been lost on the rest of American companies, which search persistently for new models for doing business.

The decline of many formerly exemplary companies has coincided with a loss of confidence in tried-and-true management recipes. The phenomenal success of *In Search of Excellence* is ample testimony to the appetite that American business has for new ideas.[14] The management section of the average bookstore today features a steady diet of innovative theories and practices offered up, in equal measure, by academicians, popularizers, and practicing managers. Of course, fads are common in human resource management, and many come and go. Still, it is inarguable that the world of work is changing its shape and that new ideas and practices are coming together into an emerging cookbook for competitiveness.

NEW CHALLENGES

We have argued that cutting edge companies were the first to adopt new ideas about human resource management developed in the 60s and 70s and to import and adapt methods of quality management, work redesign, and work/family programming from Japan and Europe. How about the leading ideas of the 80s and 90s? Certainly new thoughts on competitive strategy and positioning have taken hold and advances in information technology and its management have influenced almost every aspect of business. The latest thinking on global management is quite influential in larger multinational firms and policy circles. And, of course, the 80s gave industry hostile takeovers, soaring corporate debt, and swollen management paychecks. It also legitimated widespread corporate downsizing, which has had consequences that we examined in Chapter 4.

Meanwhile, new human resource issues have emerged the past 12 years. Not too long ago, a nagging problem in human resource management was the mismatch between "smart people" and "dumb jobs." Concern about the "blue-collar blues" was equaled by worries over "white-collar woes." This is still a problem in companies that have not taken steps to redesign jobs and decision making to tap into the skills and ideas of production and office workers. But the opposite problem is also emerging in industry, and there are few guidelines on what companies should do to prepare poorly educated young people and retrain older workers to perform "smart jobs." The need is staggering: One estimate is that over fifty million workers (21 million new entrants and 30 million current workers) need to upgrade their skills for tomorrow's jobs.[15]

Another problem is the need for work/family programs. More women are entering and staying in the workforce, and many have high career aspirations. In turn, many men now desire to take a more active role in parenting and home life. When we add to this a "baby boomlet" and the fact that boomer parents "want it all"—good jobs, free time, family time and expect society to accommodate them—we can see what is behind the stress and overload facing two-career couples in the workforce today. Add to this the high divorce rate, increasing numbers of single-parent families, and the plethora of problems afflicting adolescents and young children and it becomes apparent that work/family assistance is vital to employee retention and productivity. Industry is only just learning what kinds of flexibility and support programs are required.[16]

What have leading thinkers in human resource management been brewing up for diffusion into practice in the 90s? First, there has been a spate of studies on corporate culture and the prospects of cultural change in companies. Second, new, sometimes esoteric, theories on organizational change, transformation, and learning are being bandied about. Finally, there has been fresh thinking about corporate social responsibility and the role of business in society. Again, cutting edge companies are pioneering these new ideas. However, they are encountering competing problems occasioned by tight economic conditions and clashing value systems. Indeed, before we can say that progressive human resource management has indeed "won out," there are at least three issues that will require close attention, in theory and practice, over the rest of the 90s.

Cutbacks and the Employer-Employee Compact

Can Companies Have a People-Oriented Culture with Continuing Cutbacks? Since the concept of corporate culture burst on the scene, many companies have issued philosophy and mission statements that speak to the values and aspirations of people.[17] Recent research confirms that strong, people-oriented companies perform better, and we have found company culture to be a strong correlate of innovative human resource management.[18] Yet seismic shifts in the economy are leading to continuing cutbacks and downsizing in corporations. What does this mean for company cultures? Surely it has shattered any notions of cradle-to-grave job security for American workers and turned the "psychological contract" between employees and employers upside down. Few companies can today ask for employee loyalty and many seem no longer to want it. In turn, employees have entered an era of "free agency," in which they are being advised to keep their skills and resumes current and be prepared to move on when and where they can.[19] We can only wonder whether the cynicism washing over the workforce might reach the point where corporate proclamations about the "value of people" are going to be perceived as "corpocrisy"—hypocrisy in corporate life.[20]

Plainly there is a need for a new kind of compact between employers and employees in this era of downsizing. There are leading companies, of course, that have avoided layoffs by investing in productivity, curbing new hires, instituting job sharing, and reducing pay rates or increases. And some that have gone through major downsizing now strive to run lean and are creating a multiskilled workforce so that people can be redeployed rather than outplaced. Still, it seems that large-scale dislocation is inevitable through the 90s. Accordingly, some firms are revising their corporate philosophies to take account of new realities. Digital Equipment and Hewlett Packard, once committed to full employment, now emphasize that they offer employees top-notch training, work/family assistance, and a good work environment and promise only that they will be honest with people about business conditions and assist them with outplacement in the event of layoffs or early retirement. This, at least, clearly redefines the corporate culture and gives employees a realistic picture of what they can expect from their employers. Good intentions aside, these firms cannot expect the kind of loyalty that they once had from employees.

Looking ahead, there are further changes in corporate staffing that promise to fray the fabric of corporate culture. Many companies, including cutting edge firms in this sample, are increasingly relying on part-time and temporary workers to stay flexible, reduce health benefit costs, and avoid full-time staff reductions. This provides valuable opportunities for people seeking this type of work but consigns many others, who wish for full-time employment, to less renumerative, secure, and meaningful jobs. It also works against the once-valued goal of full employment and substitutes "contracts" for psychological commitment as the basis of human resource management in companies. Meanwhile, companies that have made major cutbacks for financial reasons and that expect further downsizing in the future are at serious risk when it comes to human resources. They are not investing in employee retraining, and they suffer from a "brain drain" as capable people leave for other work and qualified new recruits are hard to enlist. They may be developing a "lean and mean" structure, but their organizational culture is sapping the lifeblood and competitiveness out of their workforce.

Change Management Programs

Will the Latest Ideas on Change Management Really Diffuse throughout American Industry? Longitudinal research confirms that more companies today are beginning or expanding efforts at work redesign, employee involvement, and total quality management than in the 80s.[21] This adds to the notion that human resource innovations follow the diffusion curve we have outlined. But we need to ask: Will this same diffusion pattern apply to the more encompassing approaches to organizational change being tried out today in the most progressive American companies?

The latest ideas are to be found in tracts on renewal, reinvention, and transformation as well as on organizational learning.[22] In practice, these transformation programs intend to free up people's ideas and creativity and expand the boundaries of their self-awareness. They may take initially the form of encounter groups, brainstorming sessions, outward bound programs, even exercises in poetry, journaling, and other forms of inner searching. The rationale is that personal flexibility and self-knowledge are deemed essential to adapting to change. Then the intent is to hone analytic capability and harness energy by having organization members examine their decision-making models, debate and formulate a vision, and align corporate structures, processes, systems, and mindsets along a path that some refer to as "strategic intent." This may involve search conferences, in which organization members scan the environment for trends, planning sessions, in which they explore the corporate dream, and trial periods, in which they experiment purposefully with innovations both of the sort described here and of other types.[23]

What is important to note is that these efforts take, as a starting point, images of an organization as a collective mind or biological system rather than as a machine or even a computer network. Moreover, the aim is not simply to teach people new practices and fine-tune corporate processes—the goals of organizational development and total quality management programs. Rather it is to enable people and their organization to "learn to learn." As high-minded as this sounds, we wonder about its diffusion throughout American industry.

First, we anticipate problems in the "packaging" of these theories. New ideas on human resource management spread from cutting edge firms to the mainstream once they become fully coherent and attain scientific status. Certainly these new ideas on change have a following today, but there is scant empirical evidence on the merits of, say, "action inquiry" or aligning the organization with "the natural order of things." On the contrary, academe is sharply divided on these new ways of understanding people and organizations. Furthermore, when new human resource management practices work through the mainstream and reach less innovative firms, they are typically translated into "products," such as schematics on new work designs and information flows, or into teaching cases, exercises, manuals, and the like. To complicate matters, these new organizational change practices do not lend themselves readily to packaging and delivery. As stand-alone or off-the-shelf exercises, they seem "off-beat" and can be manipulative.[24] Even when the practices are fully integrated with theory and proffered as a program of change, we think that many companies simply will not understand how to implement them, or why they should.

Second, many companies may not believe that new practices will work and so may not invest in them at all. Research on the spread of seemingly more digestible employee involvement and total quality management practices in Fortune 1000 companies reinforces a key point made in this study: Top management's inattention—and resistance on the part of middle managers, employees, and unions—can block or foredoom human resource innovations.[25] The new "change management" practices being proposed require corporations to make massive investments of time, energy, and resolve. They also depend on strong leadership, open-minded organization members, and a high degree of readiness for change within the corporate culture. Hence there is no guarantee that firms that are not already prone to innovating in human resource management can or will embrace them in a fit of competitive zeal.

Certainly hothouses of innovative thinking—Xerox, Apple Computer, GE, and the like, "smart" companies with the money and imagination to invest in the human resource frontier—will enhance their change management and learning capability and, perhaps, gain a competitive edge from these new disciplines. But fast followers, which would next be expected to try out these ideas and practices, may not grasp them so easily or capitilize on their potential so readily. Furthermore, firms that wait for these ideas to achieve scientific status and these practices to spread throughout industry may find themselves at a crucial competitive disadvantage and have neither the resources nor the residual talent needed to undertake a corporate transformation. The risk is that the rich and responsive corporations will get even richer and more responsive to change while the rest will either muddle through or wither away.

Social Responsibility

Will Business Embrace Socially Responsible Human Resource Management? The issue of corporate social responsibility has been much debated over the past thirty years. But, today, there are some signs that business is assuming important social responsibilities. More and more companies, for example, are "going green" and making environmental protection an integral part of their material sourcing, packaging, and manufacturing strategies. Cause-related marketing is also catching on as Reebok's human rights efforts and Coor's literacy campaigns have caught the attention of both the market and marketers. Indeed, surveys find that consumers are willing to pay 5% to 10% more for products produced by environmentally oriented and socially responsible companies.[26]

Socially responsible human resource management is also on the rise. At present this includes family-friendly practices, programs to hire and train disabled and disadvantaged employees, and employee involvement in public schools. In Los Angeles, as an example, 125 Arco Oil & Gas Co. employees volunteer time at the Tenth Street Elementary School. Honeywell, interestingly, sponsors a summer Teacher's Academy where high school math and science teachers team up with industry people to develop work-relevant projects for students.

What will the future bring? A few smaller companies, like The Body Shop, pay employees up to ten hours a week to work on human needs in their communities, and some bigger firms, like Polaroid, have employees "adopt" community groups and manage them as part of their jobs. Carrying this a step further, Vermont ice cream maker Ben & Jerry's regularly educates its employees on social issues and has made contributions to the firm's social mission a part of everyone's job and performance appraisal. The company also has a 7-to-1 salary ratio whereby top executives can earn only seven times more than entry hourly employees. This is part of their belief in "caring capitalism." Interestingly, these policies have had a profound effect on the employees at Ben & Jerry's where it has kindled a spirit of generosity and become a prime contributor to satisfaction and commitment.[27] There is also some evidence that companies that have a smaller gap between the pay of top executives and mainline workers achieve better results in product quality.[28] Businesses for Social Responsibility, a new kind of chamber of commerce for socially responsible firms, predicts that opportunity to do socially significant work could become a prime means of recruiting and motivating at least a segment of the workforce in the future.

It would be ennobling to see this outlook spread from a thin segment of companies to respected cutting edge firms and the mainstream of American industry in this decade and thereafter. Certainly leading theorists are exploring new models of economic behavior—reaching beyond the conventional image of people as self-interested "utility maximizers" to recognize their altruistic and moral dimensions.[29] In the same way, a "communitarian" model of social organization is being advanced as an alternative to the highly individualistic "contractual" model favored by neoclassical management theories.[30] Still, the ideas behind socially responsible human resource management are controversial, evidence of their impact on morale and performance is sparse, and they are sure to encounter resistance along the innovation diffusion curve. Indeed, it will likely take at least ten to fifteen years for a new and agreeable social compact to be devised between employers and employees, for new ideas on change management to be translated into "best practice" in mainstream companies, and for socially responsible human resource management to take hold.

WHITHER PUBLIC POLICY?

Which path corporate America will follow will depend, to some extent, on public policy and how well government, business, and labor cooperate in managing the nation's economic and social agenda in the 90s. Although this has not been a central feature of the Laborforce 2000 study, Chapters 4, 5, and 7, on entry level training, work/family programs, and health care insurance have all pointed to the need for a governmental role in these areas. A new president and administration have passed or are forging ahead on legislation providing for family leaves, apprenticeship programs, a massive retraining effort, and wholesale changes in health care coverage and cost containment. Furthermore, since corporations are likely to downsize further and industry ups and downs are likely to continue, pension reform would be useful. Portable pensions, for instance, would encourage job mobility and give people more flexibility in making their own employment decisions.

There may also be a role for government in funding research and diffusing knowledge about "best practice" in the area of human resource management. As an example, the *Work in America* study helped to crystallize knowledge about changes in the workforce back in the 70s, and the National Commission on Productivity and the Quality of Work Life sponsored research and demonstration projects that helped to prove the merits of employee involvement, joint labor-management change projects, and innovations in work design and compensation.[31] The Department of Labor/Human Institute's *Workforce 2000* study is a more recent example of government bringing a human resource issue to the attention of the nation's businesses. But, to this point anyway, government has not supported much research or provided visible leadership on how to respond to the issues identified in the report.

One potential area for action concerns research consortia. There are some notable examples of industry and the U.S. government cooperating to develop semiconductors, upgrade machine tools, and speed the development of "smart" software. But there have been no sustained attempts, so far as we know, to use the resources and auspices of the goverment to bring together academics, consultants, industry groups, and human resource managers to pool what they know and to support research on new ideas about managing workforce diveristy, retraining and redeploying older workers, and making further advances in work/family programs. A research consortium could become a focal point for developing the nation's "learn-how" about the dynamics and competitive implications of the new forms of organizational change, transformation, and learning.

Research consortia, however, will not help the nation unless it produces smarter managers and workers who are capable of "learning to learn."

Labor Secretary R. B. Reich makes the point that a "fortunate fifth" of the U.S. population—a lean cadre of managers, as well as professionals, entrepreneurs, and other "symbolic analysts"—have a bright future in the global economy.[32] By contrast, he sees the opportunities and fortunes of back-office and blue-collar workers rapidly winding down. The 80s gave the country a harbinger of this divisive development: The incomes of college graduates increased 7% in constant dollars, whereas those of high school graduates declined 15% Plainly, new investments and experiments in education at all levels are essential to prevent deeper division in the U.S. workforce.

In the area of training and employment, for example, the United States in 1988 spent half as much as Canada and one-fourth as much as West Germany as a percentage of gross domestic product on employment and training programs.[33] Meanwhile, workers over age 55, once valued for their hard-earned experience and seasoning, are now "excess baggage" in even the most progressive companies. Younger entrants to the workforce are finding that high skill/high wage jobs are simply not available. Entry salaries for those fortunate enough to find work in larger companies are declining rapidly. Most other young workers have had to settle for lesser-paying jobs in service industries—what pundits call "McJobs"—that offer little in the way of long-term career opportunities.[34]

There are more than enough signs that the nation's competitiveness is in decline. This Laborforce 2000 study provides evidence that at least some leading companies are setting an example on how to best invest in human capital and rebuild their *own* competitive workforce. In our view, however, government action and increased business-government cooperation are needed to rebuild the competitiveness of the *nation's* workforce. Whether or not the new administration will be able to move to the cutting edge of investment and innovation in human resources remains to be seen.

It is hard to imagine the country, in the near term, investing in everything we need to in order to address the nation's social ills and keep industry at pace with foreign competition. But investing in people, a time-honored American tradition and prime source of the nation's economic strength, has to be a top priority for everyone's sake.

NOTES

1. Tichy, N. and S. Sherman. 1993. *Control your destiny or someone else will: How Jack Welch is making General Electric the world's most competitive company.* New York: Doubleday/Currency.
2. Johnston, W. B., and A. H. Packer. 1987. *Workforce 2000: Work and workers for the 21st century.* Indianapolis, IN: Hudson Institute.

3. Stewart, T. A. 1991. The new American century. *Fortune.* Spring/Summer, 12–23.

4. Kotkin, J. 1992. *Tribes: How race, religion, and identity determine success in the new economy.* New York: Random House.

5. Thurow, L. C. 1992. *Head to head: The coming economic battle among Japan, Europe, and America.* New York: Morrow.

6. Rogers, E. M. 1962. *Diffusion of innovations.* New York: Free Press of Glencoe.

7. Mirvis, P. H. 1984/85. *Work in the 20th century.* Cambridge: Revision/Rudi Press.

8. Roethlisberger, F. J., and W. J. Dickson. 1939. *Management and the worker.* Cambridge: Harvard University Press.

9. McGregor, D. 1960. *The human side of enterprise.* New York: McGraw-Hill.

10. Herzberg, F., B. Mausner, and B. B. Synderman. 1959. *The motivation to work.* New York: John Wiley & Sons; Likert, R. 1961. *New patterns of management.* New York: McGraw-Hill.

11. Burns, T., and G. M. Stalker. 1961. *The management of innovation.* London: Tavistock.

12. Yankelovich, D. 1979. Work, values and the new breed. In *Work in America: the decade ahead,* ed. C. Kerr and J. M. Rosow, New York: Van Nostrand Reinhold.

13. New York Stock Exchange Office of Economic Research. 1982. *People and productivity.* New York: New York Stock Exchange.

14. Peters, T. J., and R. H. Waterman, Jr. 1982. *In search of excellence.* New York: Harper & Row.

15. *BusinessWeek.* 1988. Needed: Human capital, September 19, 100–141.

16. Forisha-Kovach, B. 1984. *The flexible organization.* Englewood Cliffs, NJ: Prentice-Hall.

17. Deal, T., and A. A. Kennedy. 1982. *Corporate cultures.* Reading, MA: Addison-Wesley.

18. Denison, D. 1990. *Corporate culture and organizational effectiveness.* New York: John Wiley & Sons.

19. Hirsch, P. 1987. *Pack your own parachute.* Reading, MA: Addison-Wesley.

20. Kanter, D. A., and P. H. Mirvis. 1989. *The cynical Americans.* San Francisco: Jossey-Bass.

21. Lawler, E. E., S. A. Mohrman, and G. E. Ledford. 1992. *Employee involvement in America: An assessment of practices and results.* San Francisco: Jossey-Bass.

22. Ackerman, L. 1986. Development, transition, or transformation: The question of change in organizations. *OD Practitioner,* December, 1–8; Naisbitt, J., and P. Aburdene. 1985. *Re-inventing the corporation.* New York: Warner Books; Senge, P. 1990. *The fifth discipline: The art & practice of the learning organization.* New York: Doubleday; Tichy, N. M. 1983. *Managing strategic change: Technical, political, and cultural dynamics.* New York: Wiley Interscience; and Weisbord, M. 1987. *Productive workplaces: Organizing and managing for dignity, meaning, and community.* San Francisco: Jossey-Bass.

23. Mirvis, P. H. 1990. Organization development part II: A revolutionary perspective. In *Research in organizational change and development Vol. 4*, ed. R. Woodman and W. Pasmore, Greenwich, Ct.: JAI Press; Torbert, W. 1987. *Managing the corporate dream: Restructuring for long term success*. Homewood, IL: Dow Jones-Irwin.

24. Mirvis, P. H. 1993. Human development or depersonalization: The company as total community. In *Personal development programs in corporations: The fatal embrace?*, ed. L. Nash, New Brunswick: Transaction Publishers; Nelson, L., and F. Burns. 1984. High performance programming: A framework for transforming organizations. In *Transforming work*, ed. J. Adams, Alexandria, VA: Miles River Press.

25. Lawler, Mohrman, and Ledford, Employee involvement in America.

26. Clancy, K. J. 1991. *The green revolution: Its impact on your pricing decisions*. New York: Yankelovich, Skelly, and White/Clancy; Gary, L. 1990. Consumers turning green: J. Walter Thompson's Greenwatch survey. *Advertising Age* 61 (41): 74.

27. Mirvis, P. H., A. S. Sales, and D. Ross. 1991. Work life at Ben & Jerry's. In *Management live!*, ed. R. Marx, T. Jick, and P. Frost, Englewood Cliffs: Prentice-Hall.

28. Cowherd, D. M., and D. I. Levine. 1992. Product quality and pay equity between lower-level employees and top management: An investigation of distributive justice theory. *Administrative Science Quarterly* 37: 302–320.

29. Kohn, A. 1990. *The brighter side of human nature*. New York: Basic Books.

30. Etzioni, A. 1988. *The moral dimension*. New York: Free Press.

31. U.S. Department of Health, Education, and Welfare. 1973. *Work in America*. Cambridge: MIT Press.

32. Reich, R. B. 1991. *The work of nations: Preparing ourselves for 21st century capitalism*. New York: Alfred A. Knopf, Inc.

33. *BusinessWeek*, 1990. Can you compete?, December 17, 62–93.

34. Magnet, M. 1992. The truth about the American worker. *Fortune*, May 4, 48–65.

Index